D1384499

U.S.A. 20/21

STUDIES IN RECENT AMERICAN HISTORY

NUMBER THREE

AMERICAN CHOICES

AMERICAN CHOICES

Social Dilemmas and Public Policy since 1960

Edited by Robert H. Bremner,

Gary W. Reichard, and Richard J. Hopkins

OHIO STATE UNIVERSITY PRESS: COLUMBUS

Library of Congress Cataloging in Publication Data

Main entry under title:

American choices.
  (U.S.A. 20/21; no. 3)
  Includes bibliographies and index.
    1. United States—Social policy—Addresses, essays, lectures.
2. United States—Social conditions—1960– —Addresses,
essays, lectures. 3. United States—Economic conditions—
Addresses, essays, lectures. 4. Social problems—Addresses,
essays, lectures. I. Bremner, Robert Hamlett, 1918–. II.
Reichard, Gary W., 1943–. III. Hopkins, Richard J., 1939–.
IV. Series.
HN65.A6815 1986   361.6′1′0973   85-25833
ISBN 0-8142-0368-X

491895

Contents

Introduction

The essays in *American Choices* deal with domestic social concerns since the 1960s. The volume is intended as a companion to *Reshaping America: Society and Institutions, 1945-1960* (1982) and, as in that work, the essays are interpretive rather than encyclopedic. Since the emphasis of the volume is on domestic problems, foreign policy issues, including the Vietnam War, are dealt with only indirectly. In view of the divisive effect of the war on American thought and conscience and because of the increasing importance of the youth of the 1960s in policy decisions of the 1980s and 1990s, the volume concludes with an essay viewing the Vietnam generation in retrospect and prospect.

Following the example of the volume that inaugurated the forerunner of this series, the essays address both continuity and change.[1] The persistence of problems such as protecting the poor, advancing the rights of women and minorities, determining the proper relation between business and government, and establishing workable relations among various levels of government provide the continuity in American history. Change, however, is also a constant, reflected in the new circumstances in which the problems arise, the altered shape and dimensions they may assume, new views of their causes and consequences, and recognition of the need to attack them in new ways. Homelessness, for example, is an old story in the United States, but the cast of characters is different in the 1980s from that in the 1880s or 1930s, and the actors in the drama must assume new roles or responsibilities, even though some of them continue to repeat the old lines.

In choosing contributors to *American Choices*, the editors enlisted authors who have done and are doing important work in the areas assigned to them and who still have much to say on the subject. Each contributor has been asked to consider the social issues and dilemmas involved in his or her topical field and to discuss policy debate about the choices available and decisions taken. Unfortunately, the volume does not include individual studies on every important area; for various reasons projected essays on the problems of an aging population, immigration and ethnicity, and criminal punishment and deinstitutionalization did not materialize. Yet taken together the essays illuminate some of the general problems encountered in making choices and decisions on social issues in recent and contemporary America.

The role of partisanship in decision-making, always taken for granted, can be praised as an essential element in American democracy or decried as inimical to the general welfare. We need parties for individual voters to register their choices. We expect them to be broad enough to represent various interests and points of view, to be united, disciplined, and responsive to strong leadership. We expect them to be committed to a particular stance on public issues but to be ready to compromise and, when necessary, to accept defeat gracefully. On the other hand, we condemn unswerving party loyalty on the part of voters and the avoidance, distortion, or confusion of issues by politicians for the sake of partisan advantage. Almost a century ago, Lester Frank Ward, a civil servant as well as a savant, complained that "in the factitious excitement of partisan struggles" the real interests of society were lost sight of with the result that "nations continue in the hands of mere politicians who are easily managed by the shrewd representative of wealth."[2] At present symbol and image loom larger in politics than all but a few issues, blur party loyalty, and provide "shrewd representatives of wealth" with opportunities to shape national policy to accommodate their own interests.

It would be foolish to ignore the many factors other than reason, prudence, and self-interest that influence public as well as private decisions. It would be equally foolish to ignore the importance of trying to bring the forces of intelligence to bear on all decisions. Unfortunately the application of intelligence to social problems is likely, at least in the short run, to make their resolution harder rather than easier, by introducing new considerations into the debate and by showing up the fallacies or disadvantages in solutions at first thought to be simple and clear. Moreover, there is no guarantee that reason will lead different people to the same conclusion. Since public issues are complex, conscientious and rigorous application of intelligence to the same problem by people of comparable ability and benevolent intention often produces contradictory recommendations.

By definition a dilemma, if it is to be resolved, requires a choice between equally undesirable alternatives. In education or employment policy, for example, the choice may be between alternatives one of which seems, not better, but less objectionable. In other cases the choice may entail advancing one favored principle, such as the right of privacy or the rights of children, at the expense of another cherished ideal, such as freedom of the press or the authority and autonomy of the family. Faced with such difficult decisions, legislators and citizens may be reluctant to act, and their indecision may be justified as expedient.

Some varieties of American conservatives advocate nonintervention by public agencies in social problems not just in specific cases but as a general rule. No matter how grave the problem and whatever suffering and hardship it entails (according to this view), public action, that is, "state interference," is unwarranted and unwise. William Graham Sumner, a pioneer sociologist whose bleak view of nature and pessimistic attitude toward human nature made him suspicious of projects of social reform, asserted that private virtue and individual initiative were the only remedy for problems like poverty. Admitting to "extreme prejudice against State Interference" with the laws of nature and market place, Sumner declared public efforts at social amelioration were bound either to fail or, at best, do more harm than good.[3]

Sumner's noninterventionist position, shared by the neoconservatives of the 1970s and 1980s, goes in and out of fashion like styles in dress and decoration. So too does the rival interventionist philosophy, based on a benign view of nature and optimistic appraisal of human capacities, which makes social reform a prime duty of statesmen and citizens. Henry George, a contemporary and antagonist of Sumner, called laissez faire "the gospel of selfishness, soothing as soft flutes to those who, having fared well themselves, think everybody should be satisfied," but utterly inadequate as a means of social advance.[4] In 1937, in a message to Congress recommending adoption of a federal minimum wage and maximum hour bill, Franklin D. Roosevelt took issue with "exponents of the theory of private initiative as the cure for deep-seated national ills." No matter how well-intentioned such people were, said Roosevelt, they too often resisted social progress which, "in actual practice . . . has been effectively advanced only by the passage of laws by state legislatures or the National Congress."[5]

The split between opponents and supporters of state interference is one of the continuing divisions of American politics. The difference between them, however, is not absolute but a matter of degree. Parties and presidents opposed to governmental intervention in principle do not hesitate to use the power of office to promote causes they favor or suppress those they dislike. Conversely, a staunch supporter of government intervention, Franklin D. Roosevelt, for example, may refuse to push measures whose adoption seems dubious. In practice it is not endorsement of "little government" or "big government" but the ways and ends for which intervention is used that determine the character of an administration.

For many years Americans have taken it for granted that in matters like presidential elections, trade policy, defense, and diplomacy American choices have an impact on people in nearly every part of the world. More recently, especially since the oil embargo of 1973-74, Americans have had to acknowledge their own vulnerability to events and decisions in parts of the world over which they have no or little control. Problems related to energy, population, pollution, raw materials, human rights, and human development are not peculiarly or uniquely American but global in sweep and solution.[6]

In recent years, to a much greater extent than before the 1960s, legislators and public officials have had to consult and take into consideration the wishes not only of established pressure groups such as business, labor, and agriculture but also the desires and demands of "new" interest groups: women, blacks, Jews, the aging, Hispanic-Americans, homosexuals, and others who feel a sense of group identity and a certain alienation from the rest of the country. This infusion of new concerns exacerbates debate and makes consensus harder to reach. In the long run it may produce more equable decisions; in the short run it intensifies the feeling of betrayal and frustration on the part of those whose views do not prevail.

While the stakes at issue and the interests involved have been increasing, the options have seemingly been contracting. "As our problems grow constantly larger," the historian David Donald warned in 1977, "the chances of solving them drastically diminish."[7] Among the reasons for constriction of choice are commitments already made in treaties, executive agreements, long-standing policies and programs, and, in particular, the cost of national defense, which since 1960 has ordinarily taken precedence over outlays for other needs. In 1985, as *American Choices* went to press, at least three factors further restricted freedom of choice: the disinclination of the Reagan administration to consider options or viewpoints inconsistent with the President's philosophy; a huge national deficit that made restoration or expansion of social programs unlikely in the foreseeable future; and a tendency to define national security so broadly as to overshadow or eliminate concern for other issues such as individual freedom and security. When one issue becomes all-consuming, anything else is Hobson's Choice.

Even when choices are made and decisions reached after debate, negotiation, and compromise, the decisions may prove to be less than binding. Legislative intent may be narrowed or nullified by court rulings; court decisions may be threatened by constitutional amendment or sidestepped by revised legislation. Although a legislative act may inaugurate broad changes in public policy, the agency charged with enforcing it may not receive sufficient funds to put the program into full operation. State and local governments can and do drag their feet in putting into effect new federal policies (for example, deinstitutionalization of status offenders) or in implementing unpopular court decisions. State laws on matters like highway speed and drinking age are subordinated to national policy by denial of federal funds to states that do not comply with federal regulations. A chief executive doggedly opposed to agencies and programs instituted by earlier administrations—or even approved by Congress during his own term of office—can undermine their effectiveness by appointments, administrative orders, and withholding of funds.

These introductory remarks cannot touch on all the trials and tribulations of making and realizing choices on social issues. These problems are spelled out in more specific ways in the essays that follow. In some areas action taken since 1960 may strike readers as less comprehensive and decisive than circumstances warrant. If so, those who believe making history is as important as studying it will find the unresolved issues cause for anticipation rather than recrimination.

1. John Braeman *et al, Change and Continuity in Twentieth Century America* (Columbus, Ohio, 1964).

2. Lester Frank Ward, *The Psychic Factors in Civilization* (Boston, 1893), 326. In this and the following paragraphs quotations from late-nineteenth century thinkers are used not as authoritative statements but in the hope that observations by figures from the past will be more helpful in putting present problems in perspective than pronouncements by contemporary writers.

3. William Graham Sumner, "Sociology" (1881) in Perry Miller, ed., *American Thought, Civil War to World War I* (New York, 1954), 87, and Sumner, "State Interference," *North American Review* 145 (1887): 109-19.

4. Henry George, *Social Problems* (Chicago and New York, 1883), 20.

5. "The President Recommends Legislation Establishing Minimum Wages and Maximum Hours, May 24, 1937." Samuel I. Rosenman, comp., *The Public Papers and Addresses of Franklin D. Roosevelt* (New York, 1941), 6: 209-10.

6. Theodore M. Hesburgh, *The Humane Imperative, A Challenge for the Year 2000* (New Haven, Conn., 1974), 107.

7. David Herbert Donald, "Our Irrelevant History," *New York Times*, 8 September 1977, 27. Donald continued: "Unlike every previous generation, we face impossible choices. If we have guns, we cannot have butter. If we reduce unemployment, we produce inflation. If we hire women, we must fire men. If we give blacks preference in admission to colleges and professional schools, we exclude whites."

PART ONE

THE INDIVIDUAL, THE STATE, AND SOCIAL RESPONSIBILITY

Elevating or Ignoring The Underclass

Mark I. Gelfand

In the 1960s and 1970s, Americans rediscovered the poverty in their midst—rediscovery made painful not only by the moral dilemma posed by the persistence of material want in a society marked by widespread affluence, but also by the fear that besides inadequate incomes the poor suffered as well from a poverty of the spirit. During the very decades that the United States landed men on the moon and celebrated the bicentennial of its birth in freedom, the nation confronted the harsh fact that there were millions of Americans, white and black, rural and urban, who shared in neither its good life nor its ambitions. Contrary to every cherished belief of the American ideology, there had emerged an American underclass: people "stuck more or less permanently at the bottom, removed from the American dream."[1]

The terms *poor* and *underclass* are used interchangeably in this essay to refer to a particular segment of America's poverty population—those of working age, along with their children, who are physically capable of employment but, for the most part, do not work. Many are entirely dependent on welfare for their subsistence; for the others the income they earn is barely adequate to get by on. The underclass is America's "long-term poor"; if the vast majority of the nation's impoverished are a shifting mass that floats above and below the officially prescribed poverty level, a small fraction of this group have experienced poverty for most of their lives. A disproportionate number are black and female. Assigning a figure to the size of the underclass is fraught with statistical perils, but 5 percent of the total population is generally accepted as the outside limit.[2]

Earlier generations had possessed similar anxieties about such a social class, but their handling of these concerns was quite different from the response of governmental leaders in the 1960s and 1970s. If nineteenth and early twentieth century Americans accepted poverty as inescapable, indeed biblically ordained, their descendants proved less fatalistic, at least for a while. The economic pie had so expanded following World War II that it seemed possible, given wise management of available resources, to expand it still further so as to supply all with healthy slices. As regards the poor themselves, nineteenth and early twentieth century learned opinion tended to find the source of their difficulties in their personal characteristics; the underclass lacked the virtues of thrift, sobriety, and pluck that were at the root of the American success story. By mid-century this emphasis on individual deficiencies had been displaced, though certainly not destroyed, by a focus on environmentalism. The poor were the victims of structural defects in social organization and whatever ills society had created it could also remedy. In contrast to the earlier reliance on private charitable and educational groups, with some limited state and local government assistance, to care for the poor, the 1960s and 1970s handed the problem over to the federal authorities. It was the national government that first diagnosed the difficulty, and it would be up to Washington to solve it. By the end of the latter decade, however, this assignment of responsibility, as well as the other "modern" assumptions about poverty and the poor would be under severe challenge.[3]

Between the inauguration of John F. Kennedy and Ronald Reagan's second term in the White House, the federal government pursued a series of policies to dissipate what Gunnar Myrdal in 1963 described as the "ugly smell rising from the basement of the stately American mansion."[4] First it would be a services strategy that attempted to equip the underclass with the skills, outlook, and opportunity that would enable the poor to enter the mainstream of American society. Then it would be a welfare reform program that tried to accomplish what turned out to be two impossibly contradictory objectives: providing the poor with a decent standard of living through income transfers that recognized and respected their dignity; and quieting middle class discontent about the high costs of subsidizing a welfare population of promiscuous deadbeats. This would be followed by a half-hearted and futile effort to supply the underclass with jobs. Finally, in the early 1980s the executive branch resolved to wipe the slate clean of what it considered nearly twenty years of abject failure on the part of government by looking to the private sector for answers. With each successive policy the frustrations mounted and the visions of aiding the underclass became narrower and narrower. As the nation entered the election year of 1984, about all that the underclass had going in its favor was the "fairness" issue: the deep-seated American conviction that the poor, like everyone else, deserved an even break. But no one had been able to translate this conviction into concrete action—and so the "ugly smell" remained.

Services and Opportunity: The War on Poverty

A century before Lyndon Johnson declared "unconditional war on poverty," Abraham Lincoln had provided the rationale for this 1960s belligerency. In his Independence Day message to Congress in 1861, Lincoln proclaimed, "On the side of the Union, it is a struggle for maintaining in the world, that form, and substance of government, whose leading object is to elevate the condition of men—to lift artificial weights from all shoulders—to clear the paths of laudable pursuit for all—to afford all an unfettered start, and a fair chance, in the race of life." This was the American gospel of equal opportunity, adopted in Lincoln's lifetime and passed on through successive generations as one of the unique features of American democracy. As with so many of the nation's hallowed doctrines, rhetoric bore little relation to reality. But so imbedded was the creed that when Lyndon Johnson undertook to reestablish its validity, he began with the utmost confidence that it could be achieved without the domestic conflict Lincoln had encountered.[5] Johnson's optimism would not be vindicated.

By stressing equal opportunity Johnson could draw on a long reform tradition, but his methods and aims represented bold departures from previous effort. For most of the nineteenth century and well into the twentieth, it was government action itself that was often seen as the major obstacle to true equality of opportunity. With few exceptions, free public education among them, legislation and other forms of official intervention tended to create privileges for the few at the expense of the many. "Curb government and allow the market free play," went the classical liberal argument, "and the race would both be fair and go to the swift." During the New Deal years the Democratic party had repudiated many old Jacksonian nostrums in responding to the economic crisis of the 1930s, but not until the War on Poverty did a national administration consciously discard them in pursuit of equality of opportunity. Over the decades the increasing complexity of urban industrial society had forced some people, for reasons beyond their power to control, out of the race completely. More, not less, government was needed, and specific groups had to be singled out for favored treatment. That these targeted groups came from the very bottom of the economic ladder also distinguished the approach taken in the 1960s. Despite its populist connotations, the principle of equal opportunity had historically been used to defend and promote the interests of the middle class. When, during the Progressive Era, Woodrow Wilson spoke of breaking up the trusts in order to open broadened avenues to the "man on the make," his appreciative audience was composed of those who had already gained a firm foothold and were looking to advance still further. A half-century later, with the middle class contentedly entrenched in corporate America, Lyndon Johnson tried to extend equality of opportunity to those who were outside looking in. It would be an endeavor fraught with political danger.

Johnson understood the risks. After the holdover officials from the Kennedy administration presented their preliminary plans for an anti-poverty offensive to the new Chief Executive, veteran members of Johnson's staff reminded him, as if the master legislative tactician of this era needed any reminding, that the political rewards were greater and more immediate in programs that aided the middle class. After all, the middle class—besides being larger—voted, and the underclass did not, it was as simple as that. No one had gone very far politically by taking up the cause of the desperately poor.[6]

Social critic Dwight Macdonald, although more cynical than most, captured the prevailing attitude when he wrote: "There is a monotony about the injustices suffered by the poor that perhaps accounts for the lack of interest the rest of society shows in them. Everything seems to go wrong with them. They never win. It's just boring.'"[7] But for Johnson the chance to become the spokesman and advocate of this inarticulate minority was too alluring to resist.[8] In addition to the obvious humanitarian considerations, all too easily passed over in most analyses of Johnson's behavior, there were the personal and political aspects. Here was an opportunity for Johnson to establish a record of reform that could rank with that of his political idol, Franklin Roosevelt.[9] The patrician farmer from New York had saved capitalism and provided the middle class with a large measure of security. With his War on Poverty, this rough-and-tumble native of the Texas hill country would attack a problem Roosevelt had barely considered: raising the underclass, reviving the American dream and, thereby, putting the Communist economic and propaganda challenge to rout. The mood of the country was right, Johnson believed, for him to identify with such a noble struggle. The fight for civil rights had awakened the country to its shortcomings, and

Kennedy's assassination had seemingly stiffened the nation's resolve to remedy them. It would be Johnson's war.[10]

Among the plans being offered for waging that war, the equal opportunity strategy appeared the safest politically. For those who argued that the existence of the underclass revealed basic flaws in the American socioeconomic edifice and that a major overhaul was necessary, Johnson had nothing but contempt. He did not accept that radical critique, and he knew the public would not buy it either. Reform, not revolution, would get the job done. Nor did Johnson have any use for those who claimed that the quickest way to abolish poverty was to hand the poor sufficient money to pay for decent housing, clothing, and food. Income guarantee proposals not only smacked of socialism, but also would treat the symptoms rather than the roots of poverty. The country would be signing blank checks that would undermine its moral and economic fiber. It made no sense, Johnson believed, "simply to support people, to make them dependent on the generosity of others." Furthermore, declared the President's Council of Economic Advisers, "Americans want to earn the American standard of living by their own efforts and contributions."[11] All they needed was a chance.

The economists who were the prime movers behind the antipoverty campaign also saw positive virtues in the equality-of-opportunity approach. Fulfilling the Democratic party's pledge to "get the country moving again," to accelerate the rate of economic growth, required an increase in the productivity of the poor. In its current state, the underclass, with its crime, illness, and dependency, constituted a drag on the economy; this could not continue if the United States was to maintain its economic superiority over the rapidly expanding Soviet system. Johnson made his pitch in a way all American taxpayers could appreciate: "One thousand dollars invested in salvaging an unemployed youth today can return $40,000 or more in his lifetime." Open "the gates of opportunity" to the underclass and their despair would evaporate—and the whole nation would profit from their emancipation.[12]

Two important assumptions underlay this design of the War on Poverty. The first predicated a culture of poverty, or "The Other America," as social critic Michael Harrington had called it. Because of weaknesses in the structure of American society, such as racial discrimination, a shortage of good housing, and inadequate health care and educational facilities, the poor were caught in a cycle of menial jobs, insufficient income, and despair. Young people grew up in an environment that destroyed all incentive to improve their condition; this alienation was handed down from one generation to the next, becoming ever deeper with the passage of time. The inhabitants of "this other nation with its own way of life" lacked the skills and outlook to succeed in the fast-paced economic marketplace. Break this stupor, recast the poor in middle-class molds, and the President would win his war.[13]

The second premise was an unbounded faith among the social scientists in their ability to create whatever social circumstances were desired. Macroeconomics would provide good jobs for the emergent underclass, the educators and manpower experts would equip the underclass to fill them, and a wide range of community-based services would create the climate that would motivate the underclass to respond positively to these opportunities. Everything was in place: the goal was right, the plan correct, and the execution assured.[14]

The political wisdom of the equality-of-opportunity strategy was demonstrated by swift congressional approval of Johnson's legislative proposals. Although it would require some of the President's fabled wheeling-and-dealing to assure victory, his skill in wrapping the program in the American flag badly splintered the conservative opposition. How could anyone be against ending poverty? How could anyone oppose investment in human capital that would strengthen the nation and fulfill its historic mission? But Johnson made many promises and Congress would be watching closely to see they were kept.[15]

The Economic Opportunity Act of 1964 authorized less than $1 billion, but it bestowed great discretionary power upon the Office of Economic Opportunity (OEO) to carry out its assignment. Of the four programs discussed below, only the Job Corps was spelled out in some detail by the enabling legislation. A second, the Community Action Program, was mentioned in the 1964 Act, but the nature of the community organization and the content of its program were left vague. The two others, Head Start and Legal Services, originated within OEO and only later received congressional sanction. Together they represented the main thrusts of the War on Poverty and their experiences revealed the strengths and weaknesses of the equality-of-opportunity ideal in the real world.

It was no accident that Title I of the 1964 Act established the Job Corps. More than any other single program, it expressed the War on Poverty's central idea of preparing poor people, by concentrated education and vocational training, to do the kind of labor for which society would pay them a decent wage. The Job Corps offered school dropouts a chance to live, learn, and work in a completely fresh setting where the poverty cycle could be broken. By focusing on the 16-to-21-year age group, the Job Corps could relieve the immediate problem of juvenile delinquency and establish the base for permanent elimination of deprivation.[16]

Expectations outran accomplishments. Part of the difficulty stemmed from administrative mishaps. Even before it had opened its training center, the Job Corps embarked on an extensive national advertising campaign to interest young people. Unfortunately, the response far exceeded the Corps' ability to process inquiries, with the resulting delays dampening the enthusiasm of potential enrollees. In time, as the Corps' problems multiplied, it would have trouble recruiting trainees. Limited to sites on abandoned military installations, many of the training centers were located near small communities unhappy with the influx of unruly big-city youths. Widely reported accounts of violent encounters between Corpsmen and local residents seriously damaged the program's public image. The question of how much discipline the government could and should impose upon the Corpsmen remained a sore spot.

But the woes of the Job Corps ran deeper than uncertain management. A basic concern was money. In 1967 the annual cost of supporting a Corpsman ran to more than $8,000, higher than the expense of sending a student to Harvard. Conservative critics of the program were quick to charge boondoggle, but as the director of the Job Corps pointed out, the comparison was unfair. Indeed, he offered to pay personally for any Job Corps enrollee accepted by Harvard; no occasion arose for him to make good. Total remediation of the underclass did not come cheap, and the public enthusiasm for equal opportunity definitely cooled when the bills started to come in.

Support for the Job Corps might have continued if evidence of substantial progress could have been produced, but it could not. Dropout rates were high, and most who finished were only marginally better off in terms of jobs and wages than applicants who had decided not to enroll. The Corps' lack of success stemmed from the types of training it offered recruits. Working with educationally deprived individuals, the Corps could prepare them only for jobs in service-related fields where pay and stability were low. Despite promises about new careers and lives, the Job Corps was unable to move into skilled occupations or anticipate the coming opportunities in high technology. Even friends of the Job Corps were hard pressed to defend its performance: "Some rather heroic assumptions are required to demonstrate a positive rate of return on the Job Corps investment."[17]

If the Job Corps proved to be a jammed gun in the War on Poverty's arsenal, the Community Action Program (CAP) became its loose cannon. What had originally been touted as an instrument for more efficient local coordination of extensive federal effort turned into a federally supported device for challenging the local political and welfare federally supported device for challenging the local political and welfare structure. The ruckus CAP created was blown far out of proportion to the threat it actually posed, but the bad publicity dealt the War on Poverty a blow from which it never recovered.

The economists and management experts who were responsible for the inclusion of the community action idea on the agenda of the presidential task force that drafted the 1964 bill envisioned CAP as a way to bypass the creaky federal bureaucracy. Working under a White House mandate to get results without spending much money, these officials were in no mood to see the War on Poverty strangled in the Washington department-bureau-division-agency maze. The localities knew better than any desk-bound federal bureaucrat about their own specific needs and what would perform well in the field. Proponents of CAP envisaged it mainly as a planning agency; to the extent CAP also included administrative responsibilities, its supporters, without giving the matter much thought, assumed that the local Community Action Agency (CAA) would function as an adjunct of the existing political and service establishment.[18]

Others involved in the 1964 task force—including Richard Boone and Sanford Kravitz, who were to assume key posts in the agency, and Richard Cloward and Lloyd Ohlin, authors of an influential work on delinquent gangs—saw CAP in a different light. Planning and coordination were fine as long-range objectives, but what CAP really should do was shake up the establishment. If the culture of poverty was to be destroyed, the poor had to take control of their own lives. Politicians exploited the underclass, and the traditional public welfare and voluntary social service agencies victimized them. Only by confronting these sources of community pathology and by forcing significant institutional change could the underclass hope to improve its position. Conflict, not cooperation, ought to be CAP's *modus operandi*. Three words, "maximum feasible participation," referring to the role of the poor in the program, inserted into the 1964 Economic Opportunity Act with virtually no discussion among the bill drafters and with no debate at all during congressional consideration of the measure, supplied the rationale for this reorientation of CAP's activities. Community action agencies were not simply to provide the poor with better services; they were to involve the poor in every phase of their operations.[19]

Circumstance and personnel favored the challenge approach over the coordination mission. Congress dispersed antipoverty funds to several different old-line agencies with no mandate to link their activities to CAAs; OEO itself further undermined CAP by moving directly into program administration, giving short shrift to local determination. Bereft of any managerial function, CAP became a magnet for those who saw its potential for organizing the poor along political and direct-action protest lines. The temper of the times was certainly favorable. The civil rights movement, with its grass-roots mobilization of a subordinate racial minority, had taken to the streets to stir the white majority out of its social complacency. Using similar tactics the poor could shake up affluent America to bring about a fairer division of the economic pie—except that in this fight, the mobilization of the oppressed group would take place under the auspices of the federal government.[20]

It did not take long for local politicians to recognize and respond to the threat. Accustomed to dealing with the underclass through middle-class and professionally dominated charity and welfare groups, the mayors were extremely unhappy with demands from CAP administrators that the poor themselves sit in representative numbers on CAA boards of directors. Nor were the mayors pleased to find CAP encouraging CAAs to become actively involved in politics and to organize demonstrations against municipal agencies. As the direction of CAP's policies became evident in 1964 and 1965, local political leaders descended upon Washington insisting that CAP be reined in.

The President and Congress obliged. Neither branch of the federal government had foreseen CAP's rabble-rousing activities (it was ironic, a top official of the 1964 task force later observed, that "in a community as sensitive to the problems of the distribution and transmission of power as Washington, the power potential—constructive and destructive—of the poor themselves was largely overlooked"), and when apprised of what was happening they put pressure on OEO to tame CAP.[21] Although the maximum feasible participation requirement continued, CAP accepted the primacy of local governmental structures in the antipoverty war. When in 1967 the Congress gave City Hall the option of taking over and operating CAAs, few mayors took advantage of the opportunity—they had already neutralized them.[22]

Before being brought under control, CAP had done the War on Poverty irreparable harm. The strategy of confrontation, as much as it riled politicians and bureaucrats, disturbed the affluent majority even more. It was one thing for southern blacks to protest against a morally indefensible system of legally enforced segregation; it was quite another for northern urban blacks to attack those very institutions that were trying to help them. The underclass were ingrates—and worse. The outbreak of rioting in black ghettos was associated in the white, middle-class mind, unfairly to be sure, with the provocative behavior of the CAAs; arousing the poor, it seemed, only reinforced their proclivity for anti-social action. Instead of being intimidated by the violence, the political system maintained sharp restraints on the funds to be spent on providing opportunity.[23]

Nonetheless, CAP still had some virtues. Although many of its architects had been guilty of a "certain amount of naive and sentimental projection of spontaneous capacities among the poor,"[24] CAP served as an important training ground for the development of an indigenous leadership for the underclass, particularly blacks. Many participants would find it difficult to avoid being coopted by the establishment, but others would provide the cause of the poor with the authentic and articulate spokesmen it had previously lacked.[25] CAP also supplied a forum for previously invisible issues: How, in fact, did the government function? Were charitable and public welfare agencies really doing the poor a favor? Finally, CAP had exposed a dark side of American life. No sensitive person could ever again look at American political and social institutions with an unshakable presumption of their beneficence.

The Community Action Program's campaign to create equality of political opportunity gave the generals in the War on Poverty endless headaches; by contrast, Head Start provided the antipoverty effort with perhaps its one unblemished public relations triumph. Unfortunately for the poor, these rave press notices were not matched by substantial gains in equality of educational opportunity. Probably more than any other program, Head Start demonstrated the limits of the services strategy.

Head Start represented another step in the evolution of American public education. Free primary and secondary schools and compulsory attendance laws reflected the traditional American belief that education laid the groundwork for personal success and, therefore, should be available to all. What researchers had discovered by the early 1960s, however, was that, although poor children might attend classes, they got little out of them because of cultural and physical disabilities. Compensatory education for those already in school would certainly help (Title I of the Elementary and Secondary Education Act provided federal funds for this),[26] but an even better strategy was to strike at poverty where "it hits first and most damagingly—in early childhood." By taking preschoolers (age 3-6) away from their underprivileged surroundings, giving them good health care, feeding them nutritious meals, and exposing them to intellectual stimulation, Head Start would promote the emotional, social, and cognitive development of the children of the poor so that they would have a better chance to succeed in school. Under pressure from Congress, and needing a program to spend the antipoverty money already appropriated, OEO gave the go-ahead in early 1965 for this "prep school" for poor kids. In terms of popular opinion, OEO soon found it had a winner on its hands, and Head Start funding and enrollments grew dramatically. [27]

Unlike the Job Corps and CAP, which quickly fell from public and political grace, Head Start maintained its favored status all through the Johnson years and beyond. But social scientists began to have their doubts about the program before the 1960s were over. Research results released in 1969 disclosed that, although Head Start participants entered first grade with greater learning readiness than children of the same socioeconomic status who had not been in Head Start, by the third grade these advantages had "faded out." In the absence of highly structured "follow through" programs, Head Start returned practically no benefit. Later studies came to only slightly more positive conclusions, leading one early childhood educator to observe: "An effective early intervention program for a preschool child, be it ever so good, cannot possibly be viewed as a form of inoculation whereby the child is immunized forever afterward to the effects of an inadequate home and a school inappropriate to his needs." Head Start could not break the cycle of poverty alone, but it could help and, since its very young clients were not the disturbers of the peace who moved into Job Corps and CAP, it would be allowed to carry on. [28]

Not only did the War on Poverty fight to revive equality of opportunity in the familiar areas of economics, politics and education, but it also extended the crusade into a new field that in the American framework might even be considered the most basic of all: the legal system. Proud to be a nation not of men but of laws, the United States had long before committed itself to the principle of equal justice. But as Attorney General Robert F. Kennedy told a law school audience in the spring of 1964: "To the poor man, 'legal' has become a synonym simply for technicalities and obstruction, not for that which is to be respected. The poor man looks upon the law as an enemy, not as a friend. For him the law is always taking something away." [29] If the culture of poverty was to be shattered, the poor had to have respect for the law, and for that to happen the legal process would have to begin treating the poor fairly.

This front of the antipoverty war could not bring total victory on its own, but it witnessed some of its most notable successes and would furnish the redoubt for continuing the struggle in the 1970s.

The activities of OEO's Legal Services Program fell into two distinct categories. The first, and less glamorous, type consisted of providing poor people with assistance in civil matters, including sales contracts, wage garnishments, housing rental agreements, and domestic relations. Because of their deficient education and strapped financial condition, the poor were easy prey for unscrupulous merchants and landlords who supplied them with shoddy goods and accommodations at inflated prices. The poor were caught in a web of debt, broken-down merchandise, and legal entanglements that only added further to their deprivation and despair. By supplying the poor with expert advice on a case-by-case basis, the Legal Services Program could redress this imbalance in the judicial process.

The other dimension of Legal Services stresses law reform as "bringing about changes in the structures of the world in which poor people live in order to provide a legal system in which the poor enjoy the same legal opportunities as the rich." Instead of merely alleviating the immediate problems of the poor, legal reform sought to design new tools that would emancipate the poor from their economic, social, and psychological imprisonment. Through class-action suits, advocacy of legislation, and appearances at all sorts of administrative hearings, Legal Services lawyers pushed to expand the constitutional and statutory rights of the underclass. Those few people who kept close watch on public affairs were treated to the extraordinary spectacle of one part of the federal government suing and lobbying other parts of the governmental apparatus—federal, state, and local. Because these decorous confrontations occurred in courtrooms and legislative chambers, unlike the dramatic and often violent CAP-backed demonstrations, the Legal Services challenges largely escaped public notice. Politicians and bureaucrats grasped rather quickly the dangers legal reform posed, but it took some time for them to mobilize forces to stop it at the source. In the meanwhile Legal Services scored some important victories.[30]

At the United States Supreme Court the most impressive breakthrough came in the field of welfare law. The prevailing legal doctrine in the early 1960s held that as recipients of charity, people on welfare were subject to virtually any restriction that program administrators might wish to impose. Hence in 1966, when welfare clients sought a federal court order barring District of Columbia welfare officials from using "harsh, illegal and humiliating methods" of investigating eligibility, the

District judge dismissed the suit, in part, because "payments of relief funds are grants and gratuities. Their disbursement does not constitute payment of legal obligations that the government owes. Being absolutely discretionary, there is no judicial review of the manner in which that discretion is exercised."[31] But in a 1970 case brought by Legal Services lawyers, the Supreme Court ruled that, under the Fourteenth Amendment, welfare recipients were entitled to certain due-process safeguards, such as notice and hearing, before benefits could be terminated. "It may be realistic today," declared the Court, "to regard welfare entitlements as more like 'property' than a 'gratuity.' Much of the existing wealth in this country takes the form of rights [as examples the Court cited the licenses issued to doctors and lawyers permitting them to practice, the broadcasting licenses granted to radio and TV stations, and Social Security pensions] that do not fall within the traditional common law concepts of property. . . . Public assistance is not mere charity, but a means 'to promote the general welfare, and secure the Blessings of Liberty to Ourselves and Our Posterity.' " The same governmental interests that "counsel the provision of welfare," concluded the Court, "counsel as well its uninterrupted provision to those eligible to receive it; pretermination evidentiary hearings are indispensable to that end."[32] At about the same time, Legal Services attorneys also won Supreme Court decisions overturning state laws imposing residency requirements for welfare aid and the man-in-the-house rules in effect in many states.[33] The poor had found their advocates, and the legal system responded.

But there were limits to the Supreme Court's activism. In a 1970 ruling, the Court rejected the contention of Legal Service lawyers that the Equal Protection clause of the Fourteenth Amendment required the states to provide welfare recipients with a decent level of support. Sweeping aside the argument that the state classification scheme under challenge violated the Constitution because it resulted in inequality, the Court upheld the states' fundamental right to set and change welfare standards: "The intractable economic, social and even philosophical problems presented by public welfare assistance programs are not the business of this Court."[34] The following year the high court held that, the Fourth Amendment notwithstanding, a state could terminate welfare benefits because a recipient refused to allow caseworkers entry into her home.[35] Although hardly a complete return to the old idea of welfare as a privilege, these decisions revealed the fragility of an antipoverty strategy based on judicial lawmaking.

The courtroom triumphs of the California Rural Legal Assistance (CRLA) program provoked a political controversy that eventually insured the survival of Legal Services, but also narrowed its scope. Through a series of suits, CRLA forced the state of California to restore a $210 million cut in the program furnishing medical care to the poor, required the Department of Agriculture to institute food stamp programs in twenty-one counties that had not signed up for this aid (thus making California the first big state to have food stamp programs in every county), won new regulations liberalizing eligibility rules for the free school lunch program, and blocked the Department of Labor from allowing the entry of nonunion Mexican farm workers. Outraged by this legal assault on his conservative economic and social agenda, California Governor Ronald Reagan attempted to halt federal funding for CRLA in late 1970 by exercising his provisional veto authority. The final decision, however, lay with OEO headquarters in Washington, which appointed a special panel to study Reagan's charges of "massive irregularities" in CRLA; after this group concluded that the allegations were "unfounded and without merit," OEO kept the federal support coming.

But at heart the Nixon administration was not friendly toward Legal Services; in addition to freezing its budget, the Nixon White House sought to strip Legal Services of its reformist instincts. Important areas of public policy would have been declared totally off-limits and the class-action technique all but eliminated. The "equal justice" appeal of Legal Services, however, still held on Capitol Hill, and the program continued in the form of an independent national corporation whose prime function was to bring legal aid to the poor, but whose ability to challenge the establishment, while restricted, remained.[36]

When Lyndon Johnson left the presidency in 1969, the War on Poverty, as he had conceived it, went with him. The equality-of-opportunity approach, which at the start struck strong ideological chords and demonstrated solid political appeal, proved weak in action. Some of its problems stemmed from external sources, most notably an expensive and divisive war in Southeast Asia, but the basic difficulties arose from within. What had seemed so traditional and simple turned out to be beyond the competence of the American system. "Having the power" to eradicate poverty, Johnson had told the nation in 1964, "we have the duty." Neither the power nor the duty were much evident over the next five years.

In seeking to elevate the underclass, the War on Poverty took on more psychological and sociological variables than it could capably handle. Although sometimes unfairly criticized as a "war against the poor,"[37] the Johnson program nevertheless envisioned significant behavioral changes among the poor. But there was no precedent for direct governmental promotion of this type of individual reform on a mass scale and, despite the optimism of the experts, social science did not possess all of the answers or even most of them. There may, indeed, have been a culture of poverty, although many were challenging that assumption by the end of the decade, but there were no easy answers for breaking it. Little was known, for example, about the subject of urban black poverty and no one involved in the drafting of the 1964 Act foresaw that blacks would be the focal point of their efforts. The War on Poverty was playing with fire; with the long hot summers of the mid-1960s, fueled in part by the rising expectations of the poor, it got burned.[38]

Entranced by the rightness of equality of opportunity, the framers of the War on Poverty overlooked its limits. Education and training sounded great, but even if these endeavors had proven more productive than the Job Corps and Head Start experiences actually were, could they solve the underlying problem that the American economy did not offer enough jobs at incomes above the poverty level? The overheating of the economy caused by the Vietnam War would help push some beyond the poverty line, but these gains would often prove temporary. And could equality of opportunity be separated from equality of result? Could there be true equality of opportunity as long as there remained wide disparities in regard to housing, jobs, and income? Massive government spending could bridge the gap, but the taxes to fund it would have to come from somewhere. In the beginning Johnson had promised, and may well have believed, that victory in the War on Poverty would cost the middle class nothing; by the close of his tenure, with the Poor People's Campaign having come and gone, practically no one believed it, and the fight for equality of opportunity died.

The struggle for equality of opportunity faltered because the American people and their government could not break old habits. Johnson had caught them both in a moment of weakness in 1964 and pushed through an innovative and tightly targeted program. But even at this peak of compassion for the poor, the traditional mechanics of politics prevailed. The President's legislation was "not a choice among policies so much as a collection of them"[39]: each of the departments with a clear stake in the War on Poverty received some of the benefits the measure bestowed. As the War settled in, protection of bureaucratic turf was joined by defense of the large, well organized interests in society, including big business.[40] The poor would have to share with their more fortunate fellows.

The fate of the Elementary and Secondary Education Act of 1965 illustrated how politics and callous administration distorted the War on

Poverty. It was the formula of using federal funds to help educate the children of the poor that finally broke the decades-old logjam blocking federal aid to the nation's schools, but once local school boards had their hands on the money, they rarely directed it toward compensatory education for the poor. The funds were used to finance general expenditures or to underwrite special programs that serviced children of all backgrounds. Rather than assisting the culturally deprived, the 1965 Act helped keep local taxes down.[41] In 1963 a staff member, Robert J. Lampman, wrote to the chairman of the President's Council of Economic Advisers: "Can we imagine spending twice as much public money on the education and health of poor children as we do on non-poor children? Perhaps it is fair to say that until we do we aren't dedicated to the eradication of poverty."[42] The nation did not and was not.

Although the War on Poverty proved to be deeply flawed and its concrete achievements all but impossible to measure (social science still lacks good evaluative tools), it did leave at least one very important legacy. After 1964 virtually no domestic policy could be debated without asking the question: "What does it do for the poor?" There were no assurances that the responses would be positive; indeed, there would be few positive responses in the years to come. Nevertheless, the underclass, however it might be mistreated, was no longer invisible.[43]

WELFARE REFORM: THE FAMILY ASSISTANCE PLAN

The underclass would not be invisible partly because by the close of the 1960s it was costing the American taxpayer billions of dollars in welfare payments. What had started out in the 1930s as a temporary program to tide over those physically unable to support themselves had, three decades later, turned into an administrative nightmare that seemingly cursed recipient and benefactor alike. The persistence of the welfare system actually reflected the failure of the whole range of social institutions (for example, education, health care, minimum wage legislation) that were designed to protect people from dependency, but with collapse of the equality-of-opportunity strategy, welfare became the only game in town. Perhaps because no one had anything good to say about it, welfare served as the vehicle for one of the most revolutionary proposals in modern American reform.

At the heart of the welfare mess of the 1960s was the program of Aid to Families with Dependent Children (AFDC). Begun by the New Deal to assist families who by disability or death of the breadwinner were without means, the program was supposed to be phased out as the social insurance system reached maturity. This scenario reflected the belief that poverty was only transitory, that with the end of the Depression and the return of prosperity, everyone would be employed and their families protected. But when prosperity returned, AFDC hung on. Instead of a West Virginia miner's widow, the typical—or so it seemed—welfare client of the early 1960s was a black, usually unmarried, mother in an urban ghetto. Concluding that the problems of the new welfare population sprang not from permanent physical misfortune but from general cultural deprivation, the Department of Health, Education and Welfare (HEW) urged a services strategy to rehabilitate the poor. Adopted by Congress in 1962, this approach prefigured the far more ambitious War on Poverty. Neither effort lived up to expectations.[44]

As the nation's mood turned increasingly sour in the mid-1960s, Congress moved away from casework to putting welfare mothers to work. Mirroring the popular view that many, if not most, on AFDC's rolls were sponging off the taxpayers, Congress in 1967 enacted a measure requiring AFDC parents and children over sixteen to find employment or join a job training program. Congress also provided an incentive by allowing welfare recipients to keep part of their earnings without losing public assistance. But neither the stick nor the carrot proved particularly effective: many on AFDC were truly unable to work and those who could found themselves in dead-end jobs or training. And in the meantime the AFDC rolls continued to increase as the poor became more assertive in their rights and welfare administrators exhibited greater willingness to bend rules.[45]

When Richard Nixon moved into the White House in 1969, the nation seemed swamped in a welfare crisis. For the first time in the nation's history, welfare had been an issue in the 1968 presidential campaign, and the new Chief Executive had pledged himself to overhaul a system with almost no defenders. Nixon's natural political allies, conservatives, attacked AFDC for its spiraling costs and encouragement of fraud and promiscuity. On the other side stood liberals who criticized welfare's failure to provide adequate monetary assistance to the needy and deplored the system's incentives for dissolution of families. Somewhere in between were the policy analysts in HEW and OEO who saw AFDC undermining work incentives. Because welfare recipients paid no taxes on their assistance payments but anyone else earning income had to pay some taxes, the AFDC system took away from its clients any desire to improve their situation and to start moving their way up the ladder of achievement. Out of this universal dissatisfaction with welfare there emerged a presidential decision to support a federally guaranteed income.[46]

Proposals for various forms of income maintenance had been advanced within the Johnson administration, but had been repeatedly rejected by the man at the top. In 1965 OEO submitted to the White House plans for a negative income tax that would establish a national income floor for poor families without a breadwinner and supplement the wages of the working poor. Such a program, OEO advised in 1966, could eradicate poverty in a decade, so that by 1976 the country could celebrate its 200th anniversary of political independence with a "new freedom from want." Interagency task forces, staffed by the Council of Economic Advisers, also supported the idea during the latter years of the Johnson presidency. The Chief Executive, however, would have none of it. Personally opposed to anything that smacked of a "handout," he also feared the political fallout the program would produce; Democrats were always sensitive to charges of expensive giveaways. Before leaving office Johnson appointed a blue-ribbon commission to study the subject, but its report, which endorsed a guaranteed income, would be delivered to his successor.[47]

What Lyndon Johnson would not do Richard Nixon did—thanks largely to the efforts of Daniel Patrick Moynihan. An academician with credentials in both sociology and political science, Moynihan attempted to frame social issues in a way politicians could appreciate. He had been involved, as an Assistant Secretary of Labor, in some of the planning for the War on Poverty, but he made his major mark on the Johnson administration with his 1965 analysis, "The Negro Family: The Case for National Action." Equal opportunity for blacks, Moynihan contended, did not hold out the promise of equal results with whites as long as the lower-class black family remained so unstable. Although Moynihan identified Depression-level unemployment among black men and archaic welfare rules as the primary source of this social catastrophe, his discussion of the Negro's mental health touched a raw nerve in the psyches of blacks and liberals; the study ignited a firestorm of criticism that divided the civil rights movement and hastened Moynihan's return to academia (after a brief unsuccessful fling into electoral politics).[48] From there Moynihan launched a savage assault on the services strategy of the War on Poverty (especially Community Action) and began developing his ideas about a national system of family allowances to all parents who lived with their children.[49] Unacquainted with the latter but immensely pleased by the former, Nixon invited Moynihan to join his White House staff as his chief adviser on social issues.

In moving the President in the direction of a guaranteed-income policy, Moynihan struck three major themes. First, he reinforced Nixon's dislike for the services approach of the War on Poverty by arguing that the Johnson program had subsidized middle-class professionals better than it served the poor. If money was to be spent to improve the condition of the underclass, the most efficient way was to funnel it directly to the intended beneficiaries with the fewest possible strings attached. Indeed, Nixon had little regard for social workers and was willing to accept a more expensive government program (within "reason") in place of welfare if it interfered less with the manner in which individuals ran their own lives. Second, Moynihan stressed that, however much a guaranteed income departed from the American work ethic, it would buttress a basic institution of American life: the nuclear family. Given adequate support the family (particularly the black family) could provide the framework for eliminating not only poverty but also most of the other ills afflicting society. And finally, Moynihan played to the President's sense of history. Here was an opportunity for Nixon to dominate public debate, to go ahead of Congress and the nation, to gain the attention of the whole world, to be the American Disraeli. It was all too enticing for Nixon to resist and, in the face of strenuous opposition from some of his top aides, he decided to proceed.[50]

The President's announcement, in a televised address in August 1969, of his Family Assistance Plan (FAP) set off a three-year legislative struggle that ranks among the most bitter and most confusing in the annals of American politics. It was bitter because the questions FAP raised went to the heart of affluent America's dilemma about the underclass and its lifestyle: What exactly did the affluent majority owe to the impoverished minority? Who was to blame for the plight of the poor—society as a whole or the poor themselves? Did the poor require greater externally imposed discipline or greater freedom? Conflicting answers were thrown back and forth with far greater passion than ever before because during the 1960s a strong sense of guilt had developed on one side and an equally strong sense of disgust on the other. And not only was FAP setting the customary middle-class disputants at each other's throats, but it also brought a new fighter into the arena: the underclass. For the first time the poor, through the grass-roots-based National Welfare Rights Organization, were playing an active role in the legislative process; but whatever advance this represented for the democratic system, it did not aid the fortunes of FAP. Given to overblown rhetoric and uncompromising stands, not at all surprising inasmuch as it was their future that was being debated and this was their initial foray into the corridors of power, the poor made accommodation extremely difficult.[51]

The confusion flowed from FAP's source, Nixon, and the way in which the President introduced his proposal. It was awfully hard for the poor and their middle-class liberal supporters to accept Nixon's advocacy of a guaranteed income at face value. Nothing over the decades had prepared them to view the President as a great reformer; rather they had come to expect tricks and deception—they simply did not trust him. Partisanship was another complication. Democrats who were sympathetic to the guaranteed-income approach, but had dared not promote it because of the anticipated political backlash, were thrown off balance by the President's initiative and never really recovered. With the executive and legislative branches controlled by opposing parties, posturing became as important as achievement. And then there was the television address in which Nixon had stressed FAP's "workfare" provisions: all able-bodied heads of recipient families, except mothers of preschoolers who could not get child care, would be required to accept work or training. But in the draft legislation he sent to Congress, the President proposed to keep AFDC and add food stamps as a supplement to FAP, thereby raising the income floor. Where then was the President's program to lead: to getting more people off welfare or to higher federal spending on the poor? Would the poor be forced to take low-paying jobs that would depress wage scales, as organized labor and liberals feared, or would the poor find in FAP a way to avoid menial employment, as businessmen and conservatives feared? With so much uncertainty, and with liberals demanding higher income guarantees, conservatives seeking tougher work rules, and the poor pushing both sides to more intransigent positions, FAP died in Congress.[52]

Nixon's hesitant direction of the lobbying effort for FAP had created doubts as to his commitment to that reform. But no such ambiguity surrounded his feelings and actions regarding federal efforts to open up the suburbs to low-income families. Since the establishment of federal housing programs in the 1930s, an essential feature had distinguished the assistance going to middle-income families from that flowing to the poor. Whereas the subsidies (for example, FHA and VA insured mortgages) received by the first group could be freely transmitted to every locality in the country through basically private mechanisms, those designed for the poor (such as public housing) were available only through the consent of local government. To break up the resulting concentration of the poor in central cities and to move them to healthier environments in suburban communities closer to jobs, the Johnson administration in 1965 urged a program of rent supplements that would operate independently of local governments. The measure barely squeaked through the House of Representatives, only to have no appropriations voted. When funds were approved the following year, an amendment had been added giving localities a veto over such projects. Two new subsidy programs contained in the 1968 Housing Act again raised the prospect of putting housing for the poor in the suburbs, but implementation of this Act would be the responsibility of the Nixon regime.[53]

Under the strong leadership of Secretary George Romney, the Department of Housing and Urban Development (HUD) attempted to use its popular water, sewer, and urban renewal assistance programs to persuade suburban communities to accept low-cost housing. HUD's operation began without publicity, but in the summer and fall of 1970, when officials of the Detroit suburb of Warren rejected the Department's demands that they alter their housing policies, and hundreds of angry protesters mobbed the Secretary's car after a meeting with the town's leaders, the matter became headline news. With Romney's policies undermining the G.O.P.'s strategy of wooing suburban voters, President Nixon announced in late 1970 that he believed that "forced integration of the suburbs is not in the national interest." The Chief Executive followed this up early in 1971 with the declaration that it was unconstitutional to use federal power to "break up [a] community . . . from the economic standpoint, because homes are too expensive for some people to move into." Nixon's stance effectively eliminated HUD's leverage, and in 1973 the newly reelected president ended all threat of "forced economic integration of neighborhoods" by dismissing Romney and terminating the 1968 subsidy programs.[54]

Like the President, the Supreme Court found no constitutional protection for the poor. In 1971 a 5-3 majority upheld an amendment to the California constitution requiring local referenda on government-financed low-income housing projects; in the absence of any evidence of racial discriminatory intent, the Court ruled, there was no basis for challenging the provision. Writing for the minority, Justice Thurgood Marshall pointed out that the amendment treated the poor differently than other groups, such as the aged, veterans, state employees, and persons of moderate income: none of the publicly assisted housing for these classes of citizens had to be submitted for voter approval. The measure "explicitly singled out low income persons to bear its burden" and, declared Marshall, "it is far too late in the day to contend that the 14th Amendment prohibits only racial discrimination; and to me, singling out the poor to bear a burden not placed on any other class of citizens tramples the values that the 14th Amendment was designed to protect."[55]

Marshall dissented again two years later when the Court refused to interfere with the system of local property taxation used to finance education in forty-nine of the fifty states. In 1971, in a suit argued by Legal Services lawyers, the California Supreme Court had ruled that the vast disparities between school districts as to tax resources and per student expenditures denied equal protection of the law under both the United States and state constitutions. But in a 1973 Texas case that relied solely on the Federal Constitution, the United States Supreme Court, by a 5-4 margin, refused to extend such protection. The core of the majority opinion was that education was not a fundamental right deserving of special safeguards, but it also contended that no specific group had suffered unfair treatment. Since the correlation of district property values and per capita district wealth was imperfect, the discrimination was not against the poor but against "a large, diverse and amorphous class," including even wealthy families living in property-poor districts. Such a class, unlike racial minorities or aliens, or women, was entitled to no exceptional consideration by the Court. For Marshall the decision represented "a retreat from our historical commitment to equality of educational opportunity."[56]

Equality of opportunity, educational or otherwise, was not a concept dear to the Nixon administration. The President dismembered and finally abolished OEO in 1974, thereby depriving the underclass of the one instrument of the federal government that had consistently fought for the poor. Most of the War on Poverty programs continued, but usually under the supervision of agencies serving other, better organized clienteles. As part of his proposed New American Revolution in 1971, Nixon also sought to lump funds for antipoverty programs with those for other federal endeavors into "block grants" that states and communities could spend pretty much as they wished. This dismantling of the categorical aid system was designed to service Nixon's white, middle-class, suburban constituency; if it had been widely accepted by Congress, it would have left the poor to the mercy of local majorities. But though the legislature was hesitant about tampering with the long established structure of federal aid, it was also unwilling to embark down the revolutionary road of income redistribution as marked out by FAP. The nation had not been prepared to spend the sums necessary to make equality of opportunity a reality; not surprisingly, it proved even less eager to favor the underclass with a program that lacked ideological legitimacy. The end of the 1960s and start of the 1970s witnessed a greatly expanded food stamp program and some liberalizing of welfare benefits, particularly for the aged and disabled, but the overall message of the Nixon period for the underclass was a negative one. Even more negative messages were to follow.

JOBS: CETA AND THE
FULL EMPLOYMENT AND BALANCED GROWTH ACT

The War on Poverty began in the rising tide of a robust economy. When Nixon presented his guaranteed-income plan in 1969 there was still talk of a peace dividend once the Vietnam War had ended. But two years later the War was still on, FAP was all but dead and the President had instituted wage and price controls. The 1970s were to be a decade of economic shocks for Americans: the conflict in Southeast Asia came home not only in the shape of thousands of coffins but also in the form of inflation; then the 1973 Yom Kippur War led to an oil embargo that jacked up energy prices and contributed to a worldwide recession; and ever increasing competition from foreign nations in overseas and domestic markets sharply reduced business profits and payrolls. If the affluent 1960s could at least consider helping the underclass, the hardpressed 1970s would see Americans too caught up trying to protect those who already had a stake in society to give much thought to those who did not. Stagflation sent the government into an area—direct job creation—not visited since the Great Depression; as in the 1930s, the poor would pick up only some crumbs.

The New Deal had inaugurated programs of public employment in order to sustain a dispirited working class; Lyndon Johnson's War on Poverty rejected such an approach to the underclass. Having just embarked on an expansionary fiscal policy, the President and his economic advisers were committed to the notion that a growing economy would supply the poor with jobs; any increase in federal taxes to finance a public employment program for adults would only be counterproductive. The urban ghetto riots and the resulting studies that stressed the unemployment and underemployment of neighborhood residents did not shake Johnson's conviction that "make work" endeavors were not the way to go. To the end he placed his faith in fostering employability rather than in assuring employment.[57]

Nixon shared Johnson's distaste for public jobs, but deteriorating business conditions caused him to change his stance. In 1970 the Democratic-controlled Congress, which in the late 1960s had been more sympathetic than Johnson to public employment, passed a bill setting up a jobs program to counter the rise in unemployment. The President vetoed the measure, mocking the "WPA-type jobs" that would have been created. The following year, with the economy still stagnant, Nixon signed public employment legislation. As with the 1930s effort, this program attempted to help those already in the work force who had suffered prolonged joblessness while it ignored the underclass. This oversight was partially rectified in the Comprehensive Employment and Training Act (CETA) of 1973. Satisfying Nixon's request that the numerous manpower training programs, including the Job Corps, be consolidated into a block-grant package, CETA also provided for extension of the 1971 public employment program with new eligibility rules giving special consideration to those on welfare.[58]

CETA served as the federal government's major economic stimulant for the rest of the decade. In view of the uneven performance of the economy over that period, it was something less than a cure-all. If CETA's macroeconomic effects were marginal, so too were its specific effects for the underclass. Thousands of the poor did get on CETA payrolls, but their employment tended to be temporary. Like the Works Progress Administration before it, CETA tried to spread too few jobs among too many people and, compared to WPA, probably fell victim to greater patronage abuses. Congress continued to fund CETA despite President Ford's opposition because it saw no alternative, and the underclass got some help, but it was a stop-gap and little else.[59]

The mid-1970s witnessed one legislative attempt to regain control of the economy and assist the underclass: the Full Employment and Balanced Growth Act, better known as the Humphrey-Hawkins bill. Initially proposed in 1974, the measure gained political steam in the presidential election year of 1976. Humphrey-Hawkins proposed to commit the federal government to achieving an unemployment rate of 3 percent within four years and to establish the federal government as the "employer of last resort" for all Americans "able, willing and seeking to work." It also required the President to prepare a comprehensive program to reduce the chronic under-utilization of human resources in especially depressed areas of the country and among targeted groups in the labor force. This was to be a new war on poverty through jobs.[60]

As a candidate for the White House, Jimmy Carter (unlike Nixon's successor, Gerald Ford) had embraced the goals of the Humphrey-Hawkins bill, but once in office he scuttled its specifics. Carter had his own legislative priorities, including energy, welfare and tax reform, and government reorganization, which left little room for an intensive executive push for full employment. Nor was Carter prepared to accept the perils that an expensive jobs program would pose to his anti-inflation plans. By the time the President and Congress had finished manhandling the Humphrey-Hawkins bill, it had been turned into a collection of hollow promises that Carter and his successor ignored.[61]

Although rendered toothless, Humphrey-Hawkins had at least become law; not so with Carter's welfare reforms. Neither so ambitious nor so radical as FAP, the Carter proposals nevertheless struck the same themes of simplification, pro-family, and pro-work. They called for the setting of national minimum benefits, the consolidations of programs with an emphasis on cash payments, and the creation of jobs for the poor. The old FAP battlelines quickly reappeared, with liberals demanding higher benefits and conservatives stiffer work rules. Significantly, the poor themselves were not major participants. Years of frustration and hardship had taken their toll on the underclass, and it no longer had its own voice. Nor did welfare reform have a strong champion in the White House. Overwhelmed by the complexity and dilemmas of the system (how, for example, to raise benefits without destroying work incentives, while also making sure that no one got hurt by the changes) and unwilling to spend the funds to overhaul it, Carter let welfare reform die a quick and quiet death in congressional committee. Whatever passion the problem and sins of the underclass had generated a decade earlier had given way to a sense of helplessness.[62]

TRICKLE DOWN: REAGANONOMICS

Whereas the 1970s had been marked by indecision, the 1980s began with a renewed sense of mission. In electing Ronald Reagan, the American people chose a Chief Executive whose philosophy of government ran counter to the trends not just of the previous fifteen years but also of the past half-century. Reagan believed the federal government should do less, not more, claiming that to a greater degree than any other culpable party the national government was responsible for the economic difficulties of the 1970s. For the underclass this meant the new president not only would cut back assistance programs in the name of free enterprise, but would also blame the poor and the government for their poverty. If Johnson, Nixon, and Carter had accepted the idea that social and economic conditions beyond the control of the underclass were the main cause of its distress, Reagan focused on individual failings and argued that the underclass would never rise until it ceased its dependence on public handouts and stood on its own two feet.[63]

Demonstrating the same drive and leadership Lyndon Johnson had shown in constructing the Great Society, Reagan set about destroying it. Both presidents relied upon tax cuts to advance their designs, but whereas Johnson's fiscal policy looked forward to higher revenues to finance expanded social programs, Reagan's trickle-down strategy required big slashes in domestic spending to keep deficits manageable. Almost no social program was immune to Reagan's budget axe, including those that aided middle class families, but the underclass suffered disproportionately. Congressional Democrats put up some resistance to Reaganomics, but generally the President prevailed. CETA jobs were eliminated, welfare rules tightened, food stamp eligibility curbed, the Job Corps abolished, Head Start and educational appropriations cut back, the remnants of community action interred, and legal services (in an act of political revenge) shackled. Sensitive to the lingering compassion of the 1960s, the President defended his policy by insisting that a "safety net" remained in place. But for all practical purposes Reagan had returned the problem of the underclass to where it had been before 1900: the private sector.[64]

WHITHER THE UNDERCLASS?

In the public mind, the label "American underclass" has always been a contradiction in terms. For a country as rich as the United States and so imbued with the ideals of liberty and justice, it was inconceivable that there might exist millions of people who enjoyed little of the nation's wealth or constitutional blessings. Even as the country's political institutions attempted to deal with this group and its problems, there was scant popular perception of what elected leaders and their expert advisers were doing. Neither of the two innovative approaches advanced during this era, Johnson's War on Poverty or Nixon's guaranteed income, flowed out of any significant public discussion. Both emerged full-blown from the heads of social scientists with access to the Oval Office. The first cleared its legislative hurdles before anyone quite knew what happened, but in the field the absence of strong popular support would deny the War on Poverty any important victories. Nixon's initiative ran into such intense crossfire that it never left Capitol Hill, revealing once again the huge gap that separated the politicians and the public. If Reagan's handling of the underclass should continue to receive popular approbation, then finally the government and the people would, after nearly twenty years, be back on the same tack: believing the underclass really does not exist, and if it does it must shift for itself.

Although the War on Poverty and guaranteed-income strategies differed greatly, they shared a common problem: they asked too much of the overwhelming majority of Americans who were not part of the underclass. Despite the historical commitment of Americans to equality of opportunity, when the promises had to be kept, there was little public willingness to make the necessary sacrifices. Perhaps things might have been different if the war in Vietnam had not drained both the nation's resources and its spirit, but it is also possible that Vietnam served as a convenient excuse for not facing up to the very real changes that true equality of opportunity would entail. The War on Poverty at least had mythology on its side for a while. The guaranteed-income plan had little beyond its pledge to get the underclass off the welfare rolls on to the work rolls. If FAP had been only this it might have passed, but it also had redistributive consequences that proved too radical for the American political system to accept. In 1968, on the eve of the great debate on FAP, a liberal policy analyst wrote that it would be "unsound public policy to deprive multitudes of children of the sustenance they require to grow into healthy and self-sustaining adults in their own time in order to punish those of their parents' generation who may be considered to deserve such punishment in our time."[65] But the Puritan ethic prevailed, and punishment took priority over sustenance. The G.O.P. platform in 1972 rejected as "unconscionable the idea that all citizens have a right to be supported by the Government."

Even the goal of providing jobs proved unattainable. At the crux of the plight of the underclass was the lack of relatively stable, decent paying employment within their levels of skill. There had never been enough such jobs, even in the flush times of the 1960s. The 1970s would find them in even shorter supply. And with the general economic malaise of the latter decade, the special problems of the underclass received scant attention. Looting in New York City during an electrical black-out in the summer of 1977 revealed the anger still smoldering along economic lines in the urban ghetto, but the middle class was too caught up in its own concerns to care much. If the racial disorders of the 1960s had helped seal the fate of the War on Poverty, then the middle-class tax revolt of the late 1970s, highlighted by California's Proposition 13, demonstrated that for the mass of Americans the provision of social services took second place to the protection of individual gains. Ronald Reagan rode the crest of this middle-class resentment against overbloated government to the White House.

In 1985, twenty-one years after Lyndon Johnson declared "unconditional war on poverty," the underclass is still with us. Why it is there and whether it is any better off than two decades ago remain disputed issues. It is widely accepted that by most physical yardsticks (for example, relative numbers, nutrition, health, and housing) the underclass has experienced improvement, although the Reagan cutbacks have certainly reduced some of the gains. Less susceptible to statistical analysis is the state of mind of the underclass. What damage have broken promises and unfulfilled expectations inflicted on American's outcasts? Are they even more unreachable than when this all started? Certainly the continuing rise in the proportion of black families headed by low income women is a sign that instead of catching up with mainstream America the underclass is falling further out of step.[66] And if the poor have suffered psychological losses, so have their would-be saviors. The optimism of the 1960s is long gone. Widening the avenue of opportunity proved tougher than anyone had imagined and experiments with guaranteed-income plans have shown very mixed results. Only the free enterprisers of the 1980s remain confident, and for them the underclass is an American anomaly best treated by being left alone.

1. "The American Underclass," *Time* 110 (29 August 1977): 14.

2. Ken Auletta, *The Underclass* (New York, 1982), xiii-xviii, 24-30.

3. For a good overview of how poverty has been seen in the United States, written on the eve of the developments described in this chapter, see Robert H. Bremner, "Poverty in Perspective," in *Change and Continuity in Twentieth-Century America*, eds. John Braeman *et al.* (Columbus, Ohio, 1964), 263-80. Also Michael B. Katz, *Poverty and Policy in American History* (New York, 1983).

4. Gunnar Myrdal, *Challenge to Affluence* (New York, 1963), 49.

5. See Stephen Thernstrom, *The Other Bostonians: Poverty and Progress in the American Metropolis, 1880-1970* Cambridge, Mass., 1973), 256-58; Oscar Handlin, "The Idea of Opportunity," *Public Opinion* 5 (June/July 1982): 2-4; Howard P. Chudacoff, "Success and Security: The Meaning of Social Mobility in America," *Reviews in American History* 10 (December 1982): 101-12.

6. Lyndon B. Johnson, *The Vantage Point* (New York, 1971), 71.

7. Dwight Macdonald, "Our Invisible Poor," *New Yorker*, 19 January 1963.

8. Not that Johnson ignored the middle class. His vision of the Great Society was essentially framed with improving the quality of life for middle class America.

9. See William E. Leuchtenburg, *In the Shadow of FDR* (Ithaca, New York, 1983), 134-47.

10. The most complete account of the origins of the Johnson program is Carl M. Brauer, "Kennedy, Johnson, and the War on Poverty," *Journal of American History* 69(1982): 98-119.

11. *Public Papers of the Presidents: Lyndon B. Johnson, 1963-1964* (Washington, 1965), 1:114, 376; *Economic Report of the President, 1964* (Washington, 1964), 77.

12. Lester Thurow, "Discussion," in *A Decade of Federal Antipoverty Programs*, ed. Robert H. Haveman (New York, 1977), 118; James Tobin, "The

Political Economy of the 1960s," in *Toward New Human Rights: The Social Policies of the Kennedy and Johnson Administrations,* ed. David C. Warner (Austin, Texas, 1977), 33-36; *Public Papers,* 1963-1964, 1:114.

13. Michael Harrington, *The Other America* (New York, 1962), 15-18; *Economic Report of the President,* 1964, 55, 69-71. For a critique of the "culture of poverty" approach, see James T. Patterson, *America's Struggle Against Poverty, 1900-1980* (Cambridge, Mass., 1981), 115-25.

14. See Lance Liebman, "Social Intervention in a Democracy," *Public Interest,* no. 34 (Winter 1974): 14-15.

15. A good overview of the politics of congressional action is James L. Sundquist, *Politics and Policy* (Washington, 1968), 145-49.

16. Adam Yarmolinsky, "The Beginnings of OEO," in *On Fighting Poverty,* ed. James L. Sundquist (New York, 1969), 39, 50; Brauer, "War on Poverty," 106-7.

17. Sar A. Levitan, *The Great Society's Poor Law* (Baltimore, 1969), 273-306; Sar A. Levitan and Robert Taggert, *The Promise of Greatness* (Cambridge Mass., 1976), 144-46, quote on p. 146.

18. Brauer, "War on Poverty," 110-11.

19. The literature on the origins of CAP and the "maximum feasible participation" requirement is voluminous. An excellent summary is Allen J. Matusow, *The Unraveling of America: A History of Liberalism in the 1960s* (New York, 1984), 107-26.

20. Paul E. Peterson and J. David Greenstone, "Racial Change and Citizen Participation: The Mobilization of Low-Income Communities Through Community Action," in *A Decade of Federal Antipoverty Programs,* 242-56.

21. Yarmolinsky, "Beginnings of OEO," 50.

22. For CAP's rise and fall, see Matusow, *Unraveling of America,* 243-70.

23. See James W. Button, *Black Violence: Political Impact of the 1960s Riots* (Princeton, 1978), 42-44.

24. Kenneth Clark, "Community Action and the Social Programs of the 1960s," in *Toward New Human Rights,* 104.

25. Robert A. Levine, "An Overview of the Policies and Programs to Guarantee a Decent Standard of Living," in *Toward New Human Rights,* 68-70; Peterson and Greenstone, "Racial Change and Citizen Participation," 269-76.

26. Title I of the Elementary and Secondary Education Act of 1965, which Johnson considered an integral part of his War on Poverty, provided Federal funds for remedial education; see below, pp. 122-25.

27. Levitan, *Great Society's Poor Law,* 133-63, quote on p. 135.

28. Henry M. Levin, "A Decade of Policy Developments in Improving Education and Training of Low-Income Populations," in *A Decade of Federal Antipoverty Programs,* 153-55, quote on p. 155.

29. Quoted in Henry P. Stumpf, "Law and Poverty: A Political Perspective," *Wisconsin Law Review,* 1968: 696.

30. Earl Johnson. *Justice and Reform: The Formative Years of the OEO Legal Services Program* (New York, 1974), 128-34.

31. Cited in Rand E. Rosenblatt, "Legal Entitlement and Welfare Benefits," in *The Politics of Law*, ed. David Kairys (New York, 1982), 265.

32. *Goldberg v. Kelly*, 397 U.S. 254 (1970).

33. *Shapiro v. Thompson*, 394 U.S. 618 (1969); *King v. Smith*, 392 U.S. 308 (1968).

34. *Dandridge v. Williams*, 397 U.S. 471 (1970).

35. *Wyman v. James*, 400 U.S. 309 (1971). For the view that the Court's decision reflected a desire to protect a dependent child from a negligent and perhaps abusive mother, see Robert H. Bremner, "Other People's Children," *Journal of Social History* 16 (1983): 94.

36. Marlise James, *The People's Lawyers* (New York, 1973), 46-55; Ellen Jane Hollingsworth, "Ten Years of Legal Services for the Poor," in *A Decade of Federal Antipoverty Programs*, 297-98, 311-14.

37. See, for example, Michael Lewis, *The Culture of Inequality* (Amherst, Mass., 1978), 59-63.

38. Daniel Patrick Moynihan, *Maximum Feasible Misunderstanding* (New York, 1969), pp. 191-93; Henry Aaron, *Politics and the Professors: The Great Society in Perspective* (Washington, 1978); Charles R. Morris, *The Cost of Good Intentions* (New York, 1980), 61.

39. Moynihan, *Maximum Feasible Misunderstanding*, xv.

40. Samuel F. Yette, *The Choice: The Issue of Black Survival in America* (New York, 1971), 35-72.

41. Marion Wright Edelman, "Title I of ESEA: Is it Helping Poor Children?" in *Toward New Human Rights*, 347-49; Julie Roy Jeffrey, *Education for the Children of the Poor* (Columbus, Ohio, 1978).

42. Quoted in Brauer, "War on Poverty," 107.

43. Robert J. Lampman, "What does it do for the poor?—a new test for national policy," *Public Interest*, no. 34 (Winter 1974): 66-82.

44. See Patterson, *America's Struggle Against Poverty*, 67-71, 85-91, 129-33.

45. Ibid., 171-83.

46. Vincent J. and Vee Burke, *Nixon's Good Deed: Welfare Reform* (New York, 1974), and Daniel Patrick Moynihan, *The Politics of a Guaranteed Income* (New York, 1973) are the major sources for the discussion of the background to and debate over the Family Assistance Plan.

47. Tobin, "The Political Economy of the 1960s," 46; U. S., President's Commission on Income Maintenance, *Poverty and Plenty: The American Paradox* (Washington, D.C., 1969).

48. See Lee Rainwater and William L. Yancey, *The Moynihan Report and the Politics of Controversy* (Cambridge, Mass., 1967).

49. *Maximum Feasible Misunderstanding* (New York, 1969).

50. Richard Nixon, *RN: Memoirs* (New York, 1978), 424-27; Rowland Evans and Robert Novak, *Nixon in the White House* (New York, 1971), 223-30.

51. Nick Kotz and Mary Lynn Kotz, *A Passion for Equality: George A. Wiley and the Movement* (New York, 1977), 261-78.

52. For a good brief impressionistic account of the conflicting currents

around FAP, see Jonathan Schell, *The Time of Illusion* (New York, 1975), 47-49. Also Patterson, *America's Struggle Against Poverty,* 192-97.

53. Michael N. Danielson, *The Politics of Exclusion* (New York, 1976), 205-13.

54. Ibid., 213-36.

55. *James v. Valtierra,* 402 U.S. 137 (1971).

56. *Serrano v. Priest,* 5 Cal. 3d 584 (1971); *San Antonio Independent School District v. Rodriquez,* 411 U.S. 1 (1973); Robert W. Vennett, "The Burger Court and the Poor," in *The Burger Court,* ed. Vincent Blasi (New Haven, 1983), 53-55. In 1982 the New York Court of Appeals followed the Supreme Court's approach in interpreting that state's constitution; *New York Times,* 24 June 1982, A1.

57. Patterson, *America's Struggle Against Poverty,* 63-67, 141. James L. Sundquist, "Jobs, Training, and Welfare for the Underclass," in *Agenda for the Nation,* ed. Kermit Gordon (Washington, 1968), 54-55.

58. Levitan and Taggert, *Promise of Greatness,* 234-36.

59. Bernard I. Page, *Who Gets What From Government* (Berkeley, 1983), 83.

60. *National Journal* 8 (12 June 1976): 813.

61. *Ibid,* 9 (7 May 1977): 724; 9 (10 December 1977): 1930.

62. In his memoirs Carter mentioned his welfare reform program just once—in passing; *Keeping Faith* (New York, 1982), 84. For a critique of Carter's leadership, see Laurence E. Lynn, Jr, and David deF. Whitman, *The President as Policymaker: Jimmy Carter and Welfare Reform* (Philadelphia, 1981). An insider's view is provided by Joseph A. Califano, Jr., *Governing America* (New York, 1981), 320-67.

63. Ronnie Dugger, *On Reagan* (New York, 1983), 285-312; Laurence I. Barrett, *Gambling with History* (Garden City, N. Y., 1983), 401-14. See George Gilder, *Wealth and Poverty* (New York, 1981).

64. Sheldon Danziger and Robert Haveman, "The Reagan Budget: A Sharp Break with the Past," *Challenge* 24 (May/June 1981): 5-13; John L. Palmer and Isabel Sawhill, *The Reagan Experiment* (Washington, 1982); *New York Times,* 22 July 1983, A23; 26 August 1983, A12; 4 April 1984, A1.

65. Sundquist, "Jobs, Training, and Welfare for the Underclass," 74.

66. *New York Times,* 20 November 1983, 1; 27 November 1983, 4:4. For signs of growing interest in the problem by black organizations, nearly two decades after the Moynihan study, see *New York Times,* 7 May 1984, 8.

E Pluribus Unum: Civil Rights and National Unity

Steven F. Lawson

In early 1960 four black college students in Greensboro, North Carolina, challenged Woolworth's to serve them equally alongside whites at its lunch counter. The demands for justice seemed relatively simple then. If treated without regard to color, blacks were expected to take advantage of the available opportunities to free themselves from the bondage that had lasted a century beyond the end of slavery. The matter proved to be more complex. Although blacks would obtain equality before the law, they discovered that the law did not automatically confer equality. The barriers of racism fell, but the remnants of Jim Crow in political, social, and economic institutions kept blacks from competing equally with whites for positions of power and prestige. In seeking remedies for this vexing problem, blacks called into question the meaning of traditional notions of equality and suggested answers that inflamed anew racial animosities in the country.

The movement galvanized by the lunch counter sit-ins was a special kind of revolution. Southern blacks, segregated by law and custom and subject to unequal treatment, merely sought to gain the rights and privileges exercised by other Americans. They aspired not to overturn the system—unless it was the one that maintained apartheid—but, rather, to enter it as fully as possible. Desiring integration into American life, they pressed the nation to live up to its own democratic ideals of equal opportunity and justice for all. A charter member of the Student Non-Violent Coordinating Committee (SNCC), the interracial organization created in 1960 following the sit-ins, summed up the attitude of activists at the time. "The ache of every man to touch his potential is the throb that beats out the truth of the American Declaration of Independence and the Constitution, "Marion Barry declared. "We seek a community," the future mayor of Washington, D.C., asserted, "in which man can realize the full meaning of self which demands open relationship with others."[1]

No one expressed a greater commitment to interracial fellowship than did Martin Luther King, Jr. Having risen to prominence as a leader of the Montgomery bus boycott in 1955, the Reverend King moved on to his native Atlanta to guide the Southern Christian Leadership Conference (SCLC), a group dedicated to "achieving full integration of the Negro in all aspects of American life." From a variety of Christian and secular sources, including Jesus and Karl Marx, Walter Rauschenbusch and Reinhold Niebuhr, Friedrich Hegel and Mahatma Gandhi, Frederick Douglass and A. Philip Randolph, Dr. King constructed a set of strategic aims from which he rarely wavered. At the center of his objectives was the establishment of "the 'beloved community' in America where brotherhood is a reality." In working toward this end, SCLC had as its "ultimate goal genuine intergroup and interpersonal *living—integration.*"[2]

Martin Luther King's value to the civil rights movement came not so much as a philosopher but as a translator and communicator of ideas. He spoke to the intensely religious mass of southern blacks in language they could easily understand. His sermons took the message that blacks would find redemption for their suffering in the next world, the traditional preaching of black ministers, and transformed its meaning to the here and now. "One day the South will know that when these disinherited children of God sat down at lunch counters," he wrote, "they were in reality standing up for the best in the American dream and the most sacred values in our Judeo-Christian heritage."[3] At the same time, King's religious homilies contained soothing words for whites. Their emphasis on nonviolence, redemption, and reconciliation offered whites an opportunity to cleanse themselves of the sickness of racism and to live up to their democratic faith. This creed, which placed the main burden of suffering and loving one's enemies on blacks, posed little threat to white sensibilities. The historian August Meier attributed much of the influence of Dr. King to his "combination of militancy with conservatism and caution, of righteousness with respectability."[4]

In striving for inclusion into the mainstream of American life, blacks did not intend to relinquish their racial identity. W. E. B. Du Bois pro-

vided the classic analysis of the black yearning for assimilation and preservation. "One feels his twoness," Du Bois wrote in 1903,

> an American, a Negro, two souls, two thoughts, two unreconciled strivings;
> two warring ideals in one dark body, whose dogged strength alone keeps it
> from being torn assunder. . . . The history of the American Negro is the
> history of this strife,—this longing to attain self-conscious manhood, to
> merge his double self into a better and truer self. . . . He simply wishes to
> make it possible for a man to be both a Negro and American, without being
> cursed and spit upon by his fellows, without having the doors of Opportunity
> closed roughly in his face.[5]

The civil rights movement highlighted each element of this dualism. In
directly confronting racist institutions, blacks not only demanded full
equality as American citizens, but in the process they also heightened
their sense of worth individually and collectively. Franklin McCain, one
of the four students who originally sat in at the Greensboro Woolworth,
remarked: "I probably felt better that day than I've felt in my life. I felt as
though I had gained my manhood . . . and not only gained it, but
. . . developed quite a lot of respect for it."[6]

The tactics employed by the protesters enhanced the feeling that they
could determine their destiny. Customarily the objects of white-
controlled decision-making processes, Afro-Americans became active
participants in shaping events that directly affected them. As lawyers
and lobbyists working mainly through the National Association for the
Advancement of Colored People (NAACP), they had already won some
noteworthy judicial and legislative battles against discrimination in education, transportation, and the suffrage. By 1960, however, the South
had manufactured ways to contain these victories, and the majority of
blacks still endured segregation and disfranchisement. The adoption of
nonviolent direct-action campaigns enabled southern blacks to regain
the offensive. Such protest activities built grass-roots support among
blacks, thereby maximizing the human and financial resources available
to keep the challenges going. In addition, on the local level they circum-
vented the existing channels of communication between white elites and
traditional black leaders that had brought changes in race relations
gradually, paternalistically, and within a segregated context. Demonstrations forced white officials to deal with black demands that they
previously had not heard and would rather have avoided considering.[7]

Initially, the practitioners of nonviolent civil disobedience aimed their
efforts at convincing white southerners to abandon their Jim Crow
ways. Their optimism proved unfounded, and whites frequently reacted

with more brutality than brotherhood. Anne Moody, a black student at Tougaloo College in Jackson, Mississippi, described the perils that awaited demonstrators attempting to integrate Woolworth's lunch counter there. "We kept our eyes straight forward and did not look at the crowd except for occasional glances to see what was going on," she recalled.

> We bowed our heads, and all hell broke loose. A man rushed forward . . . and slapped my face. Then another man who worked in the store threw me against an adjoining counter. . . . The mob started smearing us with ketchup, mustard, sugar, pies, and everything on the counter. . . . About ninety policemen were standing outside the store; they had been watching the whole thing through the window, but had not come in to stop the mob or do anything.

She came away with this painful lesson: "After the sit-in, all I could think of was how sick Mississippi whites were."[8]

In areas of the region where civil rights activists did not encounter such vicious displays of prejudice, they found more sophisticated means of preserving white hegemony. In contrast with Jackson, civic leaders in places like Greensboro succeeded in moving protests off the streets and resolving disputes around a negotiating table. "Somewhere a Southern community must find a way to deal with civilities as well as civil rights," the Greensboro *Daily News* editorialized. Toward this end white officials hoped to avoid the violence that had plagued other cities, maintain the progressive image of their town as they pursued an economic and cultural renaissance, and preserve control over the pace of racial change. Led by influential businessmen in cooperation with moderate black leaders, these local communites dismantled some of the machinery of segregation, but only as much as necessary to keep the peace and head off a new round of disruptive protests. Such was the case in Tampa, Florida, one of the first cities in the South to create a biracial committee to settle disputes amicably. Reflecting the attitude of civic leaders, its principal newspaper asked: "What new industry would decide to go into a city which seethes with murderous racial conflict?" Nevertheless, not until passage of the 1964 Civil Rights Act were black Tampans permitted equal access to most of the "Cigar City's" hotels, restaurants, bowling alleys, and hospitals.[9]

This "middle way" did more to ensure peace and harmony than to promote justice. In raising their voices for moderation, white elites intended to continue exercising responsibility for local governance and not allow decisions to be dictated by civil rights militants or their extremist opponents. Although these enlightened urban communities discarded some of their blatantly racist practices, progress came unevenly.

Except for municipal facilities and large chain department stores, public accommodations remained segregated or off limits completely to black customers. Nowhere more than in education were the narrow bounds of voluntary cooperation exposed. Despite the historic *Brown* decision in 1954, most school districts in the South operated a dual system of education. States with progressive reputations, such as North Carolina, led the way in devising techniques that followed the letter of the law while violating its spirit. Attempting to present the illusion of desegregation, they adopted pupil placement regulations that permitted black students to apply for admission to previously white schools and allowed local school boards the option of turning them down for reasons other than race. In practice these so-called "freedom of choice" plans left the overwhelming majority of blacks to attend segregated schools as they had in the past.

Reliance on voluntary cooperation and goodwill had not brought blacks very far toward achieving their goals during the early sixties. If their situation had improved in a handful of progressive cities, it remained as bleak as ever in the rest of the South. Experience had proven that thoroughgoing social changes would not come without outside intervention. Since World War II the federal government had moved slowly and somewhat unsurely to the side of civil rights. Presidential orders by Harry Truman and Dwight Eisenhower had desegregated the armed forces and facilities on federal military installations in the South; Congress had enacted two civil rights laws dealing with disfranchisement; and the Supreme Court had toppled the doctrine of "separate but equal" in public education. However, by 1960 the national government had yet to use its powers forcefully enough to demolish racial discrimination in the South. Civil rights advocates, hoping to involve the federal government more fully in their cause, turned their attention increasingly to Washington.

The election of John F. Kennedy was auspicious. During his presidential campaign, Kennedy had staked out some advanced positions on civil rights. He threw his support behind the black protesters whose activities were shaking up the South. "It is in the American tradition to stand up for one's rights," he declared, "even if the new way is to sit down." Hurling criticism at Eisenhower for not providing moral leadership against racial bias, Kennedy remarked that "moral persuasion by the President can be more effective than force in ending discrimination against Negroes."[10] Not content to rely on rhetoric alone, he drew up a specific agenda to have ready if elected to the White House. It included the desegregation of federally-assisted housing "by the stroke of a presidential pen" and the drafting of legislative proposals to attack discrimination in education and the suffrage. Late in the campaign, the Democratic nominee dramatically portrayed his sympathy with the civil rights struggle. After Martin Luther King was arrested for a minor traffic offense following his participation in a demonstration in Atlanta, Kennedy telephoned the minister's wife to console her, and his aides helped secure her husband's release.[11] With this gesture Kennedy cemented the allegiance of the black electorate, which became a major factor in his slender margin of victory.

Once in office President Kennedy did not immediately translate his lofty campaign pledges into action. The chief executive backed away from incorporating into his legislative program the civil rights measures that had been drawn up at his initiative, and a bill to limit abuses in the administration of literacy tests for voting died on the congressional floor for lack of White House support. For nearly two years, the president failed to issue the promised executive decree against housing discrimination, prompting black skeptics to send him pens lest he had forgotten. Finally, in late November 1962, Kennedy issued an order, albeit a very limited one. Needless to say, his early record brought disappointment to black leaders who had been led to expect much more from the new president. Martin Luther King, previously the recipient of Kennedy's favor, nevertheless concluded that the White House "waged an essentially cautious and defensive struggle for civil rights."[12]

King's assessment hit the mark. Although Kennedy continued to express sympathy for the goals of the civil rights movement, he chose mainly to react to events rather than provide the kind of forceful executive leadership he had pledged. His priorities were elsewhere. He devoted much of his energy to matters of foreign policy, playing his role on the world stage with a daring he did not exhibit at home. In domestic affairs Kennedy felt hamstrung by the conservative coalition of southern Democrats and northern Republicans whose strategic grip on the legislative machinery had long frustrated reform. Furthermore, in waging the Cold War against the Soviet Union, Kennedy needed the support of these powerful lawmakers, and, thus, he sought to avoid offending their racial sensibilities. When the administration did move in a liberal direction on the legislative front, it preferred to fight for expansion of existing social welfare measures—such as minimum wages and social security—that would benefit blacks economically without directly raising the controversial racial issue.

However much Kennedy would have liked to postpone dealing with troublesome civil rights problems, he could not set the timetable for action. The struggle for black equality had gained a momentum all its own. Although five major organizations—NAACP, the Urban League, SCLC, SNCC, and the Congress of Racial Equality (CORE)—directed legislative and legal strategies, the impetus behind the demonstrations came at the local level. The Greensboro sit-in had given birth to hundreds of others, and these indigenous movements had devised wade-ins, kneel-ins, drive-ins, and other imaginative techniques to confront segregation directly. Building on this ferment from below, the NAACP, CORE, SCLC, and SNCC mobilized their forces to pressure the national government and to prick the consciences of whites throughout the nation to guarantee black emancipation.

The Kennedy Administration responded warily to the racial conflicts sparked by heightened black protests. Although believing in integration and worried that vicious displays of racism tarnished America's international image, the president nonetheless counselled moderation in handling civil rights disputes. Preferring reason to coercion and order to agitation, Kennedy hoped to persuade southern officials to act responsibly and to convince civil rights activists to refrain from participating in disruptive confrontations. "Tell them to call it off. Stop them," President Kennedy responded upon first hearing about a proposed interracial freedom bus ride through the South in 1961, and he remarked privately, "I don't think we would ever come to the point of sending troops."[13] The chief executive eventually did dispatch federal marshals to protect the freedom riders when they came under attack in Alabama, and in 1962 he mobilized the armed forces to quell an uprising at the University of Mississippi following the matriculation of its first black student, James Meredith. However, he did so only as a last resort. In such instances Kennedy hardly showed a greater willingness to throw the full weight of federal power behind the civil rights cause than had Eisenhower in Little Rock, and when he did react it was more to restore law and order than to recognize the justice of black demands.

As an alternative to disruptive civil disobedience campaigns, the Kennedy Administration offered the conventional enterprise of voter registration drives where the laws protecting the right to vote were clearly on the activists' side. Guaranteed by the Fifteenth Amendment, the suffrage was considered the cornerstone of the nation's democratic foundation. Furthermore, the franchise would foster racial progress in the orderly fashion that Kennedy found acceptable. The ballot also had great appeal for black strategists who believed that it might provide the key to unlock the door to liberation. "Give us the ballot," Martin Luther King declared in 1957, "and we will no longer have to worry the Federal government about our basic rights."[14] In 1962, to promote enfranchisement, the Kennedy regime encouraged the formation of the Voter Education Project, thereby bringing together white liberal philanthropic foundations and civil rights organizations to conduct suffrage drives in the South. At the same time, the Justice Department stepped up litigation in the courts against discriminatory registration practices.

The voting rights campaigns met with neither much success nor tranquility. Less dramatic than direct action protests, door-to-door canvassing of prospective registrants nevertheless aroused the same kind of white hostility that accompanied sit-ins and freedom rides. A virtual reign of terror existed in much of the rural southern black belt, where whites firebombed civil rights headquarters, cracked the skulls of suffragists, and jailed them for minor infractions of the law. The prospects in the judiciary were only slightly better. Although the Kennedy Justice Department brought suits against biased electoral practices, unsympathetic federal judges in the South threw them out of court or delayed processing them as long as possible. The civil rights forces felt this hurt even more because President Kennedy had appointed several of the most obstructionist judges. Although the efforts of the executive branch did increase the number of black names on the registration lists, the majority of blacks were still unable to vote.

By 1963 civil rights leaders had concluded that federal intervention would come primarily in response to crises. "Civil rights workers knew that so long as there was no disorder," the historian Catherine Barnes has noted, "the administration would not move vigorously."[15] Consequently, in May 1963 Martin Luther King led demonstrations in Birmingham to provoke a confrontation that would increase the pressure for federal action. His strategy worked. "Bull" Connor's police force broke up nonviolent protest marches with excessive force, and the use of attack dogs, water hoses, clubs, and cattle prods created an ugly scene. Racial tensions reached a breaking point when the home of Martin Luther King's brother and the headquarters of SCLC became the targets of firebombers, and in retaliation rampaging mobs of blacks temporarily abandoned nonviolence and assaulted white people and property. In June the situation was much the same in Jackson, where NAACP Field Secretary Medgar Evers was ambushed and killed by a sniper, precipitating a near riot by black mourners. Attempts by the Kennedy Administration to mediate these conflicts produced an uneasy peace but did not redress black grievances.

For two and one-half years, President Kennedy had tried to maintain a delicate balance between his personal commitment to the objectives of the civil rights movement and his political obligations to powerful southern leaders within his party. With racial turbulence rapidly rising, the president finally asked Congress to enact a comprehensive civil rights measure that would go a long way toward toppling discriminatory racial barriers and moving unruly demonstrations off the streets. Identifying the issue as essentially a moral one "as old as the Scriptures and . . . as clear as the American Constitution," he repeated the question that blacks had been raising for years as to "whether all Americans are to be afforded equal rights and equal opportunities, [and] whether we are going to treat our fellow Americans as we want to be treated."[16] Kennedy's answer was a bill to desegregate public accommodations, authorize the Justice Department to file school-desegregation litigation, allow the national government to withhold funds from federally-assisted programs that operated discriminatorily, and create a Community Relations Service to mediate racial disputes. Although these proposals were more extensive than ever before, Kennedy hesitated to request the establishment of an agency to challenge job bias for fear of further angering southern lawmakers. Nevertheless, liberal legislators succeeded in adding a provision for a permanent Equal Employment Opportunity Commission.[17]

Proponents of the bill waged an intensive lobbying effort on its behalf. The chief executive summoned to the White House business, civic, and religious leaders to rally their support. While the president maneuvered quietly in the Oval Office, civil rights activists dramatically mobilized their forces at a massive demonstration in the nation's capital. Fearing that such a mammoth gathering would "create an atmosphere of intimidation" for uncommitted congressmen, Kennedy had urged black leaders not to hold it. Once assured by the architects of the March on Washington of their peaceful intentions and willingness to forego acts of civil disobedience, Kennedy swung his approval behind the idea. The subsequent rally at the Lincoln Memorial on 28 August attracted nearly a quarter of a million people and much favorable publicity. In a dignified manner, it spotlighted the interracial vision of brotherhood that had characterized the early years of the struggle for civil rights. Eloquently reciting his dream of freedom and justice for all, Martin Luther King, in the words of the historian Harvard Sitkoff, "transformed an amiable effort at lobbying Congress into a scintillating historic event."[18] Nevertheless, neither the rhetoric of the popular president nor that of the charismatic civil rights leader was sufficient to secure passage of the bill. On

22 November the measure was still tied up in the House of Representatives.

The assassination of John F. Kennedy did not kill hope for enactment of the bill, and the battle for the proposal went on without him. Despite his limitations as a presidential advocate of civil rights, Kennedy had inspired youthful idealism in pursuit of racial justice. Even his critics acknowledge that there was greater progress in civil rights because Kennedy rather than Richard Nixon had been elected to the White House in 1960. Yet the civil rights movement had preceded Kennedy and would persist beyond his death. Indeed, the president could never quite catch up to the advancing civil rights forces and the demands they made, although he was getting closer when he died.[19]

Kennedy's successor took up where he had left off. A southerner from Texas, Lyndon Johnson had broken away from the segregationist positions taken by fellow politicians from the region. By the time he reached the White House, he displayed a moral fervor for civil rights that exceeded Kennedy's. Immediately upon taking office, President Johnson urged Congress to write the slain chief executive's epitaph by enacting the pending civil rights measure. A nation's grief alone, however, could not break the legislative logjam. After some eight months of painstaking efforts by the administration and its liberal allies on Capitol Hill, a bipartisan coalition finally overcame southern opposition to put through the law that President Johnson signed on 2 July 1964.

The successful outcome represented a stunning triumph for the principle of equal opportunity and the liberal faith in a color-blind society. Emphasizing integration, the 1964 law sought to foster the movement of Afro-Americans into the mainstream of economic and civic life by tearing down the most pernicious obstacles standing in their path. The lengthy debate on the bill reinforced the viewpoint that once the stigma of race was removed black citizens would be judged by virtue of their talents and abilities. Having maintained white supremacy throughout their history, southern opponents of the measure wanted assurance that racial classifications would not be imposed to benefit blacks. In response, the bill's supporters stressed that all individuals must be treated equally before the law regardless of race. Whether relating to school desegregation or job discrimination, the prevailing attitude could be described as favoring racial neutrality. Expressing this position Hubert Humphrey, the Senate floor manager of the legislation, acknowledged that the proponents were not seeking to achieve "racial balance" through "preferential treatment" or quotas.[20] Despite this sentiment the question had yet to be settled whether the federal government had to ignore racial considerations in fashioning remedies to remove the effects of past bias in education and employment.

Although victorious, the civil rights movement increasingly suffered from dissension within its ranks. During the summer of 1964 civil rights workers who gathered in Mississippi to promote voter registration wound up feuding among themselves and with the federal government. Racial and political concerns accounted for this friction that produced a growing strain between white and black fieldworkers. Many of the 700 college student volunteers who participated in the Freedom Summer came from white middle-class backgrounds and were better educated than their black compatriots from the South. Members of SNCC, the militant group in the forefront of the campaign, complained about white paternalism and questioned the commitment of college students who would return to their comfortable northern campuses after the summer. "Look at these fly-by-night freedom fighters bossing everybody around," a SNCC worker declared. Making matters worse, sexual relations between black males and white women aroused the ire of black females who considered their rivals "neurotic whites who sought to ease their guilt by permitting blacks to exploit them sexually and financially." Even the murder of three civil rights workers, two of whom were white, did not hold in check the burgeoning racial resentments.[21]

The rising anti-white feelings of black activists also extended toward their liberal allies in Washington. The Kennedy and Johnson administrations raised great expectations that remained unfulfilled, and the gap between promise and reality added to the physical and psychological pain inflicted upon civil rights workers in the South. The issue of federal protection of voter registration canvassers reflected this problem. The Kennedy Justice Department had encouraged civil rights organizations to undertake suffrage drives and had led them to believe that the government would provide protection. Justice Department officials did try to carry out their obligation but within narrow bounds. They preferred the cumbersome process of litigation and the use of Federal Bureau of Investigation agents as neutral observers rather than the deployment of federal marshals and the assignment of the FBI to an active role in combating racial harassment. Although the federal government retained the authority to intervene in local affairs when constitutional guarantees were threatened, it hesitated to do so for fear of creating a national police force. In contrast, civil rights groups argued that the Kennedy-Johnson regimes refused to act more forcefully for political reasons and accused them of holding back because they did not desire to alienate influential southern officials. Civil rights activists insisted that, having encouraged them in the first place, the federal government had a moral duty to ensure their safety. As the killings, beatings, and intimidation mounted, so did black disillusionment with white liberals.[22]

The abortive attempt of the Mississippi Freedom Democratic Party (MFDP) to gain recognition at the Democratic National Convention in 1964 accentuated the difficulties. Emerging from grassroots organizational efforts during Freedom Summer, the MFDP challenged the exclusionary racist practices of the regular state Democratic party and sought to replace it as the representative of the national party. Although the predominantly black Freedom Democrats made a strong moral case at the convention, and many thought a valid legal argument as well, President Johnson orchestrated a compromise that left them bitter. They were denied status as the official delegation from Mississippi, but two members of the group, one white and one black, were selected to sit as honored guests of the convention. Branding this a "back of the bus" sell-out, the MFDP was particularly unhappy with what it saw as white paternalism in naming the delegates to represent it.[23] Angry with a solution that elevated political over moral and even legal considerations, many of the black activists returned to the South with ever-increasing suspicions about alliances with white liberals.

These hostilities did not keep the interracial coalition from achieving one of its greatest triumphs. Behind the controversies over federal protection and seating the MFDP loomed the suffrage issue. By 1965 the imposition of literacy tests and poll taxes, reinforced by the application of physical and economic intimidation, had resulted in only 35 percent of eligible blacks signing up to vote. The Mississippi Freedom Summer had amply demonstrated the tenacity of southern officials in reinforcing these obstacles. Following enactment of the 1964 Civil Rights Law, President Johnson turned his attention to the suffrage problem and instructed the Justice Department to prepare legislative proposals for the next congressional session. The chief executive believed strongly in the right to vote, and he thought that once southern blacks were permitted to cast their ballots "many other breakthroughs would follow and they would follow as a consequence of the black man's own legitimate power as an American, not as a gift from the white man."[24]

Civil rights leaders also shared this premise. For several years SNCC fieldworkers had been operating a voter registration drive in Dallas County, Alabama, an area with a black population majority but virtually no black voters. Headquartered in the county seat of Selma, the civil rights group had met with much resistance and scant success. The recalcitrance of local officials, especially Sheriff Jim Clark, made Selma a prime target for provoking a confrontation to publicize the plight of disfranchised blacks. With this in mind, in January 1965 Martin Luther King spearheaded a series of demonstrations in Dallas County to focus attention on the system of oppression that treated blacks as second-class citizens. These protest activities yielded the expected, if regrettable, results. Peaceful marchers were met with arrest, demonstrators were beaten by law enforcement agents, and a sympathetic white minister from the North was bludgeoned to death on a city street. The climax came with a march scheduled to proceed from Selma to Montgomery. Hardly had the civil rights crusaders ventured beyond the outskirts of the city when a club-wielding sheriff's posse and mounted state troopers charged into their ranks and brutally beat them back. This bloody performance did not go unnoticed as television cameras vividly recorded the event for viewers across the nation.

There was no more concerned spectator than the President. Greatly disturbed by the behavior of Alabama officials and pressed for a speedy response by civil rights leaders, Johnson fully marshalled the resources at his disposal to safeguard the demonstrators who still intended to march to Montgomery. Furthermore, in a nationally televised address to a joint session of Congress, the chief executive passionately urged lawmakers to demolish the barriers to black enfranchisement. The Afro-American "has called upon us to make good the promise of America," Johnson reminded his audience. "And who among us can say that we would have made the same progress were it not for his persistent bravery and faith in American democracy."[25]

Following these stirring remarks, the journey from Selma to Montgomery finally concluded, and Congress swiftly prescribed a powerful remedy to treat voting ills in the South. The bill President Johnson signed into law on 6 August 1965, suspended for five years the operation of literacy tests in states and counties where less than 50 percent of the adult population was registered or had voted in the 1964 presidential election. This formula covered the jurisdictions with the most severe suffrage abuses—Alabama, Georgia, Louisiana, Mississippi, South Carolina, Virginia, and parts of North Carolina.[26] The law also empowered the Attorney General of the United States to authorize federal examiners to enroll qualified applicants in these areas. In the future local officials had to submit all changes in electoral procedures to the Justice Department or the federal district court in Washington, D.C., before they could go into effect. Until a covered state proved that it had not sanctioned racial discrimination in voting for five years, the act would remain in force. In addition Congress instructed the Justice Department to initiate a suit challenging the constitutionality of the poll tax, and within a year the financial levy had been outlawed by the courts.

The Voting Rights Act not only provided a strong measure for expanding the suffrage, but it also offered important lessons for attacking racial discrimination in general. The law dealt with the current condition of black enfranchisement by recognizing its roots in the past. Moreover, it aimed to correct patterns of racial bias against persecuted groups rather than to rectify specific instances of discrimination suffered by individuals. Accordingly, a statistical formula was devised that automatically presumed the existence of racial bigotry and authorized the government to overcome the consequences of previously harmful practices. It did so through the concept of "freezing." The statute acknowledged that enrollment procedures historically had favored whites and ordered that prospective black registrants merely have to meet the same permissive standards operating to the advantage of whites in the past. In effect this meant the suspension of literacy tests, and because most whites were already on the rolls, the statute provided the majority of black adults with a chance to join them.[27] Within four years approximately 60 percent of eligible blacks had registered to vote in the covered states, and the newly enfranchised helped elect over 200 black public officials, an impressive gain from only a few years earlier when successful black candidates were extremly rare.[28]

In another important way, the Johnson administration had articulated the necessity of taking positive steps to destroy the remnants of racial injustice. In an eloquent commencement address at Howard University in June 1965, the President had asserted: "We seek not just freedom but opportunity—not just legal equality but human equality—not just equality as a right and theory, but equality as a fact and as a result." He recognized that changes in the law alone did not place blacks at the same starting line with whites in the race for material success. Equality of opportunity was restricted for Afro-Americans as long as they competed with whites who benefited from the economic, political, and social advantages accumulated through centuries of racial supremacy. The chief executive realized the magnitude of the problem, which he likened to "converting a crippled person into a four minute miler."[29]

Having steered two monumental civil rights bills into law, President Johnson sought to explore new directions toward achieving full equality. For this purpose he convened a White House Conference on Civil Rights that met in Washington in early June 1966. This gathering of government officials, businessmen, liberal academics, and civic, religious, and black leaders spent two days discussing programs designed to implement the rights blacks had only so recently obtained.[30]

By 1966 the national consensus that the president had previously counted on was quickly eroding. Outwardly, the conference of some 2500 delegates came off without a hitch. The representatives produced a 100-page document, *To Fulfill These Rights*, calling for legislation to ban racial discrimination in housing and the administration of criminal justice, and they also suggested increased federal spending to improve the quality of housing and education. Despite agreement on these proposals, the meeting revealed deep fissures within the civil rights coalition. The tensions that had been building since the 1964 Freedom Summer rose to the surface. Some of the participants attacked the Johnson administration for failing to do more to protect civil rights workers in the South; others questioned the traditional emphasis on integration and expressed their belief in the need to control the levers of economic and political power within black communities; and a few condemned the president's escalation of the war in Vietnam as a racist and imperialist policy. In fact the divisive nature of these issues had become evident even before the meeting had begun, when SNCC decided to boycott the conference. Several months earlier the organization had issued a statement condemning the United States for waging a "murderous policy of aggression in Vietnam."[31] Within a year Martin Luther King, the most popular black leader in the country, loudly denounced Johnson's widening of the Southeast Asian hostilities.

Meanwhile, the warring tensions within black souls and the civil rights movement erupted dramatically during James Meredith's march through Mississippi. In June 1966 the first black graduate of the University of Mississippi undertook a 200-mile pilgrimage to challenge fear and encourage black voter registration. Shortly after starting out, Meredith was ambushed and wounded by a white sniper. While he recovered the march continued under the leadership of SCLC, SNCC, and CORE. Along the route Stokely Carmichael, the newly elected chairman of SNCC and a veteran of civil rights protest in the South, seized the opportunity to call for black solidarity and active resistance to oppression. He wanted the trek through Mississippi to "deemphasize white participation" and "highlight the need for independent black political units." The SNCC leader urged black Mississippians to secure power for themselves and not to "beg the white man for anything [they] deserve." In one electrifying moment, Carmichael issued a clarion call for a new departure in the civil rights movement. "The only way we gonna stop them white men from whippin' us," he shouted to a rally, "is to take over. We been saying freedom for six years and we ain't got nothin. What we gonna start saying is Black Power."[32]

This black power doctrine was forged out of personal experience, the model of the African liberation struggle, and the idea of cultural pluralism. Borrowing from each, Carmichael advocated black separatism over assimilation, retaliatory violence over passive suffering, and group power over individual rights. SNCC fieldworkers had come to scorn nonviolence and integration as psychologically debilitating in light of their savage treatment by southern racists and the paternalism they found in white liberals. In seeking freedom from mental and physical oppression, Carmichael urged black communities, like African colonies, to throw off the yoke of white imperialism and achieve "self-determination." Although speaking in revolutionary terms, including calling for the overthrow of capitalism, Carmichael also presented his ideas within a traditional conceptual textbook framework. "For each new ethnic group," he asserted in classic textbook fashion, "the route to social and political integration into America's pluralistic society has been through organization of their own institutions with which to represent their communal needs within the larger society."[33] However disparate the various parts of this ideological amalgam may have been, they added up to a powerful longing of an oppressed minority for acceptance as both blacks and Americans.

Not all blacks responded favorably to Carmichael's message. Martin Luther King believed the slogan of "black power" was an unfortunate choice of words, sounding too inflammatory and suggesting "wrong connotations." He accepted Carmichael's contention that other ethnic groups had advanced by mobilizing their economic and political resources and that blacks "must work to build racial pride and refute the notion that black is evil and ugly." But, King asserted, the black power phrase gave "the impression that we are talking about black domination rather than black equality."[34] Unlike the leaders of SNCC and CORE, Dr. King refused to believe that promotion of a healthy black consciousness depended on excluding white liberals from the struggle for racial justice.

As King feared the positive aspects of black power were lost on most whites. This was especially true in the wake of the bloody urban riots sweeping the North during the mid-1960s. The reasons for the uprisings were complex, but in general black northerners sought to gain what the American Dream had promised but the ghettos lacked—decent housing, jobs, and personal security. Justifiably proud of the accomplishments of the civil rights movement in the South, blacks in the North were letting government officials know that all the legal rights they had long possessed still had not brought them economic and political power. Although Carmichael and his associates were not responsible for the spontaneous outburst of violence consuming cities throughout the country, their bellicose rhetoric fanned the flames of racial discord. After a riot broke out in Cleveland, Carmichael declared: "When you talk about black power, you talk of building a movement that will smash everything Western civilization has created."[35]

Such menacing words together with the ghetto violence frightened whites at a time when the national consensus in favor of black advancement was already beginning to crack. Even before the riots became a prominent feature of the urban landscape, signs of a white backlash had emerged. Convinced that the major aims of the civil rights struggle had been achieved by mid-decade, many whites failed to appreciate the sources of enduring black frustration, favored a halt to further demonstrations, and considered as ungrateful those who continued to agitate.[36] No one played on the anxieties of whites better than did George Wallace. Having whipped up the antagonism of southerners against desegregation, the Alabama governor transported his racist messages to the North where they received a favorable reception from whites who feared that black progress came at their expense. Wallace exploited class as well as racial tensions. He appealed to blue collar workers and denounced "left-wing theoreticians, briefcase totin' bureaucrats, ivory tower guideline writers, bearded anarchists, smart alleck editorial writers and pointy headed professors" for thumbing their noses at them.[37] The racial uprisings of the late sixties added fuel to Wallace's political ambitions. Running in the Democratic presidential primaries in 1964, Wallace surprised his opponents by showing well in three northern states before withdrawing from contention; four years later, campaigning on an independent party ticket, he captured 13.5 percent of the popular vote for president in the November general election.

During that period the more intently the Johnson administration championed the goals of the civil rights movement, even those deemed most temperate, the further it angered whites unhappy with the accelerated pace of the black liberation struggle. In 1966 a well-informed presidential aide noted "that it would have been hard to pass the emancipation proclamation in the atmosphere prevailing this summer."[38] Rather than retreating, Johnson charted a moderate position between denouncing the perpetrators of violence and expressing concern for the continuing plight of blacks and offering legislative proposals to relieve it. Despite the sting of the white backlash, for two years the administration fought to obtain omnibus civil rights legislation directed at housing discrimination and bias in the criminal justice system, issues affecting both the North and the South.

Operating in an explosive political environment, lawmakers had violence very much on their minds. Civil rights supporters condemned the ghetto uprisings, but they tried to turn them to their advantage. By passing the proposed civil rights legislation, they hoped to show blacks that they could resolve their legitimate grievances in a peaceful and orderly way. A leading House Republican, William McCulloch of Ohio, suggested that the omnibus civil rights measure would succeed "in moving the struggle for equal rights and equal opportunities from the streets into the polling places and into the courts." The blade of violence cut both ways as a debating weapon. Opponents of the bill scoffed at the contention that the passage of additional legislation would bring a cease fire on racial battlegrounds. They pointed out that the ghetto rebellions had grown in number following enactment of strong civil rights laws in 1964 and 1965. Horace Kornegay, a North Carolina Democrat, spoke for many of his colleagues in noting that the "more Civil Rights bills the congress passes, the worse race relations become in the country."[39]

In 1968 a renewed round of violence helped break the legislative logjam. The White House had been working very closely with civil rights groups, especially the NAACP, to forge a bipartisan coalition behind the pending bill. Their hard work paid off as Senator Everett Dirksen of Illinois, the Republican Minority Leader, swung his support behind a compromise measure endorsed by the administration. The last legislative hurdle had not yet been cleared when, in early April, Martin Luther King was assassinated, and a wave of urban disorders swept the nation. The precise impact of King's murder and the ensuing riots is difficult to calculate, but these events provided the final push for passage of the bill. As a sign of the times, not only did the lawmakers approve the civil rights package, but they also adopted tough antiriot measures.[40]

This hard-earned victory crowned Johnson's extraordinary accomplishments in obtaining civil rights legislation. Three times in five years the president and his allies had cracked barriers to racial equality that had existed for a century. The 1968 triumph was particularly rewarding because it came against considerable odds at a time when public support for racial reform had ebbed and the civil rights movement was torn by factionalism. Although the chief executive's last years in the White House were marred by strife, Johnson's presidency constituted the high point of the Second Reconstruction. The Great Society had extended civil and political equality to southern blacks, helping them to shatter Jim Crow.

As Johnson retired from office, this phase of the civil rights struggle came to an end. The laws placed on the books, as magnificent as they were, focused on equal rights and scarcely touched the vital issues of the distribution of economic and political power. Indeed, many white liberals believed that the federal government's obligation ceased once the legal obstacles of racial discrimination had been destroyed. With these impediments removed, it remained for blacks to take advantage of the opportunities that awaited them and strive for success according to their individual abilities. However, the chance to buy a cup of coffee at a lunch counter or obtain housing in the suburbs meant little to black residents of inner city ghettos or rural plantations who could not afford a decent standard of living. In the long run, the right to vote might ease the burdens of poverty, but in the meantime blacks still had difficulty electing officials of their own race who best represented their interests.

II

In moving to the next stage of the civil rights struggle, blacks raised a fresh storm of controversy. In demanding affirmative action to improve their condition, Afro-Americans upset traditional standards of equality. Since race had been used for centuries to victimize them, blacks now argued that they would not be able to overcome the pervasive effects of past discrimination without the legal and political systems taking race into account, but this time in their favor. A rigid racial caste system had kept most blacks far behind whites in gaining a fair share of status, wealth, and power, and they would never be able to close the distance without special treatment. In public education this would require busing to ensure integration and quality schooling; in employment and admission to universities and professional schools it meant the establishment of quotas and the active recruitment of qualified minorities to fill them; and in political participation it involved the elimination of procedures that diluted the black vote. Wherever applied, affirmative action was defended by blacks as a reasonable means of compensating them for prior wrongs and the most effective way of obtaining significant results within their lifetimes. Otherwise, they believed, additional generations of Afro-Americans would be sacrificed to the ravages of discrimination.

The Johnson Administration shaped these ideas into policies. In his Howard University address in 1965, the President declared that affirmative steps must be taken to close the economic gap between blacks and whites in order to achieve "equality as a fact." Later that year he backed up his words by issuing an executive order requiring federal contractors actively to recruit and hire qualified minority job seekers. Subsequently, in 1968 the Department of Labor instructed major contractors to adopt a "written affirmative action compliance program" that included "the development of specific goals and time-tables for the prompt achievement of full and equal employment opportunity."[41] Thus, in developing affirmative action criteria, the Johnson regime began defining equal opportunity, not according to some legal abstraction, but by the actual results that were produced.

This approach generated a great deal of opposition. Many whites who had once joined blacks in challenging segregation concluded that affirmative action would lead to preferential treatment, the establishment of flexible goals would turn into the imposition of rigid quotas, and the attempt to promote proportional representation would undermine the egalitarian concept of a color-blind society. They argued that racially sensitive solutions practiced "discrimination in reverse" against whites and offended the meritocratic principle that each individual be judged by his or her qualifications. They attacked the notion that blacks were entitled to special consideration because of their membership in a racial group and contended that charges of discrimination be examined on an individual basis. Proponents of this point of view, termed "neoconservatives," condemned affirmative action for resulting in "an increasing consciousness of the significance of group membership, an increasing divisiveness on the basis of race, color, and national origin, and a spreading resentment among disfavored groups against the favored groups."[42]

The affirmative action issue polarized relations between blacks and white ethnic minorities. Jews who had risen high into the ranks of the academic, legal, and medical professions felt threatened by the assault on meritocracy. After all, they remembered that quotas had long been set to keep them out of graduate and professional schools, and they feared that in the guise of benign goals a new version of the quota system would again restrict their access to positions of prestige. Members of other immigrant groups had also experienced the pain of discrimination in struggling for upward mobility. Comfortably entrenched in civil service jobs and gaining rewards from union seniority, Irish, Italian, and Polish Americans were troubled by policies that appeared to take away some of their hard-earned advantages, redistribute them among blacks, and diminish the prospects of continued success for their children.

Ironically, the black emphasis on racial pride during the latter half of the 1960s stimulated a heightened consciousness among the members of these other ethnic groups, leading to both an increased awareness of their own heritage and a greater sense of their own grievances. As with black nationalism, the new ethnic chauvinism had positive and negative aspects. "Experiencing an appreciation for ethnic values, family loyalty, and neighborhood solidarity," historian Richard Polenberg has written, the ethnic reawakening "suggested that only when people were comfortable with their own backgrounds would they be socially and psychologically whole."[43] On the darker side, however, growing ethnic identification reinforced the political animosities of the white backlash and fueled anti-black sentiments by promoting the virtues of "turf and territoriality." Pulled apart by ethnic and racial factionalism, the descendants of black slaves and white immigrants nonetheless shared a common concern about assimilating into American culture without losing their cultural uniqueness.

Despite these deep divisions, the federal government plunged ahead with affirmative action. The main force behind implementing this policy came not from the president, as it had during the Johnson Administration, but from the Supreme Court and Congress. In fact, the election of Richard Nixon in 1968 brought to the White House a chief executive who had conducted a campaign that appealed mainly to the racial frustrations of disgruntled whites. Though he attempted to redirect racial policies in a manner that pleased the "silent majority" of whites in the North and South, he found his options narrowed by a judiciary and national legislature still supportive of black equality.

The chief executive faced his stiffest challenge in the field of education. He backed the "freedom of choice" plans that the southern states had designed to comply with the technicalities of desegregation without producing much in the way of integrated schools. Such had been the case in New Kent County, Virginia, where freedom of choice left 85 percent of black pupils in segregated facilities. In 1968 fourteen years after *Brown*, the Supreme Court ruled that it would no longer tolerate delay. The justices charged school boards operating dual educational systems with "the affirmative duty to take whatever steps might be necessary to convert to a unitary system in which racial discrimination would be eliminated root and branch."[44] The court sanctioned the use of statistics to assess the discriminatory impact of educational assignments and ordered that race be taken into account to promote integration. One legal commentator concluded: "The Constitution was, indeed, becoming color conscious as well as color blind."[45]

Nixon did not wait long to make his intentions perfectly clear. After a fierce bureaucratic battle between White House practitioners of a "southern strategy" and civil rights enforcement officials in the Department of Health, Education and Welfare, the administration decided to ask the judiciary to postpone a desegregation plan for Mississippi that was scheduled to go into effect in the fall of 1969. For the first time since *Brown*, the federal government and civil rights advocates squared off against each other on opposite sides of school desegregation litigation. When the Supreme Court heard the case, it delivered a sharp rebuke against the White House-sponsored procrastination. Emphasizing the need for less deliberation and more speed in completing the integration process, the high tribunal underscored "the obligation of every school district . . . to terminate dual school systems at once and to operate now and hereafter only unitary schools."[46]

The explosive issue of busing also came under judicial scrutiny. The use of buses to transport students to school had been a commonplace feature of American education. Students from scattered rural areas rode buses to commute to centrally-located schools as did handicapped and exceptional children who participated in special education programs. In the South black and white pupils had customarily traveled on buses to attend segregated schools, frequently passing a nearby school that was closed to them because of their skin color. Few whites had registered complaints over these traditional forms of busing; they did raise a howl, however, against busing for the purpose of achieving school desegregation. Given the judicial mandate to integrate immediately, local school boards in the South had little choice but to introduce busing and reassign pupils on the basis of race. The Charlotte-Mecklenburg County Board of Education in North Carolina had devised an innovative plan for its sprawling 550 square-mile district containing over 100 schools and eighty-four thousand students. On 20 April 1971, the Supreme Court gave its qualified endorsement to busing as a remedy in such school systems that had previously practiced segregation by law. The court refrained from approving "racial balance or mixing" as a constitutional right, but it upheld "the use of mathematical ratios . . . [as] a starting point . . . rather than an inflexible requirement."[47]

Most Americans accepted busing for traditional purposes and most favored the principle of desegregation, but the overwhelming majority disapproved of busing to promote integration. Even blacks were split over the issue. They expressed reservations about extensive busing mainly because they usually bore most of the travel burden; however, they tended to support busing to a far greater extent than did whites. A 1972 survey revealed that when asked whether they favored busing if it was *essential* for desegregation, 71 percent of blacks replied in the affirmative compared to 43 percent of whites.[48] Both groups agreed that quality education was their main concern, but they differed over how to achieve it. Blacks took pride in their schools for the contributions they had made in developing leaders and preserving cultural traditions. Nevertheless, they recognized that, within the context of a racist society, separate education had never been equal nor was it likely to become so in the near future. In contrast most whites felt that busing would harm their children's education by placing them in inferior ghetto schools, and they argued that the compulsory transportation of pupils was self-defeating because it led to "white flight" from the cities to the suburbs where there were few blacks available for integration.[49]

The Nixon administration championed the sentiment of the white majority and tried to roll back the buses. "I do not believe that busing to achieve racial balance is in the interests of better education," the president declared following the Charlotte-Mecklenburg County ruling, and he urged Congress to call a halt to further busing.[50] In 1972 Nixon proposed legislation that barred courts from ordering the transfer of elementary school pupils beyond the closest or next closest schools to their neighborhood. The bill passed the House but failed in the Senate, a pattern that was repeated throughout the Nixon years. What Nixon could not accomplish through legislation, however, he achieved through executive action. Under his regime federal agencies responsible for school desegregation eschewed the busing remedy and concentrated instead on reducing instances of racial discrimination within schools and equalizing funding between existing segregated schools. In effect the administration operated on the premise that separate schools did not necessarily have to provide unequal educational opportunities.[51]

Civil rights leaders strongly disagreed. They interpreted Nixon's actions as part of a drive to halt racial equality. Clarence Mitchell, the chief Washington lobbyist of the NAACP, called the foes of busing "the same people who are against equal treatment in all aspects of American life." In a similar vein, Vernon Jordan, Executive Director of the National Urban League, accused the Nixon administration of grossly distorting the facts in portraying massive busing as a means of achieving "racial balance." Rather, Jordan argued, "busing, as ordered by the courts and other governmental bodies, takes place for only one reason—to desegregate segregated schools."[52] Although unable to stop the executive branch from discarding busing remedies, civil rights groups kept sufficient pressure on Congress to defeat proposed constitutional amendments for ending court-ordered busing.

The opponents of busing were more successful in the North than in the South. In many of the industrialized areas of the Northeast and

Midwest the post-World War II exodus of whites from the cities to the surrounding suburbs had left most blacks behind in the urban ghettos to attend increasingly segregated schools. In the mid-1970s the city of Detroit, viewing the problem from a metropolitan perspective, came up with a workable plan to integrate its schools by transporting students across municipal boundary lines into adjacent school districts. In this case the Supreme Court, although previously approving busing within the confines of northern cities that had been guilty of officially practicing racial discrimination, greatly restricted its possible extension to surrounding suburban jurisdictions. Only if it could be proven that segregated educational patterns had resulted from intentional government action in both city and suburb, the justices ruled in *Milliken v. Bradley*, was metropolitan-wide busing across school districts permissible.[53] In practice this decision ensured that the North and the South switched positions as the most segregated regions of the country. In 1976, 47.1 percent of black students attended schools in the South with a white majority compared to 42.5 percent of blacks who did so in the North.[54] Although the schools in Dixie had to balance their student populations by race, most of those in the North were allowed to maintain a dual system of education. And in those urban areas such as Boston where the demography of the inner city permitted busing as a legal remedy for segregation, the attempt to transport students produced a violent response from whites who saw their neighborhoods under siege.[55]

Like school busing the expansion of the black suffrage also raised questions about race-conscious policies. After 1965 the Voting Rights Act had evolved from a measure primarily concerned with dismantling the formal barriers to voter registration to one that challenged dilution of black ballots. In this category were such devices as gerrymandering, multi-member districts and at-large elections, and annexation of predominantly white territory adjacent to majority black areas or those locations likely to become so. In a landmark opinion in 1969, the Supreme Court declared that the Voting Rights Act "was aimed at the subtle as well as the obvious" and broadly interpreted the right to vote to mean "all action necessary to make a vote effective."[56]

Civil rights advocates were delighted with this line of reasoning. They argued that Congress had anticipated that the southern states would devise new techniques to restrict black voting. Though the legislators could not have foreseen the exact shape these subterfuges would take, they had written the preclearance requirement (Section 5) into the Voting Rights Law to challenge biased practices as they arose. Furthermore, a few years of exercising the ballot had not erased the results of a century of disfranchisement, and civil rights supporters pointed out that continued federal vigilance was necessary. Howard Glickstein, the Staff Director of the United States Commission on Civil Rights, explained in 1971: "The Voting Rights Act was designed to provide a protective umbrella under which a viable black political tradition could begin to grow . . . [and should] be kept constantly in place until black political participation in the South develops strong roots."[57] Consequently, the 1965 law was conceived less as a means of combating registration problems and more as a tool for extending to blacks an opportunity to make their ballots count more fully. Increasingly, suffragists evaluated the success of the law by the number of blacks who won election and calculated the remaining distance to racial equality by the gap between the percentage of black officeholders and the proportion of blacks in the population.

This expansive view of enfranchisement did not go unchallenged. Justice John Marshall Harlan issued a vigorous dissent from the Supreme Court bench. He accused the majority of his colleagues of requiring a "revolutionary innovation in American government." Maintaining that in adopting the Voting Rights Act lawmakers had intended only to curtail "those techniques that prevented Negroes from voting at all," Harlan asserted that "Congress did not attempt to restructure state government" by altering the form of elections.[58] This opinion was shared by the White House. Attempting to carry out his southern strategy, President Nixon asked Congress to soften the potent enforcement features of the 1965 law and extend application of the act throughout the country. In doing so the Republican administration would be removing the regional stigma from the South and weakening implementation of the statute where it was most needed. Other critics cared less about the burdens the South had to shoulder for its past misdeeds and more about the consequences to the principle of equality of individual opportunity resulting from the new emphasis on getting blacks elected. They asked what had happened to the original civil rights goal of the color-blind society and wondered whether "group power, not individual worth is made the measure of political equality." Neoconservatives warned that the judicial redefinition of the Voting Rights Act "envisions blacks as a permanent group apart [and] . . . assumes that there is no escape from race."[59]

Congress was not prepared to agree that the day of racial neutrality had arrived and that blacks no longer were worthy of special protection to compete equally with whites for political office. On three occasions, in 1970, 1975, and 1982, lawmakers renewed the vital provisions of the Voting Rights Law and even expanded its guarantees to language minorities. Although the legislators refused to make proportional representation the constitutional benchmark for judging black political equality, they made it easier for blacks to prove that the rules of the electoral game had been stacked against them.[60] The consensus behind continued enfranchisement has been stronger than that on any other civil rights issue. Bipartisan and national, the legislative coalition in its favor attracted a majority of Democrats and Republicans and, more surprisingly, southerners as well as northerners. In contrast to the divisive racial conflicts generated by busing, a congressional observer remarked, "Everyone is for letting a guy have his full right to vote."[61]

Granting language minorities the special guarantees of the Voting Rights Act reflected the belief that non-English-speaking groups were also being deprived of equal treatment under the law. In 1975 the legislators decided that English-language requirements had disfranchised foreign-speaking citizens, and they provided relief for them, as they had for blacks, in the conduct of elections. A year earlier the Supreme Court had reached a similar verdict concerning education. In *Lau v. Nichols*, the high tribunal ruled that school districts had to take "affirmative steps" to provide instruction to non-English-speaking students in their native tongue. This opinion challenged the traditional American assumption that immigrants should learn the language of their adopted homeland, and instead it upheld bilingualism. The selection of these minority groups for compensatory action did little to soothe the antagonistic feelings of other ethnic-Americans whose ancestors had struggled to learn English several generations before without any preferential treatment.[62]

Much more controversial than the suffrage, programs that provided for special treatment of blacks in employment and higher education aroused as much white indignation as did busing. Perhaps more than any other form of affirmative action, racial goals and quotas in hiring and university admissions directly pitted the interests of blacks against those of whites. In an economy that had not yet reached full employment, the stiff competition for better-paying jobs meant that programs seeking to advance blacks would come at the expense of whites. The same was true for entry into professional schools where spaces were limited and qualified applicants were plentiful. The recessionary spiral of the 1970s and the coming of age of the postwar baby boom generation exacerbated the struggle for the limited positions available. While the economy had flourished in the 1960s, many whites could afford to take a generous attitude toward black civil rights goals, but with the harder times of the next decade, they preached the virtues of a neo-Social Darwinism. Having gained their legal right to equality, blacks were told to forget their previous history of enslavement and discrimination, prove themselves meritorious, and make it on their own without government favor or else the rewards of progress would come to an end.[63]

Even the staunchest defenders of this position nonetheless admitted that employers should make a positive effort to hire qualified minorities. A 1972 survey showed that 82 percent of whites opposed giving blacks a job promotion over an equally qualified white, but it also revealed that 77 percent favored the establishment of job training programs for blacks. Most respondents distinguished between "legitimate" compensatory action programs that helped disadvantaged minority groups compete on an equal basis and "unfair" preferential treatment that enhanced the opportunities of one group over another. The *New Republic* refused to endorse the kind of affirmative action that "guaranteed advancement for the members of a particular group" but supported policies ensuring "talented individuals, from every social group, have a chance to shine."[64]

Initially, the federal government had recognized the need for affirmative action and compensatory treatment of disadvantaged minority job applicants and workers. Although the civil rights movement had brought steady economic gains for blacks, by the late 1960s the income of Afro-American families was 60 percent that of whites, a figure that had grown slightly from approximately 53 percent in 1954. Prohibitions against discriminatory hiring did not guarantee jobs for blacks who, because of past bias, were less successful than whites in meeting employment criteria. In many instances scores on standardized tests were used to measure job qualifications, and this worked to the detriment of blacks, many of whom were victims of an inferior education. The Johnson administration had sought to relieve the persistent imbalance in the employment market by ordering federal contractors to establish affirmative hiring programs for minorities.

This approach continued during the Nixon administration, which applied it to unions as well as employers. The "Philadelphia Plan" required construction workers' unions employed on federal projects to sign up a fixed percentage of black apprentices who would subsequently be admitted to the union. Moreover, in 1971 the Supreme Court delivered a strong endorsement of affirmative action. In *Griggs v. Duke Power Company*, the justices ruled that "neutral" employment tests were not valid if they maintained the effects of prior discriminatory employment practices. They placed the onus on employers to prove that an employment exam that operated to exclude blacks was related to job performance. Thus, the *Griggs* doctrine focused on the enduring results of previous discrimination and presumed them to exist when blacks fell short of holding jobs in rough proportion to their percentage of the general population.[65]

By the mid-1970s, the Supreme Court began to retreat from this position. President Nixon had been able to turn the court in a more conservative direction. The four judges he appointed, led by Chief Justice Warren Burger, helped sound the retreat from the liberal positions taken by the Warren Court during the previous decades. In the *Griggs* case, the judiciary had based its opinion on a positive interpretation of the 1964 Civil Rights Act. When the justices examined the Equal Protection Clause of the Constitution in dealing with similar controversies over standardized employment tests, however, they found the requirements for proving discrimination to be more stringent. The high tribunal judged as constitutionally valid the administration of a federal civil service exam for Washington, D.C., police officers that blacks failed at a rate four times greater than did whites. The justices ruled that such examination standards could be nullified only if they had been adopted for a "discriminatory purpose." This opinion marked a setback for affirmative action programs because it was much harder for minorities to demonstrate a biased intent behind a law than to show its actual discriminatory effects.[66]

The Court struck another blow to affirmative action in the *Bakke* case. At issue was the special program of admission to the University of California Medical School at Davis that set aside sixteen of 100 places for entering minority students. In 1973 Alan Bakke, a thirty-four year-old aerospace engineer with a burning desire to become a physician, unsuccessfully competed for one of the eighty-four openings available to white applicants. Bakke had been turned down by other institutions because he was considered to be over the traditional age for a beginning medical student. He was not alone in feeling the pain of rejection as 42,155 applicants competed for 15,774 seats in medical schools throughout the nation. Apparently Bakke was willing to accept the customary reasons for failing to obtain one of the scarce spots—receiving lower scores on competitive entrance tests or the matter of his age. Bakke, a Vietnam veteran, did not seem to mind the preferential consideration that many institutions accorded former G.I.s. He would not leave unchallenged, however, a system that on the basis of race prevented him from competing for a fixed number of positions.[67]

In suing the Board of Regents of the University of California, Bakke sought only his admission into medical school; nevertheless, the litigation afforded the judiciary a chance to examine what limits the constitutional guarantee of equal protection of the law placed on race-conscious remedies. Those who expected the high bench to settle the affirmative action issue conclusively were sorely disappointed. Rather than presenting a united front, the badly-divided justices could agree on little else than that Bakke should receive his coveted admission. Justice Lewis Powell cast his vote with the majority of five to declare the Davis program unconstitutional because it reserved a fixed number of places based on a racial classification. Having spoken against the use of quotas, Powell then joined a different majority of five to approve a university's flexibility in considering a prospective applicant's race in order to assemble a diverse student body. Although Justice Powell provided a legal opening through which affirmative action programs could continue to exist, he attacked the basic assumption upon which they functioned. The Justice decried the notion of "benign" quotas that did not stigmatize the white majority and expressed his belief that restrictive racial categories would force "innocent persons . . . to bear the burdens of redressing grievances not of their making." Pointing out the racial and ethnic tensions that were sharpened when members of one group were preferred over another, he refused to hold individual whites to blame for the racial injustices of the past.[68]

Consequently, it remained for a minority of four to defend in full force the principle of compensatory treatment. Justice Thurgood Marshall, who had represented the black plaintiffs in the *Brown* case, spoke most fervently about the historical justification for singling out blacks for special consideration. He challenged those who suggested that Afro-Americans were just another ethnic group that had faced prejudice and must overcome it in the same fashion of hard work and individual effort. "The experience of Negroes in America has been different in kind, not just in degree, from that of other ethnic groups," Marshall declared. "The dream of America as the great melting pot has not been realized for the Negro; because of his skin color he never even made it into the pot." His colleague, Justice Harry Blackmun, summed up the practical lesson that centuries of racial discrimination had taught: "In order to get beyond racism, we must first take account of race."[69]

As the United States moved into the final quarter of the twentieth century it appeared very little inclined to heed this message. The Supreme Court that two decades before had paved the way toward establishing racial equality hesitated to go much further. In a 1979 decision, it upheld an affirmative action plan that the United Steelworkers of America and Kaiser Aluminum and Chemical Corporation adopted voluntarily to provide blacks with 50 percent of the available spaces in a craft training project regardless of whether they had less seniority than whites. In a 1984 case, however, the high tribunal declared that the Memphis Fire Department could not suspend its seniority rules by laying off whites in order to protect recently-hired blacks with fewer years of employment. Benjamin L. Hooks, Executive Secretary of the NAACP, charged that the opinion ignored the historical pattern of blacks being the "last hired and first fired" and was blind to "the reality that such discriminatory practices have had and continue to have upon excluded groups."[70]

Nor did civil rights activists find imaginative leadership in occupants of the White House after Kennedy and Johnson. Nixon and his successor, Gerald Ford, responded with either outspoken opposition to or grudging acceptance of civil rights measures. More sympathetic than his Republican predecessors, Jimmy Carter, a Georgia Democrat, was nonetheless limited in his accomplishments. Though pleased with the transformation that the civil rights movement had brought to his native south, Carter was either unwilling or unable to direct his presidential resources to carry on those changes. Carter's Justice Department had taken the affirmative action side in the *Bakke* case, but in a manner so hesitant that civil rights groups came away confused and dismayed. Still, Carter tried to boost the black cause when he could, whereas Ronald Reagan deliberately attempted to contain it. A spokesman for the forces of conservatism that equated affirmative action with reverse discrimination, Reagan called a virtual moratorium on implementing race-sensitive programs. His administration considered racial classifications "morally wrong" and intolerable in any form, and relaxed minority hiring guidelines for federal contractors, argued in the courts against employment quotas, and restructured the United States Commission on Civil Rights to reflect these views.[72] Although civil rights supporters fought against this retrenchment, they did so from a weakened position. The struggles of the late 1960s and early 1970s had cost them support from many of their former allies who felt threatened by the new definition of equality.

To a large degree, the controversy over whether or not blacks merited special treatment revolved around differing perceptions of minority progress. Most whites apparently believed that the main goals of the civil rights movement had been secured, and they resisted new measures that went beyond granting equal rights under the law to all citizens. A 1977 Harris survey revealed that only 33 percent of whites thought that racial discrimination persisted and 55 percent agreed that blacks were pressing "too fast" for equality.[73] Most blacks, however, felt that their struggle to reap a fair share of the rewards of first-class citizenship was yet to be completed. Without programs to remove the vestiges of racism, they saw little hope for entering the mainstream of American life. An exchange between Justice Marshall and Alan Bakke's lawyer during the oral argument before the Supreme Court underscored the affirmative action conflict. "You are arguing about keeping somebody out and the other side is arguing about getting somebody in?" Marshall questioned the attorney, who succinctly replied: "That's right."[74]

The intense feelings that arose from the increasing racial polarization obscured a realistic assessment of the black condition in America. The statistical indicators displayed a complicated picture that makes easy generalizations risky. Whether measuring socioeconomic or political factors, the data suggested the tremendous gains achieved by blacks since 1960. A much greater percentage of black students than ever before were completing high school, and there was little difference between the percentage of high school graduates of each race who went on to college. In addition a majority of Afro-Americans had moved into the electorate from disfranchisement, thousands of successful black candidates were holding office throughout the country, and in 1984 a black challenger made a serious bid for the Democratic Party's presidential nomination. Despite these important strides forward, blacks had not caught up to whites either educationally or politically. Their rate of graduation from college was lower than that of whites, and most blacks in 1980 attended two-year rather than four-year institutions of higher learning. Furthermore, on the average, the voter registration and turnout figures for blacks lagged behind those for whites and the percentage of black elected officials trailed considerably behind the proportion of blacks in the total population.[75]

III

Civil rights advocates had assumed that equal educational and political opportunites would relieve the economic plight of blacks. Despite notable improvements, their hopes have not been fully realized, as shown in Table 1. By 1980 a significant proportion of black families had joined the middle class and one-third of black workers were employed in white-collar jobs as professionals, managers, and clerical workers. However, the bulk of the black population remained far less upwardly mobile. In 1980 black families lived on incomes averaging 58 percent of those earned by whites, only a slight improvement from two decades earlier. Although many blacks had advanced into professional ranks, blacks still were underrepresented in better paying white-collar jobs and overrepresented in lower income positions. More ominously, during the period between 1960 and 1980, the black unemployment rate consistently was double that of whites and had reached depression-era levels by the late 1970s. Approximately 30 percent of all blacks lived below the poverty line compared with 10 percent of whites. Economists attributed this dire condition to the leap in female-headed households among blacks from nearly 24 percent in 1965 to 40 percent in 1980, and they pointed out that approximately two-thirds of impoverished black families had females at their head.[76]

To some observers black educational and political attainments along with the enlargement of the black middle class meant that race had ceased to be a significant factor in explaining continuing inequalities. They explained the gaps that remained between blacks and whites as

TABLE 1

BLACK ECONOMIC STATUS, 1964-1980

	1964-1965 %	1975-1976 %	1980 %
Black family income versus white family income	56.0[a]	62.0[a]	58.0[b]
Black unemployment	9.6[c]	13.9[c]	13.1[d]
Black families below poverty line	—	27.1[e]	28.9[e]
Female-headed black households	23.7[f]	37.0[f]	40.0[f]
Female-headed black households below poverty line	—	50.1[e]	49.4[e]
Black families earning under $5000	19.5[g]	17.7[h]	20.7[h]
Black families earning $35,000-49,999	3.8[g]	6.1[h]	7.7[h]

a. Dorothy K. Newman, *Protest, Politics, and Prosperity: Black Americans and White Institutions, 1940-1975* (New York, 1978), 269.

b. Harrell R. Rodgers, Jr., "Fair Employment Laws for Minorities: An Evaluation of Federal Implementation," in Charles S. Bullock III and Charles M. Lamb, eds., *Implementation of Civil Rights Policy* (Monterey, Calif., 1984), 105.

c. Newman, *Protest, Politics, and Prosperity,* 64.

d. *Economic Report of the President* (Washington, D.C., 1984), 259. The poverty line was devised by the federal government in 1969.

e. *Economic Report of the President,* 262

f. Harvard Sitkoff, *The Struggle for Black Equality, 1954-1980* (New York, 1981), 235.

g. United States Department of Commerce, Bureau of the Census, *Statistical Abstract of the United States, 1984* (Washington, D.C., 1983), 459. The earliest figures given are for 1967.

h. *Statistical Abstract of the United States, 1984,* 459.

stemming more from the working of the economic marketplace than from racial discrimination. With the decline of Jim Crow barriers, the proponents of this viewpoint asserted, blacks were held back from advancing for the same reasons that blocked other low income groups from getting ahead: unsteady economic growth and structural changes in the modern industrial state. Accordingly, technology and automation were supposed to have had an impact on black and white job seekers and workers alike, and it was generally argued that affirmative action could do little to remedy their problems.[77] In fact by introducing the element of race such programs split potential allies who might otherwise have joined together in fighting shared economic battles.

This analysis was certainly correct in highlighting the class dimension of inequality in the United States, but it unfortunately minimized the enduring sources of racial discrimination. One cannot easily separate race from class in an economic system reflecting long-standing discrimination against Afro-Americans. Individual acts of racism have diminished substantially, but biases remain embedded in societal institutions. Such concepts as meritocracy might have worked to ensure equality of opportunity in a color-blind nation, but in practice they operated to reinforce the injustices inherited from the past. If blacks are to continue to make progress toward real equality, white Americans must recognize the ongoing significance of race and take affirmative measures to reverse the effects of discrimination. To the extent that this is tried, this country will continue to move toward closing the gap between its democratic promise and reality.

I wish to thank Nancy A. Hewitt and Mark I. Gelfand for their assistance in the preparation of this work.

1. Harvard Sitkoff, *The Struggle for Black Equality 1954-1980* (New York, 1981), 94.

2. Southern Christian Leadership Conference, "The Ultimate Aim Is The Beloved Community," in August Meier, Elliot Rudwick, and Francis L. Broderick, eds., *Black Protest Thought in the Twentieth Century* (Indianapolis, 1971), 302-6; John J. Ansbro, *Martin Luther King, Jr.: The Making of a Mind* (Maryknoll, New York, 1982).

3. Haig Bosmajian, "The Letter from Birmingham Jail," in C. Eric Lincoln, ed., *Martin Luther King, Jr.: A Profile* (New York, 1970), 136.

4. August Meier, "On the Role of Martin Luther King, Jr.," *New Politics* 4 (Winter 1965):52-59.

5. W. E. B. DuBois, *The Souls of Black Folk* (New York, 1969), 45-46.

6. William H. Chafe, *Civilities and Civil Rights: Greensboro, North Carolina and the Black Struggle for Freedom* (Oxford, 1981), 83.

7. See Elizabeth Jacoway and David R. Colburn, eds., *Southern Business-men and Desegregation* (Baton Rouge, 1982) for a variety of responses by southern communities to racial protest during the 1960s.

8. Anne Moody, *Coming of Age in Mississippi* (New York, 1968), 265-67.

9. Chafe, *Civilities*, 100; Steven F. Lawson, "From Sit-in to Race Riot: Busi-nessmen, Blacks, and the Pursuit of Moderation in Tampa, 1960-1967," in Jac-oway and Colburn, eds., *Southern Businessmen*, 264, 280.

10. Carl M. Brauer, *John F. Kennedy and the Second Reconstruction* (New York, 1977), 33.

11. Ibid., 47-50; Harris Wofford, *Of Kennedys and Kings: Making Sense of the Sixties* (New York, 1980), chapter one.

12. Steven F. Lawson, *Black Ballots: Voting Rights in the South, 1944-1969* (New York, 1976), 289.

13. Sitkoff, *Struggle for Black Equality*, 106.

14. Lawson, *Black Ballots*, 175.

15. Catherine A. Barnes, *Journey From Jim Crow: The Desegregation of Southern Transit* (New York, 1983), 188.

16. Brauer, *John F. Kennedy*, 260.

17. Ibid., 267.

18. Sitkoff, *Struggle for Black Equality*, 164.

19. For critical accounts of Kennedy's civil rights program that share this judgment, see Bruce Miroff, *Pragmatic Illusions: The Presidential Politics of John F. Kennedy* (New York, 1976), 269-70; David Burner, "Kennedy: A Cold Warrior," in Robert D. Marcus and David Burner, eds., *America Since 1945*, 2d ed. (New York, 1977), 190-93, 195-96; Roy Wilkins with Tom Mathews, *Stand-ing Fast: The Autobiography of Roy Wilkins,* (New York, 1982), 277, 294. It should be noted that when Richard Nixon ran for the presidency in 1960 he had compiled a strong civil rights record as vice-president. Yet his campaign exhib-ited the features of his "southern strategy" that would achieve success in 1968.

20. Nathan Glazer, *Affirmative Discrimination: Ethnic Inequality and Pub-lic Policy* (New York, 1975), 45. According to Title VII of the law, employers were not required to grant preferential treatment to any individual or group on the basis of race, color, religion, sex, or national origin "or account of an imbal-ance which may exist with respect to the total or percentage of persons of any race, color, religion, sex or national origin employed by an employer."

21. Allen J. Matusow, "From Civil Rights to Black Power: The Case of SNCC, 1960-1966," in Barton J. Bernstein and Allen J. Matusow, eds., *Twen-tieth Century America: Recent Interpretations* (New York, 1972), 507, 509; Cleveland Sellers with Robert Terrell, *The River of No Return: The Autobiog-raphy of a Black Militant and the Life and Death of SNCC* (New York, 1973). On the issue of women in the civil rights movement, see Sara Evans, *Personal Politics: The Roots of Women's Liberation in the Civil Rights Movement and the New Left* (New York, 1980), chapter four. Black activists may have become cynical about whites, but they had invited their participation for tactical reasons

in the first place. The organizers of the summer project expected casualties and believed that violence against northern white volunteers would push the federal government to take stronger action against racism in Mississippi. Neil R. McMillen, "Black Enfranchisement in Mississippi: Federal Enforcement and Black Protest in the 1960s," *Journal of Southern History* 43(August 1977):367.

22. James Forman, *The Making of Black Revolutionaries* (New York, 1972), 265.

23. On this point see Joseph Rauh, Oral History, Lyndon B. Johnson, Presidential Library.

24. Lawson, *Black Ballots*, 300; David J. Garrow, *Protest At Selma: Martin Luther King, Jr., and the Voting Rights Act of 1965* (New Haven, 1978), chapters two and three.

25. *Public Papers of the Presidents, Lyndon B. Johnson, 1965* (Washington, D.C., 1966), 1:284.

26. Initially, the state of Alaska, three counties in Arizona, one county in Hawaii, and one country in Idaho were covered under the formula of the act because of the presence, not of blacks, but of Indian, Eskimo, or Asian minorities. By 1968 these jurisdictions had removed themselves through litigation. United States Commission on Civil Rights, *Political Participation* (Washington, D.C., 1968), 11.

27. Frank T. Read and Lucy S. McGough, *Let Them Be Judged: The Judicial Integration of the Deep South* (Metuchen, New Jersey, 1978), 300ff.

28. Increased black political participation produced a white counterreaction. While the number of black registrants was growing by 1.5 million during the late 1960s, the number of white registrants rose by 4.4 million. Garrow, *Protest At Selma*, 302, n. 33. Also on this point, see Numan V. Bartley and Hugh Davis Graham, *Southern Politics and the Second Reconstruction* (Baltimore, 1975), 109.

29. *Public Papers of the President, Lyndon B. Johnson, 1965*, 1:636; Harry McPherson, Oral History, Lyndon B. Johnson Presidential Library.

30. Lee Rainwater and William L. Yancey, *The Moynihan Report and the Politics of Controversy* (Cambridge, Mass., 1967) for a highly critical account of the conference.

31. *New York Times*, 7 January 1966, 2. For the transformation of SNCC and CORE into black power groups, see Clayborne Carson, *In Struggle: SNCC and The Black Awakening of The 1960s* (Cambridge, Mass., 1981) and August Meier and Elliott Rudwick, *CORE: A Study in the Civil Rights Movement, 1942-1968* (New York, 1973).

32. Sellers with Terrell, *The River of No Return*, 162, 166-67.

33. Matusow, "From Civil Rights to Black Power," 514-17. Stokely Carmichael and Charles V. Hamilton, *Black Power: The Politics of Liberation In America* (New York, 1967), 30-31.

34. Martin Luther King, Jr., *Where Do We Go From Here: Chaos or Community?* (New York, 1967), 30-31.

35. Carson, *In Struggle*, 221.

36. In 1963, 64 percent of the nation's whites thought blacks were pushing too

quickly for equality. Robert H. Wiebe, "White Attitudes and Black Rights from *Brown* to *Bakke*," in Michael V. Namorato, ed., *Have We Overcome? Race Relations Since Brown* (Jackson, Mississippi, 1979), 156.

37. William L. O'Neill, *Coming Apart: An Informal History of America in the 1960's* (New York, 1975), 389.

38. Harry McPherson to Nicholas Katzenbach, 20 September 1966, Box 21 (2), Harry McPherson Files, Lyndon B. Johnson Presidential Library. On the complexities of the riots and their varying effects on governmental policy, see James Button, *Black Violence* (Princeton, 1978).

39. McCulloch is quoted in the *Congressional Record*, 89th Cong. 2nd Sess., 17112. Horace Kornegay to James W. Morrison, 21 July 1966, Box 39, Horace Kornegay Papers, Southern Historical Collection, University of North Carolina Library.

40. For an extended treatment of the passage of the 1968 law, see Steven F. Lawson, *In Pursuit of Power: Southern Blacks and Electoral Politics, 1965-1982* (New York, 1985), chapter 3. For less favorable assessments of Johnson's role after 1965, see James C. Harvey, *Black Civil Rights During the Johnson Administration* (Jackson, Mississippi, 1973), and Allen J. Matusow, *The Unraveling of America: A History of Liberalism in the 1960s* (New York, 1984), 206-8. Matusow has emphasized the weaknesses in the enforcement provisions concerning equal housing. The act failed to give the Department of Housing and Urban Development power to issue cease and desist orders. Undoubtedly, this omission limited the effect of the law, and housing segregation remains a substantial problem today. Nevertheless, it is difficult to see how the Johnson administration could have obtained passage of a stronger housing section, given the legislative climate of opinion. The results of the law notwithstanding, Johnson's legislative achievement, in the face of serious obstacles, was extraordinary.

41. Glazer, *Affirmative Discrimination*, 46-47; Harvey, *Black Civil Rights*, 117-18. Despite these quidelines the federal government failed to live up to its promises. Allen Matusow has concluded that in the late 1960s and 1970s "the direct effects of federal enforcement on the vast and complex American job market were small." Matusow, *Unraveling of America*, 211. Also see Harvey, *Black Civil Rights*, 123-48. Besides the Department of Labor, the Equal Employment Opportunity Commission, created by the 1964 Civil Rights Act, played a major role in challenging job bias. Since 1972, when Congress expanded the EEOC's enforcement powers, it has become more effective in implementing affirmative action programs. For a history of affirmative action, see Citizens' Commission on Civil Rights, *Affirmative Action to Open the Doors of Job Opportunity* (Washington, D.C., 1984), chap. 1.

42. Glazer, *Affirmative Discrimination*, 220.

43. Richard Polenberg, *One Nation Divisible: Class, Race, and Ethnicity in the Unites States Since 1938* (New York, 1980), 246.

44. *Green v. County School Board of New Kent County*, 391 U.S. 430, 437-38 (1968).

45. J. Harvie Wilkinson, III, *From Brown to Bakke: The Supreme Court and School Integration 1954-1978* (Oxford, 1981), 117.

46. *Alexander v. Holmes County Board of Education*, 396 U.S. 19, 20 (1969).

For an insider's account of the bureaucratic struggle, see Leon E. Panetta and Peter Gall, *Bring Us Together: The Nixon Team and the Civil Rights Retreat* (Philadelphia, 1971).

47. *Swann v. Charlotte-Mecklenburg Board of Education*, 402 U.S. 1, 25 (1971).

48. Gary Orfield, *Must We Bus? Segregated Schools and National Policy* (Washington, D.C., 1978), 115-16; Polenberg, *One Nation Divisible*, 239.

49. On the complexities of white flight, see Orfield, *Must We Bus?* 100, 413, and Diane Ravitch, "The 'White Flight' Controversy," in Nicolaus Mills, ed., *Busing U.S.A.* (New York, 1979), 238-55.

50. *Public Papers of the Presidents, Richard M. Nixon, 1971* (Washington, D.C., 1972), 597.

51. Orfield, *Must We Bus?*, chapters eight to ten, 267. In the final days of the Nixon administration, Congress passed legislation restraining the courts from ordering the busing of students beyond the closest or next closest schools. After Nixon resigned, President Gerald Ford signed the bill into law. The practical effect of the measure was minimal, however, because Congress could not restrict courts from enforcing the constitutional rights of minority students through busing. The law did limit federal agencies from implementing busing by simple legislation.

52. *Congressional Quarterly Almanac*, 28 (1972), 680.

53. *Milliken v. Bradley*, 418 U.S. 717 (1974)

54. Charles S. Bullock, III, "Equal Education Opportunity," in Charles S. Bullock, III and Charles M. Lamb, eds., *Implementation of Civil Rights Policy* (Monterery, California, 1984), 72.

55. Orfield, *Must We Bus?*, 417. Two recent histories of educational desegregation disagree over the value of busing. George R. Metcalf, *From Little Rock to Boston: The History of School Desegregation* (Westport, Connecticut, 1983), finds busing an effective remedy and criticizes the federal government for not implementing it more fully. In contrast Raymond Wolters, *The Burden of Brown: Thirty Years of School Desegregation* (Knoxville, 1984), considers busing a misguided solution and condemns the judiciary for promoting its use. For the case of Atlanta, where blacks preferred increasing their control over the school district rather than supporting massive busing, see Orfield, 369-70.

56. *Allen v. State Board of Elections*, 393 U.S. 544, 565 (1969).

57. U.S. House of Representatives, Committee on the Judiciary, Civil Rights Oversight Subcommittee, *Hearings on the Enforcement and Administration of the Voting Rights Act of 1965, As Amended*, 92nd Cong., 1st Sess., 1971, 91.

58. *Allen v. State Board of Elections*, 393 U.S. 585 (1969).

59. Abigail M. Thernstrom, "The Odd Evolution of the Voting Rights Act," *Public Interest* 55 (Spring 1979):59-60.

60. *City of Mobile v. Bolden*, 446 U.S. 55 (1980), for the court opinion that made it difficult for civil rights plaintiffs to prove suffrage discrimination in at-large elections.

61. Burt Wides to Philip A. Hart, n.d. (1971), Box 185, CR 3f, Philip A. Hart MSS., Michigan Historical Collection, University of Michigan. In the area of

political party organization, however, the Democrats compiled a much better record than did the Republicans. Following the MFDP challenge, the Democratic Party adopted affirmative action guidelines to ensure blacks and other minority groups fair representation in the selection of delegates to the national convention. Although Democratic chieftains did not make quotas mandatory, they wrote guidelines that suggested proportional representation as a goal for achieving equality in selection procedures. This reform reached its peak in 1972 with the nomination of George S. McGovern. Since the disastrous defeat in the general election of that year, the Democrats have retreated somewhat from applying their earlier standards, but black participation within party affairs is at a much higher level than in the GOP. See William J. Crotty, *Decision for the Democrats: Reforming the Party Structure* (Baltimore: 1979).

62. *Lau v. Nichols*, 414 U.S. 563 (1974), involved Chinese-speaking children in San Francisco. For purposes of busing to achieve school desegregation, the Supreme Court equated Mexican-American children with black students and ordered them integrated with Anglos. *Keyes v. School District No. 1, Denver, Colorado*, 413 U.S. 189 (1973). For a discussion of bilingualism and biculturalism in the education of Hispanic-Americans, see Orfield, *Must We Bus?*, chapter 7. According to the 1975 extention of the Voting Rights Act, a jurisdiction was eligible for federal examiners and observers and subject to preclearance review if it used English-only registration and election materials on 1 November 1972 and less than 50 percent of the voting-age citizens were registered on 1 November 1972 or voted in the presidential election of 1972, and more than 5 percent of the citizens of voting age belonged to a sizable language minority group. In addition, if more than 5 percent of citizens were part of a sizable language minority and the illiteracy rate of such group was higher than the national average, then registration and election materials had to be furnished in the language of the applicable minority group as well as in the English language. To those areas already covered, the act added Texas and parts of California, Colorado, Connecticut, Florida, Hawaii, Idaho, Kansas, Maine, Michigan, Minnesota, Montana, Nebraska, Nevada, New Mexico, North Dakota, Oklahoma, South Dakota, Utah, Washington, Wisconsin, and Wyoming. The protected groups included, Spanish, American Indian, Chinese, and Filipino.

63. Joel Dreyfuss and Charles Lawrence, III, *The Bakke Case: The Politics of Inequality* (New York, 1979). For a different view, see Norman Podhoretz, *Breaking Ranks: A Political Memoir* (New York, 1980), 293-94.

64. Seymour Martin Lipset and William Schneider, "An Emerging National Consensus," *New Republic*, 15 October 1977, 8; "Disadvantaged Groups, Individual Rights," *New Republic*, 15 October 1977, 8.

65. *Griggs v. Duke Power Co.*, 401 U.S. 424 (1971); Alan P. Sindler, *Bakke, DeFunis, and Minority Admissions: The Quest for Equal Opportunity* (New York, 1978), 239; Polenberg, *One Nation Divisible*, 241.

66. *Washington v. Davis*, 426 U.S. 229 (1976); Sindler, *Bakke*, 184-86.

67. Although Bakke scored higher on the entrance qualifications than did most of the minority students admitted through the special program, he still might not have been accepted because other whites had been rejected with even higher ratings than he had.

68. *Regents of the University of California v. Bakke*, 438 U.S. 265, 298 (1978).

69. Ibid., 400-401, 407.

70. *United Steelworkers of America v. Weber*, 443 U.S. 193 (1979); *New York Times*, 13 June 1984, B12 for Hooks' statement and the opinion of the Court in *Firefighters v Stotts*. The Court has approved congressional legislation establishing a quota for granting contracts in public works projects to minority-owned firms in order to rectify past discrimination. *Fullilove v Klutznick*, 448 U.S. 448 (1980).

71. For the Carter administration's uneven performance in civil rights and the Bakke case, see Joseph A. Califano, Jr., *Governing America: An Insider's Report From the White House and Cabinet* (New York, 1981), 243; Dreyfuss and Lawrence, *Bakke*, 166ff.; and Sindler, *Bakke*, 246-51. In 1980 Carter did act forcefully in threatening to veto a bill passed by both houses of Congress that prohibited the Justice Department from seeking busing remedies in the courts. Congress backed down and the measure was withdrawn. Under the Reagan administration it was revived and passed by the Republican-controlled Senate but was defeated in the House.

72. "Quotas Under Attack," *Newsweek*, 25 April 1983, 95-96; Tampa *Tribune*, 30 April 1983, 9A.

73. Dreyfuss and Lawrence, *Bakke*, 144; Lipset and Schneider, "An Emerging National Consensus," 8-9.

74. Dreyfuss and Lawrence, *Bakke*, 198. For a prominent exception of a black who opposed most affirmative action programs, see Thomas Sowell, "A Black Conservative Dissents," *New York Times Magazine*, 8 August 1976, 15, 43.

75. Sitkoff, *Struggle for Black Equality*, 232-33. Of all the areas of civil rights, the situation had perhaps improved the least in housing. For a balanced assessment, see Charles M. Lamb, "Equal Housing Opportunity," in Bullock and Lamb, eds., *Implementation of Civil Rights Policy*, 148-83.

76. Sitkoff, *Struggle for Black Equality*, 234-36; Polenberg, *One Nation Divisible*, 275; Harrell R. Rodgers, Jr., "Fair Employment Laws for Minorities: An Evaluation of Federal Implementation," in Bullock and Lamb, eds., *Implementation*, 93-117; Dorothy K. Newman, et al, *Protest, Politics, and Prosperity: Black Americans and White Institutions, 1940-1975* (New York, 1978), passim.

77. William J. Wilson, *The Declining Significance of Race: Blacks and Changing American Institutions* (Chicago, 1978), 154-64; Thomas Sowell, *Race and Economics* (New York, 1975), 156. Sowell blames affirmative action for contributing to the economic decline of disadvantaged blacks, but Wilson discounts this as a causal factor and stresses the changing structure of the economy. See Wilson's review of Sowell's *Civil Rights: Rhetoric or Reality?* (New York, 1984), in "Hurting the Disadvantaged," *New York Times Book Review* 89 (24 June 1984):28.

The Women's Movement Since 1960:
Structure, Strategies, and New Directions

Leila J. Rupp and Verta Taylor

When feminist scholar Dale Spender interviewed Mary Stott for her book on British feminists active in the post-1920 years, she asked Stott what she had done during the time when there was no women's movement. Stott replied indignantly: "What do you mean, when there was *no* women's movement? There's always been a women's movement this century!"[1] We are convinced of the accuracy of this perception, and so it is from this perspective that we view the American women's movement since 1960 in this essay. The early 1960s should not be viewed solely in terms of the origins of the contemporary movement but rather as a period of transition from a small, isolated, elite-sustained movement to a more mass-based, publicly visible one. In contrast to scholars who have traditionally referred to the death of the women's movement in 1920 and its rebirth in the 1960s, we emphasize the historical continuity of the movement. Since at least the 1840s, the women's movement, although not always in the same form and not always with the same vigor, has raised a challenge to sexual inequality in American society.

The structural preconditions for the resurgence of a mass-based women's movement—an increase in women's educational level, a decline in fertility, and both a rise in women's labor force participation rate and a change in the patterns of that participation—existed by the 1960s, but not until women with different organizational experiences began to come together in new groups devoted to ending women's oppression and winning equality in American society did the movement take on a new shape.[2] This essay will concentrate on the nature and dynamics of the women's movement since 1960 in order to understand the contemporary movement of the mid-1980s. It will examine, first, the resurgence of the women's movement in the early 1960s. This first section is more detailed than the other two because it is based on our own research and makes the critical argument for historical continuity of the women's movement. Although other scholars have examined the activities of women in the early 1960s in order to explain the origins of the contemporary movement, no one has explored the linkages between women's movement activity in the 1950s and the events of the early 1960s.

The second section, based on the work of other scholars, describes the structure, ideology, goals, and strategies of the movement from the late 1960s to the late 1970s, by which time the movement had taken on a somewhat different shape. The third and final section charts the course of the movement since the late 1970s and explores the ways that the feminist vision and the women's movement have interacted with the larger social and political context of American society in the 1980s.

THE RESURGENCE OF THE WOMEN'S MOVEMENT

Students of social movements have traditionally depicted the women's movement of the 1960s and 1970s as having two segments, a liberal or women's rights branch and a radical or women's liberation branch. They have traced the origins of the first to the activities of the President's Commission on the Status of Women from 1961 to 1963 and the formation of the National Organization for Women in 1966, and the roots of the second to the activities of women involved in the Civil Rights and New Left movements.[3] Since scholars have for the most part assumed that there was no organized feminist activity in the period after the end of the Second World War in 1945, they have failed to recognize that an existing women's movement played a role in the activities that led to the resurgence of the movement in the mid-1960s.[4]

In 1960 the American women's movement consisted of a number of organizations and networks of women, most of them older, white, middle or upper class, well-educated professionals who had developed a commitment to feminism in the early years of the twentieth century. We call this movement "elite-sustained" because a small group of women with the time, financial means, and other kinds of resources to commit themselves to the feminist cause kept the movement alive. The movement lacked an active mass membership, but it attempted to give the appearance of a mass base and used strategies such as lobbying and letter-writing that could be carried out by the leadership and core membership without large-scale support from members. The movement, which had ties with the suffrage movement through both its personnel and its organizational history, focused its efforts primarily on passage of the Equal Rights Amendment and advocacy of women in policy-making positions.[5]

This elite-sustained movement made important connections with the emerging liberal branch of the contemporary movement. This section explores these connections through an examination of the President's Commission on the Status of Women, the struggle to include sex discrimination in the Civil Rights Act of 1964, and the establishment of the National Organization for Women.

The President's Commission on the Status of Women

When President John F. Kennedy announced the formation of his Commission on the Status of Women in 1961, he implicitly recognized the existence of gender-based discrimination in American society. If the 1950s had brought only contentment and conformity among American women, it would be hard to understand why the president would have perceived the need for such a commission. The mere establishment of the body suggest that the women's movement, as it existed throughout the 1950s, had made some impact on American society. For the Commission was to a large extent a response to the challenge of the existing women's movement and, at the same time, an important factor in the resurgence of the movement.

The concept of a commission on women's status in American society was not a new one in the 1960s. Opponents of the Equal Rights Amendment, which had been introduced in every Congress since 1923 and was the major goal of the women's movement in the period after 1945, had long supported Congressional legislation to establish such a body in hopes that it would serve as an alternative to the amendment that they believed would harm women by eliminating protective legislation.[6] ERA foe Esther Peterson, head of the Women's Bureau and the most influential woman in Kennedy's new administration, revived the idea of a commission in 1960 when the activity of ERA supporters raised the issue during the 1960 election.

Both the National Woman's Party, the core of the movement in the years after 1945, and the National Federation of Business and Professional Women's Clubs (BPW) had fought for support of the ERA by candidates and both major parties. In 1960 the Democratic platform, for the first time since 1944, carefully avoided a specific commitment to the ERA. Despite the efforts of ERA supporters, the 1960 platform supported "legislation which will guarantee to women equality of rights under the law including equal pay for equal work." Although National Woman's Party president and Democratic Committeewoman Emma Guffey Miller insisted that the plank favored the ERA, it in fact deliberately did not mention the amendment, a consequence of strong opposition from high-level Democratic women, especially Peterson. When Kennedy received the nomination at the convention, Miller forged ahead in an attempt to gain an endorsement from him, despite the fact that he had long refused to commit himself on the question, making it quite clear to other Woman's Party members that he was not a supporter.[7] Nevertheless, Miller triumphantly proclaimed his support, quoting a letter over his signature that assured her that he would interpret the platform, "as I know it is intended, to bring about, through concrete actions including the adoption of the Equal Rights for Women Amendment, the full equality for women which advocates of the equal rights amendment have always sought."[8]

This puzzling announcement of support was not, however, genuine. Esther Peterson, who worked closely with Kennedy in his campaign, had drafted his response, which did not include the phrase "including the adoption of the Equal Rights for Women Amendment" in the portion of the letter quoted above. Her files include two versions of the letter, one with and one without the offending phrase. Peterson later privately denounced the revised letter as a "forgery" and blamed it on a "mishap of the headquarters office" that she had not wanted to discuss openly because it reflected badly on the operation of the campaign. Notes in Peterson's papers from the 1970s make clear her conviction that a National Woman's Party member in the campaign office had added the phrase and taken the letter to the press.[9] According to Cynthia Harrison, who has written about women's organizations and the federal government during this period, Miller herself had amended the letter and used her connections at the Democratic National Committee to have it typed on Kennedy letterhead and signed, presumably by machine.[10] To Peterson's fury the Woman's Party took full advantage of the altered letter.

In response to this situation, Peterson, with a great deal of effort, persuaded Kennedy to appoint the Commission on the Status of Women.[11] Scholars who have written about the President's Commission agree that it represented in part an attempt to sidetrack the ERA. Peterson complained, "[A]lmost no day passes but what I have to draft some letter" about the ERA. "I will continue to do this," she wrote to one of Kennedy's aides, "but I do think you should be aware that the Equal

Righters, since they have nothing else to do, are intensifying their campaign in every State."[12]

Since Peterson hoped that a commission would "substitute constructive recommendations for the present troublesome and futile agitation about the 'equal rights amendment,' " she chose only one ERA supporter, former BPW president Marguerite Rawalt, to serve on the body.[13] Not surprisingly, the Commission, despite the efforts of ERA supporters in the women's movement and Rawalt's efforts on the Commission, concluded in its final report that a constitutional amendment was not at that time necessary in order to establish the principle of equality.

To no one's surprise, then, the Commission tried to dampen the ardor of ERA advocates, but, ironically, it gave a boost to the ERA by serving as a stimulus for the growth of the women's movement. It did this in two major ways: by raising the issue of women's status to the level of national discussion; and by creating an institutional structure that brought together women not previously involved in women's movement activity.

Katherine Ellickson, executive secretary of the Commission, reported that the work of the Commission was widely publicized throughout the country, although not so much through the media as by distribution of copies of the final report, which became a best seller. Throughout the existence of the Commission, women wrote the president or the Commission itself in praise of the national attention focused on the status of women. Such letters, included in the Commission papers, suggest that some women saw the Commission as a body able to bring change to women's lives.

Perhaps even more significant for the growth of the women's movement was the continuing institutional structure that the Commission created. Participation in the work of the Commission played a crucial role in the development of feminist consciousness for several key figures such as Catherine East and Mary Eastwood, both government employees assigned to assist the Commission, and Pauli Murray, a Black woman lawyer who served on the Civil and Political Rights Committee. Murray described the Commission in an interview as "kind of heaven for me, this was like throwing brer rabbit in the briar patch, because it was the first time in my life that I had really sat down and researched the status of women."[14] The Commission brought together women interested in women's status, raised their consciousness, and created a structure through which they could continue to meet.

In its final recommendation, the Commission asked Kennedy to establish both a permanent commission of executive department and agency heads and an advisory commitee of private citizens. These took shape, respectively, as the Interdepartmental Committee on the Status of Women and the Citizens' Advisory Council on the Status of Women. In addition the BPW developed a plan to set up state commissions on the status of women throughout the country to continue the work of the President's Commission.

Even at the time, members of the President's Commission recognized that their work had both grown out of and in turn stimulated activity among existing women's organizations. During committee discussions Pauli Murray asserted that everyone associated with the Commission in any way would act as a catalytic agent.[15] It is not surprising, then, that the Commission has been identified as a key institution in the growth of the women's movement in the 1960s. Although, as Katherine Ellickson noted, she and Esther Peterson "were not primarily concerned with feminist efforts," the Commission that they shaped in response to pressure from the existing women's movement had important feminist results.[16]

Title VII of the Civil Rights Act

Perhaps the most peculiar episode in the history of the women's movement occured in 1964, when Congress passed a Civil Rights Act that included a prohibition against discrimination in employment on the basis of sex. Title VII, the only section of the bill to include sex as well as race discrimination, continues to serve as the major piece of legislation safeguarding women's employment rights, and the issue of its nonenforcement by the government became an early rallying cry for the liberal branch of the movement in the mid-1960s. Yet most interpretations of the process by which Title VII came to include gender-based as well as racial discrimination emphasize the fact that the civil rights bill's opponents introduced and supported the amendment to include sex discrimination in Title VII. Thus, according to most accounts, the legislation that serves as a cornerstone of the women's movement originated as an attempt to ridicule and defeat the civil rights legislation by dividing its supporters. But the story, as several commentators have recognized, is much more complex and shows that Title VII was not just an unexpected gift to the women's movement.[17]

The idea of linking sex and race in the civil rights bill did not suddenly occur to Howard Smith, the conservative Virginian who introduced the amendment on the floor of the House of Representatives. The National Woman's Party had already tried to jump on the civil rights bandwagon in the 1950s, and eight years before the famous debate on Title VII, the House of Representatives had debated a similar amendment to a civil rights bill at the instigation of Woman's Party founder

Alice Paul. In late 1963, anticipating the debate on the new civil rights bill, the national council of the Woman's Party passed a resolution calling for the amendment of the proposed bill to include discrimination on the basis of sex. Two members then wrote to their representative, Howard Smith, knowing that he opposed the bill, to suggest that a sex amendment would divert some of the pressure for passage of the bill. Presumably the Woman's Party was trying to persuade Smith that a sex amendment would serve his interests. The members who wrote, although genuinely opposed to the civil rights movement, were willing to use any method to eliminate sex discrimination.[18]

Smith responded to the letters from the Woman's Party members with an indication that he expected someone to make an amendment from the floor during the debate, but he did not offer to make it himself. This in itself indicates that the idea of including sex discrimination was not such a far-fetched idea in 1964. In January he mentioned the sex amendment in a committee hearing, commenting that the "National Woman's Party were serious about it."[19] Late in January Smith appeared on "Meet the Press," where journalist May Craig, a longtime feminist activist and National Woman's Party member who bombarded presidents from Eisenhower to Johnson with questions about equality for women, asked him about the amendment. He said that he might introduce it. And, when the House took up debate of the bill, he did. Smith's presentation and the subject itself provoked a great deal of laughter, contributing to the legend of what came to be known as "Ladies' Day in the House."

Smith's motives in all of this are not totally clear. Although it is certainly true that he wanted to defeat the civil rights bill, it is also true that he had served as a sponsor of the ERA since 1943. Women involved in the fight for Title VII tend to believe that Smith may have acted in part out of a kind of southern "chivalry" toward white women.[20] Probably he hoped that the amendment would help defeat the bill but believed that, if it did not, it would be better at least to give white women the same protection accorded to black women and men.

Once Smith introduced the amendment, forces other than those hostile to civil rights jumped into the fray, and it is this support from feminists that has been ignored in the popular version of the story. Martha Griffiths, representative from Michigan and a member—if only on paper—of the National Woman's Party since 1955, had planned to introduce a similar amendment but had allowed Smith to do it since he would bring in the votes of the southern Democrats.[21] All but one of the other women members supported the amendment also. The National

Woman's Party, the BPW, and individuals who had been active in the President's Commission lobbied and wrote memoranda in support of the amendment. After victory in both the House and the Senate, the Woman's Party claimed credit, and commentators, including Marguerite Rawalt, recognized the hard work that the Woman's Party put into the Title VII fight.[22] Women involved in the struggle recognized that the small number of women in the feminist "underground" had an impact out of all proportion to their numbers. Said one: "I seriously doubt that women could have gotten Title VII without just a very small number of us. As a matter of fact I think it was a tremendous political coup, if you want to know the truth." And another: "Our guess is that the Senators did not know how few there were of us and got the feeling that this . . . would really touch off a woman's revolt and that they better not fool with it and so they went along."[23]

In 1965, at a meeting of the National Council of Women on Title VII and its enforcing agency, the Equal Employment Opportunity Commission, the significance of the legend of the passage of Title VII began to emerge. Franklin Roosevelt, Jr., head of the EEOC, suggested that the inclusion of sex discrimination in Title VII presented a problem, since the intent had been to ridicule the concept of equal employment opportunity. Feminist Miriam Holden, who attended the meeting, reported to Alice Paul that Roosevelt seemed to be indicating that the EEOC would not enforce the sex provision.[24] This is exactly what happened, and the public image of the sex amendment as "a mischievous joke" and "cumbersome irrelevancy" supported the government's decision to downplay sex discrimination.[25] As Ernestine Powell, former national chair of the Woman's Party, commented to a Columbus, Ohio, newspaper reporter: "It was a great achievement. Oh, I know most men call it a fluke, but it wasn't anything of the sort. It was a long hard fight and we won."[26] That victory, which probably could not have been won by the women's movement alone, shows how the movement could link up with diverse interests, not all of them progressive, to make progress for women. After the founding of the National Organization for Women in 1966, the enforcement of Title VII became a primary goal of the liberal branch of the movement.

The Founding of NOW

As a result of the President's Commission and the inclusion of sex discrimination in employment in Title VII, the issue of women's status began to edge into the public consciousness. The publication in 1963 of Betty Friedan's *The Feminine Mystique* had also alerted women throughout the country to the collective character of what had once seemed personal dissatisfaction.[27] Meanwhile, women continued to meet in the Status of Women organizations sparked by the President's Commission. Friedan, beginning work on another book, contacted Martha Griffiths, attorney Pauli Murray, members of the President's Commission, and staff members of the EEOC and discovered "a seething underground of women in the Government, the press and the labor unions."[28]

It was women from this "seething underground" who gathered at the Third National Conference of Commissions on the Status of Women in June 1966 and spontaneously decided to form a new organization, modeled on the NAACP, to fight for women's rights. Friedan suggested the name "National Organization for Women." The early leadership of NOW included women from the United Auto Workers; women such as Pauli Murray from the President's Commission; women from the state commissions; in-government feminists such as Mary Eastwood and Catherine East; and women who had long been involved in women's movement activity such as Marguerite Rawalt. The government unwittingly contributed to NOW's early work, since the women who wrote the early sex discrimination briefs made use of government offices, typewriters, and copy machines at night, unbeknownst to their superiors.[29] As Pauli Murray explained it, "Women did not come to the women's movement without bringing an awful lot of resources: resources in organizations we hadn't even thought about, borrowed techniques of research; and I think a lot of this had to do with why the thing exploded so."[30] This access to and cooptation of existing resources inside and outside the movement proved crucial in the development of the movement in the later 1960s.

Although most of the women involved in the founding of NOW had not identified with the women's movement in earlier decades, the old elite-sustained movement did make connections with the new. Individuals who had been active in the older women's organizations joined NOW and other of the new groups. Perhaps most important, the major issue of the elite-sustained stage of the movement—the Equal Rights Amendment—was adopted by NOW in 1967, largely as a result of prompting from National Woman's Party members.[31] The Woman's Party took the same approach toward NOW that it had long taken toward other women's organizations: it sought endorsement of the ERA, it used infiltration, and it sought to recruit members from NOW's ranks. In Alice Paul's view, "We captured the NOW people."[32]

The elite-sustained women's movement did, then, make connections with the resurgent women's movement in the 1960s and 1970s. The history of the President's Commission, the inclusion of sex discrimination in Title VII, and the early years of NOW make clear that the movement that grew in the mid-1960s consisted of new organizations and individuals who brought fresh perspectives to the question of women's status. At the same time, the elite-sustained women's movement as it had survived the 1950s played a role in the key events that marked the transition from one stage of the movement to another.

Emergence of the Radical Branch

By the late 1960s, the "seething underground" had taken shape as the liberal branch of the contemporary women's movement. At the same time, the radical branch had begun to grow from quite different roots.[33] Young women active in the Civil Rights movement in the South and the New Left movement in the North, experiencing oppression as women not only in the larger society but within the movements to which they had committed their time and energy, began to apply their radical ideas about equality and social justice to their own lives as women. Just as the older women involved in the founding of NOW used the NAACP as a model, the younger women applied the concept behind Black Power and the principles of participatory democracy to themselves: they began to insist that only a movement of women focused on the oppression of women could bring about true liberation. The personal friendship networks of women, the movement media, and movement events publicized and spread the burgeoning movement for women's liberation.

The resurgence of the women's movement, then, came from these two different sources. The radical branch at first made little connection to the historical tradition of the women's movement, since the participants, from their radical political perspective, denounced the activity of the liberal branch organizations as bourgeois reformism, but the older feminists of the elite-sustained stage of the movement were aware of the radical young women. In 1967 Ruth Gage-Colby, a peace activist and progressive Woman's Party member, attended the National Conference for New Politics, a New Left event at which women began to organize, and worked on the women's resolution presented to the body. Second generation and longtime Woman's Party member Mary Kennedy went to hear Kate Millett speak at Purdue University in 1971 and took ERA literature to hand out to the crowd. Although Kennedy felt out of place as the only one in the audience in a hat and without long hair and could not hear the speech due to a hearing impairment, she reported with satisfaction that Millett favored the ERA and that the crowd had responded enthusiastically to her speech.[34] If an old suffragist like Kennedy felt out of place at such an event, nevertheless women who, like Alice Paul, criticized the movement for taking up too many controversial issues also acknowledged that the women's liberationists "are a little like we were."[35]

By the end of the 1960s, both liberal and radical branches had taken on their distinctive structures, strategies, and goals. The next section examines the development of the movement in the following decade.

THE WOMAN'S MOVEMENT,
LATE 1960s TO LATE 1970s

When the women's movement burst onto the public scene in the late 1960s, it grabbed the attention of the media and the public. Not surprisingly, scholars writing about the women's movement have tended to focus on this period in order to explain the flurry of activity around feminist issues. This section makes use of existing scholarship in order to outline the structure, goals, and strategies of the movement during this period—a decade during which the two branches of the women's movement began to converge.[36]

Structure

The two arms of the women's movement, as they developed from the late 1960s to the late 1970s, differed primarily on the basis of origins, membership, and structure. Although both branches were comprised primarily of white, middle-class, college-educated women, the membership of the two, as already suggested, differed on the bases of age and previous organizational experience. The structure of organizations within the two branches also differed in fairly dramatic ways. The liberal branch consisted primarily of national-level, hierarchically-organized, formal organizations with officers and constitutions; the radical branch was an amorphous, decentralized network of primarily local, autonomous groups characterized by lack of formal organization and hierarchy. In addition, the ideology of the two branches differed: the politics of both branches were predicated on the belief that women disproportionately occupy peripheral positions in society and men are more frequently found in core positions, but a liberal feminist approach holds that society should make a greater effort to redistribute persons (women and men) between the core and the periphery, and a radical feminist approach advocates a redistribution of rewards between the core and periphery.[37] In other words the liberal feminist branch took a reformist stance, while the radical feminist branch advocated the transformation of the major structures of society.

Goals and Strategies

On the basis of the differences in origin, membership, and structure, the two branches used different strategies in pursuit of their related goals. The liberal branch in its early years focused on legal change. The immediate impetus for the founding of the National Organization for Women in 1966 was the refusal of the Equal Employment Opportunity Commission to enforce the provisions of Title VII as they applied to women. The women involved in the founding of NOW at the Third National Conference of the State Commissions on the Status of Women took their first action when they sent telegrams protesting the EEOC guidelines permitting the continuation of sex-segregated want ads in newspapers. NOW's purpose was "to take action to bring women into full participation in the mainstream of American society *now*, exercising all the privileges and responsibilities thereof in truly equal partnership with men."[38]

At its 1967 conference, the organization debated a Bill of Rights that specified particular areas of concern. Most had to do with employment: enforcement of Title VII, maternity leave rights, tax deductions for child care expenses, child care centers, education, and job training. Only two "rights" aroused heated disagreement: the Equal Rights Amendment and reproductive rights. The first met opposition from the United Auto Workers union women who could not support the amendment, whatever their personal opinions, while their union continued to oppose it. The issue of reproductive rights alienated women who did not believe that abortion was a women's issue and who feared that advocacy of abortion would destroy whatever credibility the organization might have. Women from the old elite-sustained stage of the movement, who worked to win an endorsement of the ERA from NOW, were infuriated by NOW's endorsement of reproductive freedom for women. When Betty Friedan, as president of NOW, spoke at the Democratic convention in 1968 in favor of both the ERA and abortion rights, Woman's Party members considered it sabotage of the ERA.[39] Conflicts within NOW in the early years resulted in the exodus of members who, from both conservative and radical positions, found the goals and structure of the organization uncongenial. When NOW endorsed reproductive freedom, a group of women walked out and formed the Women's Equity Action League, a liberal branch organization that focuses primarily on the issue of discrimination in education. At the next meeting, part of the New York branch left NOW after failing to restructure the organization along nonhierarchical, more participatory, lines.

In its first years, NOW tended to focus on issues of legal change, but it did not confine its activities to the courts. In contrast to the women's movement in the years after the suffrage victory in 1920, NOW began to make use of militant tactics such as picketing EEOC offices throughout the country in 1967 and organizing a national Women's Strike on the anniversary of the suffrage victory in 1970. Ironically, when NOW began to propose militant tactics in support of the ERA struggle, the National Woman's Party, heir of the militant suffragist tradition, opposed such actions. By the late 1970s, when NOW had become the established leader of the ERA forces, a new group, taking the name "Congressional Union," the original name of the group that became the Woman's Party in 1916, in turn took up militant tactics, much to the dismay of both the Woman's Party's and NOW's leadership.

In contrast to organizations like NOW, the radical branch groups that formed in the early years had more diverse and amorphous goals. Women in New Left organizations came together to engage in consciousness-raising and to begin to develop a theory of women's oppression. Women active in the civil rights and New Left movements had already accepted a radical—in most cases Marxist—critique of American society, but they had also begun to meet with other women because not only did they experience oppression within the movement as women but also because movement theory made no place for the oppression of women. That is, not only did women find themselves confined to traditional women's roles—making coffee and making love—but they also found that New Left men ridiculed their early attempts to apply their radical perspective on liberation to their own lives. The ambiguity of this position—making use of the theory, structure, personal contacts, and media of movements that women were essentially leaving—led to conflicts within the radical branch. Some women attempted simply to extend the analysis and action of the New Left to women, but others broke away by putting women's oppression at the center of their analysis. These tendencies solidified into two positions: what early commentators called "politicos" and "feminists" and later ones called "socialist feminists" and "radical feminists."

In accord with their emphasis on theory-building and consciousness-raising, small groups in major cities began to publish newsletters and engage in "actions" that called their existence to the attention of the media. The most famous of these actions was the 1968 Miss America protest, at which members of Radical Women, a New York group, joined with other women in Atlantic City during the famous pageant to crown a sheep Miss America and deposit symbols of women's objectification—including bras, giving rise to the myth of "bra-burning" in the movement—in a "freedom trashcan." Other public actions occurred as well. Both the Redstockings, which was founded by a group of women who split off from Radical Women, and the Feminists, another New York group, devoted their first public activity to the abortion issue. In 1969 the Redstockings disrupted hearings of the New York state legislature on the abortion laws, and the Feminists demonstrated at the trial of an abortionist and picketed the New York Marriage License Bureau to protest the institution of marriage.

Convergence of the Branches

Since the late 1960s, NOW has grown enormously and has become a kind of umbrella group for the movement as a whole. In addition, other liberal branch organizations like the Women's Equity Action League (WEAL) and the National Women's Political Caucus, founded by feminist politicians Shirley Chisholm and Bella Abzug in 1971, have grown in both numbers and political power. NOW in effect took over leadership of the ERA struggle by the early 1970s and, while expanding its focus and taking ever more radical positions throughout the years, has become the organization the media and even government is most likely to call upon to represent the women's movement as a whole. But NOW's history was stormy, as the conflict at the 1967 conference foretold. Despite NOW's success in winning a wide range of support for the 1970 Women's Strike, which focused on demands for 24-hour child care centers, abortion on demand, and equality of opportunity in education and employment, joint endeavors with other feminist organizations were rare in the first decade of renewed activism. A major conflict in NOW that gave it a bad reputation among radical feminist groups erupted over the participation of openly lesbian women in the movement. Betty Friedan was outspoken in opposition to such participation, labeling the lesbian "issue" a "lavender herring." When lesbian author and activist Rita Mae Brown joined New York NOW in 1969, the conflict erupted. In 1970 lesbian members staged a "Lavender Menace" protest at the second annual Congress to Unite Women and forced recognition of the reality of lesbian oppression both outside of and within the movement. Despite further bitter conflict, NOW at its fifth annual conference in 1971 passed a strong prolesbian resolution that recognized the unacceptability of permitting only closeted lesbians to participate in NOW and emphasized the significance of lesbian rights to feminism.

Another conflict broke out within NOW at the 1975 convention. A group designating itself the Majority Caucus called for the organization of women in sex-segregated "women's" jobs; recognition of the relationship of oppression based on sex, race, ethnicity, class, and sexual orientation; the recruitment of minority women; and the use of more militant tactics. Despite the fact that many members opposed this program, the organization as a whole adopted it and, by the 1977 convention, appeared unified.

As liberal groups, and NOW in particular, expanded their programs in the course of the 1970s, the proliferating radical groups shifted from an emphasis on theory-building and consciousness-raising to a focus on specific issues such as violence against women, women's health, reproductive freedom, pornography, and the creation of women's culture through the production of women's music and the establishment of alternative institutions such as bookstores, coffee houses, and festivals. Liberal branch groups took up some of these issues, such as violence against women and reproductive freedom, while radical groups alone worked on others. As Jo Freeman has pointed out, it is ironic that the radical branch has increasingly taken on what we tend to think of as maintenance or service activities, such as the creation of shelters for battered women, the establishment of rape crisis centers, the publication of newspapers, and the production of cultural events, while the liberal branch focuses its efforts on bringing about change in the laws and policies of our society. In a sense this represents a reversal of what are ordinarily thought of as "radical" and "liberal" activities. Of course, what lies behind the service activities of the radical branch are two convictions: that the provision of alternative structures for women is one means of transforming society, and that working within these structures results in and sustains fundamental changes in individual women's consciousness that, in turn, is another means of changing society.

Although the women's movement as a whole grew throughout the 1970s—NOW numbered almost sixty thousand members in 1977 and small groups had formed in cities and towns across the country—the movement remained relatively homogeneous. Although individual women of color and working-class women had participated in the founding of NOW and in the early protests against sexism in the civil rights movement, the movement continued to attract primarily white middle-class women. This was not because other women experienced no oppression as women. The 1972 Virginia Slims Poll showed clearly that black women as a group were more likely than white women to support the women's movement. Forty-eight percent of the female population at large favored efforts to strengthen or change women's status in society; the comparable figure for black women was 62 percent. And 67 percent of black women, compared to 39 percent of all women, were sympathetic toward women's liberation.[40]

Yet the movement remained predominantly white and middle class, because of the continuation of the historical tradition within the women's movement of defining its goals with regard to the concerns of white middle-class women and because black women and other women of color believed in the necessity and importance of working with men of their own communities toward their own collective interests. From the very beginnings of protest within the civil rights movement, for example, black women's experiences had been different from those of white women. Although Ruby Doris Smith Robinson, a black woman, had been involved in protest within the Student Non-Violent Coordinating Committee over the relegation of women to traditional women's work, the major complaints came from white women. Sara Evans quotes Cynthia Washington, a black woman who directed her own project within the Student Non-Violent Coordinating Committee, on black women's attitudes toward the white women's protests: "What . . . white women seemed to want was an opportunity to prove they could do something other than office work. I assumed that if they could do something else, they'd probably be doing it. . . . It seemed to many of us . . . that white women were demanding a chance to be independent while we needed help and assistance which was not always forthcoming. We definitely started from opposite ends of the spectrum."[41] The contradiction between black women's supportive attitudes and the predominantly white composition of the women's movement resulted, in 1973, in the formation of the National Black Feminist Organization, which numbered one thousand members by the end of the year. Other groups, too, like the Combahee River Collective, a group of black feminists formed in 1974, came together in response to the situation.[42] By the late 1970s, the women's movement had begun to explore the realities of its racism and class bias, even if sometimes only superficially, and to attempt to confront the institutionalization of racism in the movement. For example, the 1981 National Women's Studies Association conference, entitled "Women Respond to Racism," was a response to the demands of women of color within the association that the women's movement address its own racism.

In the same way, the class bias of the women's movement has made working-class and poor women unlikely to participate in sizable numbers. It should not be forgotten, however, that union women played a significant role in the formation of NOW and in fact supported the fledgling organization by providing office space and clerical services until the group's endorsement of the ERA forced the United Auto Workers women to withdraw such support. Women committed to both feminism and the union movement eventually formed their own organization, the Coalition of Labor Union Women, in 1974. CLUE claimed sixteen thousand members by 1982 and had made progress in its fight to win AFL-CIO support for feminist issues.

Throughout the 1970s, then, the women's movement grew and expanded its focus. The composition of the movement may have remained predominantly white, middle-class, and well-educated, but it began to recognize the need to expand the definition of "women's issues" to include problems of central concern to women of color, working-class and poor women, and lesbian women. Despite the continued differences in the structure of national mass-membership organizations and small local groups, the goals and strategies of what began as two quite distinct branches began to converge. By the late 1970s, the differences in movement organizations were not nearly as significant as they had seemed in the 1960s, even though ideological disputes continued to be fierce. The ERA, for example—once too controversial for some women and too insignificant, if not downright counterrevolutionary, for others—received support from a variety of organizations throughout the movement. When NOW sponsored a national march in Washington in support of the ERA in 1978, civil rights groups, left-wing groups, labor unions, and a wide range of other organizations and individuals turned out to support the cause. Despite the failure to win ratification of the ERA by the 1982 deadline, the show of support and unity was impressive.

In the same way, reproductive freedom, once a goal of the early radical groups and a source of bitter dispute in NOW, became a rallying cry for the entire movement. Since the 1973 Supreme Court decision that legalized abortion by making it a private issue between a woman and her doctor, the women's movement has been fighting to preserve existing reproductive rights and to extend those rights to the women denied them.[43] The National Abortion Rights Action League, established in 1969 as the National Association for the Repeal of Abortion Laws, is typical of the special interest groups that have emerged in the 1970s. Organizations like New York's Committee for Abortion Rights and

Against Sterilization Abuse link the problem of sterilization abuse of poor women and women of color to the issue of abortion and fight against legislation like the Hyde Amendment, which forbids federal funding of abortion through Medicaid. The continuing threat of the Human Life Amendment, supported by the New Right and the Reagan administration, has brought together groups that cannot easily be labeled "liberal" or "radical."

The final section of this essay addresses the movement since the late 1970s, considering how it has changed and how it fits into the larger social and political context of American society in the 1980s.

THE WOMEN'S MOVEMENT SINCE THE LATE 1970s

By the late 1970s, the American women's movement had begun to confront issues of racism, class bias, and heterosexism within its own ranks, but at the same time it continued to work to bring about change in the larger society. The movement since the late 1970s has, paradoxically, grown at once increasingly radical and increasingly institutionalized. There has been a tendency in the social movement literature to view moderation and accomodation as invariably accompanying institutionalization. Accepting benefits from established groups, it is assumed, entails compromise. Yet the consequences of increasing institutionalization may in fact be more complex.[44] What follows is a consideration of the increasingly radical analysis of the women's movement and its success in working through established institutions to accomplish some of its goals, as well as reflections on the challenge that the New Right, as an antifeminist countermovement, has offered to the women's movement.

Radicalization

Although contemporary feminist ideology is diverse and complex, radicalization is the most important trend in feminist ideology today. Participation in liberal feminist reform organizations and work on "women's issues" such as rape or woman-battering in the context of established organizations has raised women's consciousness, increased their feminist activism, and contributed to their radicalization.[45] Women have also become radicalized in the process of working through personal experiences with sexual harassment, divorce, abortion, employment discrimination, incest, and rape. Radicalization, as we have already seen, is evident at the group level also. In 1979 NOW included in its program not only the ERA and reproductive freedom, but also such issues as nuclear energy, lesbian and gay rights, homemakers' rights, the exploitation of women in the home, the sexual segregation of women in the workplace, and the influence of corporate, patriarchal, and hierarchical models of organization on its own activities.

Contemporary feminist thought encompasses diverse beliefs and is by no means a monolithic perspective, but as an ideology feminism generally has become far more comprehensive in its analysis of the institutions that perpetuate and sustain male dominance than in any other period of history. Feminism in the 1980s is a transformational politics, a comprehensive ideology that addresses nearly every issue in the world, from international peace to the economic policy of the United States. Because feminist ideology has become a tool for linking social issues, it has become threatening to the established order. For example, the belief in a woman's right to control her own body, extended to other issues, raises the questions not only of rape, incest, and sexual harassment, but also of job safety, the destruction of life through starvation, poverty, chemical dumping, nuclear proliferation, and the exporting to the Third World of unsafe drugs banned in this country.[46] In some ways the radicalization of feminist ideology has brought the women's movement back into alliance with other progressive movements for social change in this country and around the world. The movement that grew in the 1840s out of the abolition movement and emerged reinvigorated from the civil rights and New Left movements of the 1960s is beginning to consider how American society can be changed according to feminist principles so that it is a just and fair society for all people regardless of sex, race, class, sexual orientation, or any other social characteristic.

The decentralized structure of the movement has made possible the expansion of goals associated with increasing radicalization. Independent feminist groups continue to proliferate and work toward such goals as the reintroduction of the ERA; provision of services for displaced homemakers; elimination of pornography; the right of women to options, including home delivery, in childbirth; support for women with substance abuse problems; lesbian rights; the elimination of racism and anti-Semitism; workplace organizing of clerical workers; and other new and continuing goals. These different organizations recruit from different sectors of the population, develop their own organizational styles, and have their own specific goals and means. The two branches of the women's movement have converged not because there are no longer any differences between groups on the basis of ideology, structure, goals, and strategies, but because it is more likely to be age and social network that determine how an individual woman will participate. For example, in Columbus, Ohio, in the late 1970s, the local NOW chapter became involved in a series of radical and militant actions around the issue of violence against women. A small group of women who identified as radical feminists made NOW, considered a liberal feminist organization on the national level, into a radical feminist group on the local level. The radical feminist NOW members shared a common political perspective with the members of a local radical feminist group, the Women's Action Collective, but they were older than the predominantly student or student-age membership of the Collective and moved in different social networks. As a result they focused their energies into NOW. While NOW members were arrested for spray-painting antirape slogans on a freeway sound barrier, members of constituent groups of the Women's Action Collective had, with financial support from a federal grant, instituted a court watch program to help rape survivors within the legal system and developed a child assault prevention project that sent speakers into the schools. In other words, the group that would be identified as a radical feminist one was working within the system while the organization considered a liberal feminist one was making use of militant, even illegal, tactics on the local level. What is significant about all of this is that the old distinctions beween the branches have less meaning in the 1980s.

Institutionalization

At the same time that the women's movement as a whole has become more radical in its ideology, it has also become more institutionalized. Although the movement failed in its attempt to win ratification of the ERA by the 1982 deadline and is fighting an increasingly fierce battle over reproductive freedom, it has also succeeded on a number of fronts in institutionalizing both organizations and goals. In the realm of politics, for instance, both NOW and the National Women's Political Caucus have become organizations whose endorsements of issues and candidates are regularly sought within the established political process. They have, in effect, become the "interest group" representatives of women in the arena of politics. But even groups that developed within the radical branch of the movement have established institutional contacts and won support for their goals within the system. For example, groups working on rape prevention have received financial support from government agencies such as the National Institute of Mental Health and private foundations at the local level and have begun to provide programs and workshops on rape prevention within public schools and universities. In fact, the widespread acceptance of the feminist analysis of rape as an act of violence and power rather than a strictly sexual act attests to the impact of the feminist antirape movement in

American society. Likewise, the battered women's shelter movement has grown in less than ten years from a small group of radical feminists to a movement supported by agencies such as the United Way and, in some states, by a tax on marriage licenses.[47]

The same kind of development is evident in almost every area of the women's movement: the growth of women's studies within high school, colleges, and universities; the development of the women's culture industry, including women's music and feminist publishing; and the success of feminist legal groups in expanding women's legal rights and charting future directions for the movement. The distinctions between "working outside the system" and "working within the system," so important in the late 1960s, no longer have the same significance in the 1980s. Women working to organize clerical workers, to educate children about sexual assaut, to win legal recognition for the principle of equal pay for work of comparable value, or to organize a "Women Take Back the Night" march are all working toward the same goal of dismantling the complex structural base of patriarchy and ultimately transforming society.

The fact that collective action by the women's movement has both created new institutions and moved into almost every major institution of society suggests that the feminist challenge today has a significant impact on every facet of social life and on the lives of many individuals as well. If this is the case, then the decentralized structure and diverse strategies of the contemporary movement would seem to be effective in helping the movement to survive and to reach its ultimate objectives. At the same time, however, the movement has generated countermovement activity that represents a challenge to the further progress of the women's movement. We turn now to a brief examination of the actions and activities directed against feminist activism in the early 1980s, actions that can be viewed in part as a response to the momentum achieved by the women's movement in the decade of the 1970s.

Antifeminism and the New Right

Almost any movement as long-standing and pervasive as the feminist movement gives rise to waves of countermovement activity. In the 1970s the New Right, a highly organized movement with a broad program, took up the banner of antifeminism. It began as a coalition of groups opposed to busing, abortion, and the ERA, later took up opposition to gay rights and developed an interest in foreign policy issues, and in the 1980s includes in its program a concern with economic policies and opposition to social policies designed to regulate business, such as affirmative action and health and safety programs.[48] Included in the New Right, although this list is by no means comprehensive, are such explicitly antifeminist groups as Stop-ERA, the National Pro-Life Political Action Committee, the National Right-to-Life Committee, the Phyllis Schlafly Report, along with other groups such as the Moral Majority, Fund for a Conservative Majority, American Conservative Union, Young Americans for Freedom, National Right to Work Committee, National Rifle Association, God Bless America, Inc., the Conservative Caucus, the Heritage Foundation, the Ku Klux Klan, the John Birch Society, and the central political wing of the Right, the National Conservative Political Action Committee. Its principal strategies are lobbying and electoral campaigns, and it relies on a small cadre of professionals, most often ministers and conservative politicians, to mobilize its constituency through preexisting institutional networks, primarily churches.

Antifeminist women in the 1980s are in some ways responding to the same set of experiences and changing circumstances that feminists are encountering, but they have fashioned a rather different sort of response. In joining anti-ERA, antiabortion, and other groups of the New Right, they are in some ways responding to their own oppression as women.[49] According to feminist writer Deirdre English's research on the antiabortion movement, the women of the Right are mostly white, middle-class, older homemakers with few employment options, married to men whose salaries are no longer adequate to support their families. Like feminists, they fear the consequences of abortion and divorce for women. They believe that legalized abortion has often meant the abdication of any male responsibility for pregnancy; and they deplore the fact that most families cannot survive without two wage-earners, that half of all divorced men default on child support within the first year, and that a single woman often cannot support her children on her own. As English suggests, these women accurately sense that feminism has freed men and may never get around to freeing women. The difference between feminists and the women of the Right lies not in the problems they face but in their approach to solutions. Antifeminism is reactionary, expressed in the desire to return to the simple solutions of the past. It blames feminists for the new complexities and hardships of women's lives.

Ironically, as English points out, participation in the antifeminist movement offers women opportunities similar to those offered by the women's movement. Women find the possibility of organizing and working collectively in a female, almost sisterly, setting where they can affirm their political power. Unlike the feminist movement, however, the New Right is led almost exclusively by males.

The growing political activity and power of the New Right has meant that antifeminism has reached a national audience. The 1984 Republican platform, for example, did not mention the Equal Rights Amendment, endorsed a constitutional amendment banning abortion, opposed the concept of equal pay for work of comparable value, and opposed affirmative action programs as "reverse discrimination." The women's movement and its demand for equality has become one of the New Right's scapegoats for many of the problems confronting American society today. New Right leaders blame the women's movement, either directly or indirectly, for the increase in divorce, the rise in teenage pregnancy, unemployment among white men, the decline of Christian morality, the increased visibility of homosexuality, the failure of American business, and the lack of a "tough" foreign policy. Echoing the traditional conservative critique, the New Right characterizes liberalism as having the same kinds of subordinate traits ascribed to women and disparaged by the larger society: liberalism is "soft" on Communism, "passive" in its exercise of military power, "permissive" with the poor, "submissive" in relations with Third World countries, and has developed policies guided by "emotion"—by the "bleeding heart" approach—rather than by reason.

In this context the women's movement faces serious challenges. But the opposition of the antifeminist countermovement may in fact lead to a flourishing of feminist recruitment and activism. Immediately after Ronald Reagan's election in 1980, feminist groups reported that formerly complacent women were swelling their ranks. Eleanor Smeal president of NOW, reported that new memberships began to roll in at the rate of nine thousand to ten thousand a month—two or three times the average in previous years.[50] By the end of the unsuccessful ERA campaign in June of 1982, NOW alone had raised approximately eight million dollars, more than any political action committee spent in the 1982 congressional elections, and the organization had built a giant political machine with a staff of 300. As already suggested, feminist groups have begun to join forces with each other and with other progressive organizations, even male-led ones, to block the efforts of the Right to end reproductive freedom and to eliminate social programs that largely serve women and minority groups. Should the Right succeed not only in blocking the passage of the ERA as it has already done, but also in rolling back some of the gains already made by women, especially those supported by women who do not identify as feminists, it is likely that more women, and perhaps more men as well, might come to accept women's claims of injustice and develop greater sympathy for feminist demands. It is significant that even on the controversial issue of abortion, which a 1981 Yankelovich poll shows 56 percent of American women feel from their personal point of view is morally wrong, 67 percent of women believe that any woman who wants an abortion should be permitted to obtain it legally. Furthermore, 70 percent of women were bothered that decisions about abortion are often made by politicians and judges who are men.[51] This suggests a feminist perspective on the part of women who would certainly not be likely to identify as feminists.

Since the late 1970s, then, the women's movement has continued to develop a more radical ideology even while its organizations and goals have become more institutionalized. The success of the women's movement in affecting American society has stimulated countermovement activity in the form of anti-ERA and antiabortion organizing. What the outcome of movement-countermovement conflict will be is an open question. But the history of the women's movement suggests that the movement, no matter how it may change, is not likely to disappear.

CONCLUSION

The women's movement has taken different shapes at different points of time since its origin in the mid-nineteenth century, but it has clearly been a continuing presence for the expression of women's grievances. The failure of historians and other observers of the American scene to recognize the existence of a women's movement in certain periods has resulted in part from a tendency to think of social movements as having a well-defined mass membership, a monolithic leadership and ideology, and central and hierarchical direction. But there is another model: the multigroup model of social movements, developed by sociologists Luther Gerlach and Virginia Hine and applied to the women's movement of the 1960s and 1970s by anthropologist Joan Cassel.[52] This model views social movements as comprised of a number of relatively independent movement organizations that differ in ideology, goals, and tactics, are characterized by a decentralized leadership, and are loosely connected by multiple and overlapping membership, friendship networks, and cooperation in working for common goals. The women's movement since 1960 seems to conform to this latter model, although it has changed from a relatively centralized elite-sustained movement with a limited membership base, to a more mass-based movement with two distinct branches, and, finally, to a decentralized movement comprised of a multitude of organizations, many of them with a single-issue focus, that has become both more radicalized and more institutionalized.

Social movement theorists John McCarthy and Mayer Zald have

argued that social movements in the 1960s and 1970s have increasingly taken the form of professional social movements—movements characterized by full-time leadership whose actions are often carried on without, but in the name of, a mass membership base; and financed by contributions from a constituency the leadership purports to represent and from outside sources, including government agencies, foundations, and churches.[53] McCarthy and Zald attribute this emergence of professionalization to a number of conditions that developed in the late 1960s and continued into the 1970s: an increase in individual income that allowed payment of membership dues, an increase in discretionary time among students and professionals, and a rise in institutional support from churches, foundations, government, and private industry for social change activity, including the development of full-time paid positions for social movement leaders.

Although this model may not describe the women's movement as a whole, since the membership base, though amorphous, is real, nevertheless some organizations within the movement are "professionalized" and the development of "careers" within the women's movement is significant. The large national women's movement organizations, because of the resources generated by their membership, are able to pay a professional staff to carry out their work, and even independent local groups employ members in movement jobs. This kind of "professionalization" accompanies the institutionalization already described. At the same time, a major consequence of antifeminist activism has been the dismantling of federal programs whose resources had been coopted to support women's movement activities.

The history of the women's movement over time is best explained by the resource mobilization perspective on social movements, which starts from the assumption that grievances and discontent alone, although necessary preconditions for the emergence of a movement, are not sufficient. In most instances discontent is more or less constant over time, and what changes, giving rise to collective action, "is the amount of social resources available to unorganized but aggrieved groups, making it possible to launch an organized demand for change."[54] The major distinguishing feature of the resource mobilization perspective, then, is its focus on the resources available to the potential movement and the structural conditions of the movement's environment that facilitate or hinder mobilization.

From this perspective we see that the movement since 1960 has been shaped not only by the larger social and political climate but in part by the amount and kind of resources available to it. The elite-sustained movement of the early 1960s, functioning in a hostile and conservative context, relied primarily on the time, commitment, and money of its members to support its relatively limited strategies of lobbying and letter-writing. This stage of the movement brought some resources to emerging organizations like NOW, but the new organizations that emerged in the mid-1960s, because of a significant change in the social and political environment affecting the opportunities for collective action, were able to mobilize a wider range of resources toward a broader range of objectives. We have seen, for example, how the federal government unwittingly contributed to NOW's early work by providing office space and equipment to employees involved in the early sex discrimination cases. Jo Freeman has explored the differential access to resources of the two branches of the movement from the late 1960s to the late 1970s.[55] Because of the different organizational experiences of participants in the two branches, they had differential access to such resources as money, space, publicity, expertise, networks, contact with decision-makers, status, time, and commitment. The liberal branch had some money, used the offices and clerical services of the United Auto Workers until the ERA endorsement in 1967, had limited access to established media, had expertise in public relations and lobbying, used the networks set up through the commissions on the status of women and professional groups, and had some access to decision-makers in government, media, and the unions. In contrast the radical branch made use of space, publicity, and networks within the New Left movement, had expertise in community organizing and pamphleteering, and had access to a great deal of time and commitment from its largely student members.

By the late 1970s, then, the movement as a whole had clearly gained greater access to resources, including the support of elites and other outside groups, through institutionalization. The movement has financial support not only from members but from the government and foundations, has created its own space for both cultural and political activities, operates its own media, and also receives relatively regular, if not mostly favorable, coverage from the established media. It has also developed specialized expertise in a wide range of activities, has access to a variety of networks and decision-makers, has increased access to status, and continues to attract the time and commitment of members.

Despite changes over time, the movement has continued. Like feminist educator and activist Alma Lutz, who hoped at the birth of her grand-niece in 1950 that the "new woman" in our family "won't still be asking for women's rights in 1970," women throughout the history of the movement have looked toward a time when there would be no need for a women's movement.[56] But in the context of the mid-1980s, there is every reason to believe that women in the 2000s will be able to echo Mary Stott's conviction that "there's always been a women's movement this century."

1. Dale Spender, *There's Always Been a Women's Movement This Century* (London, 1983).

2. See Joan Huber and Glenna Spitze, *Sex Stratification: Children, Housework, and Jobs*, (New York, 1983), chapter 1.

3. Judith Hole and Ellen Levine, *Rebirth of Feminism* (New York, 1971); Jo Freeman, *The Politics of Women's Liberation* (New York, 1975); Sara Evans, *Personal Politics: The Roots of Women's Liberation in the Civil Rights Movement and the New Left* (New York, 1979).

4. Two exceptions are Olive Banks, *Faces of Feminism: A Study of Feminism as a Social Movement* (Oxford, 1981); and Cynthia E. Harrison, "Prelude to Feminism: Women's Organizations, the Federal Government and the Rise of the Women's Movement, 1942-1968," Ph.D. diss., Columbia University, 1982. Banks employs a similar perspective to ours in her exploration of the historical continuity of the women's movement in both Britain and the U.S., but she does not examine this period in detail. Cynthia Harrison explores the activities of women's organizations in the post-1945 period, but she does not consider this women's movement activity.

5. Leila J. Rupp and Verta Taylor, *The Survival of American Feminism: The Women's Movement, 1945 to the 1960's* (in progress). See also Leila J. Rupp, "The Survival of American Feminism: The Women's Movement in the Postwar Period," in Robert H. Bremner and Gary W. Reichard, eds., *Reshaping America: Society and Institutions, 1945-1960* (Columbus, 1982), 33-65.

6. Anna Lord Strauss to Mrs. Malcolm L. McBride, 4 February 1947, League of Women Voters papers, box 689, Library of Congress; Katherine Ellickson, "The President's Commission on the Status of Women," 1976, Ellickson Papers, Schlesinger Library. See Harrison, "Women's Organizations;" and Patricia G. Zelman, *Women, Work, and National Policy: The Kennedy-Johnson Years* (Ann Arbor, Michigan, 1982).

7. John F. Kennedy to Emma Guffey Miller, 1 October 1946, National Woman's Party papers, reel 90; Alma Lutz to Florence Kitchelt, 29 July 1959, Kitchelt papers, box 7 (178), SL; Marjorie Longwell to Alice Paul, 16 July 1960, NWP papers, reel 106.

8. Emma Guffey Miller to John F. Kennedy, 3 September 1960, NWP papers, reel 106; John F. Kennedy to Emma Guffey Miller, 7 October 1960, Miller papers, box 3 (19/6), SL.

9. John F. Kennedy to Emma Guffey Miller, 28 September 1960, Peterson papers, SL; John F. Kennedy to Emma Guffey Miller, 7 October 1960, Peterson papers, SL; Memo from Esther Peterson to Claude Desautels, n.d. (1963), Peterson papers, SL; Esther Peterson, note, 17 May 1975, Peterson papers, SL.

10. Harrison, "Prelude to Feminism," pp. 345-46. See also Zelman, *Women, Work, and National Policy.*

11. Interview with Esther Peterson, conducted by Emily Williams, 26 April 1979, for the Franklin D. Roosevelt Library, Peterson papers, SL. See also Zelman, *Women, Work, and National Policy.*

12. Memo from Esther Peterson to Myer Feldman, 12 May 1961, Peterson papers, SL.

13. Memo from Esther Peterson to Secretary of Labor, 2 June 1961, Peterson papers, SL. Zelman, *Women, Work, and National Policy,* reports that Peterson herself chose the Commission members.

14. Interview, 16 June 1983.

15. Transcript of Proceedings, Committee on Political and Civil Rights, President's Commission on the Status of Women papers, box 14, John F. Kennedy Library.

16. Ellickson, "The President's Commission on the Status of Women." The President's Commission also had important consequences for the passage of the Equal Pay bill in 1963. Harrison, "Prelude to Feminism," provides an excellent analysis of the struggle for equal pay, 140-82, 294-337. See also Zelman, *Women, Work, and National Policy.*

17. Caroline Bird, *Born Female: The High Cost of Keeping Women Down* (New York, 1968), chapter 1; and Hole and Levine, *Rebirth of Feminism,* 30-44, emphasize the attempts of the bill's opponents to ridicule civil rights by including women. Caruthers Gholson Berger, "Equal Pay, Equal Employment Opportunity and Equal Enforcement of the Law for Women," *Valparaiso University Law Review* 5 (1971):326-73; Freeman, *Politics of Women's Liberation;* Betty Friedan, *It Changed My Life* (New York, 1977); and Barbara Sinclair Deckard, *The Women's Movement,* 3d ed. (New York, 1983), 322-24, present more complex, if very brief, interpretations. The interpretation given here is consistent with the most recent work, in particular Carl M. Brauer, "Women Activists, Southern Conservatives, and the Prohibition of Sex Discrimination in Title VII of the 1964 Civil Rights Act," *Journal of Southern History* 49 (1983):37-56. See also Harrison, "Prelude to Feminism," 469-83 and Zelman, *Women, Work, and National Policy,* 55-71.

18. Brauer, "Women Activists," 41-42. Brauer interviewed Butler Franklin and Nina Horton Avery, the authors of the letters.

19. Quoted in Zelman, *Women, Work, and National Policy,* 61.

20. Interviews, 15 May 1982 and 16 June 1983.

21. Brauer, "Women Activists," 47.

22. Marguerite Rawalt to Victoria Gilbert, 4 August 1967, NWP papers, reel 110.

23. Interviews, 15 May 1982 and 16 June 1983.

24. Miriam Holden to Alice Paul, 16 October 1965, Holden papers, box 1, Princeton University archives.

25. "Sex and Nonsense," in *New Republic;* quoted by Alma Lutz to Emma Guffey Miller, 11 September 1965, Miller papers, box 5, (81), SL.

26. Lucinda Klemeyer, " 'Equal Rights' is Battle Cry," Columbus *Dispatch,* 12 February 1967.

27. Betty Friedan, *The Feminine Mystique* (New York, 1963).

28. Betty Friedan, "Up From the Kitchen Floor," *New York Times Magazine,* 4 March 1973, 9; see also Friedan, *It Changed My Life,* 109-23.

29. Interview, 26 November 1982.

30. Interview, 16 June 1983.

31. Communication from Frances Kolb, who is currently writing a history of the first ten years of NOW.

32. Alice Paul, "Conversations with Alice Paul: Woman Suffrage and the Equal Rights Amendment," interviews conducted in 1972 and 1973 by Amelia R. Fry, Regional Oral History Office, University of California, 1976. Also interview, 15 May 1982.

33. Evans, *Personal Politics.*

34. Mary Kennedy to Alice Paul, 11 February 1971, NWP papers, reel 112.

35. Quoted in Kathryn Paulsen, "The Last Hurrah of the Woman's Party," NWP papers, reel 111.

36. Hole and Levine, *Rebirth of Feminism*; Sidney Abbott and Barbara Love, *Sappho Was a Right-On Woman: A Liberated View of Lesbianism* (New York, 1972); Anne Koedt, Ellen Levine, and Anita Rapone, *Radical Feminism* (New York, 1973); Gayle Graham Yates, *What Women Want: The Ideas of the Movement* (Cambridge, Mass., 1975); Freeman, *Politics of Women's Liberation;* Wlliam H. Chafe, *Women and Equality: Changing Patterns in American Culture* (New York, 1977); Joan Cassell, *A Group Called Women: Sisterhood and Symbolism in the Feminist Movement* (New York, 1977); Leah Fritz, *Dreamers and Dealers: An Intimate Appraisal of the Women's Movement* (Boston, 1979); Jo Freeman, "Resource Mobilization and Strategy: A Model for Analyzing Social Movement Organization Actions," in Mayer N. Zald and John D. McCarthy, eds., *The Dynamics of Social Movements* (Cambridge, Mass., 1979), 167-89; Deckard, *Women's Movement.*

37. This analysis of the difference between liberal and radical perspectives is developed in Verta Taylor, "The Future of Feminism in the 1980s: A Social Movement Analysis," in Laurel Richardson and Verta Taylor, eds., *Feminist Frontiers: Rethinking Sex, Gender, and Society,* (Reading, Mass., 1983), 434-51.

38. Quoted in Hole and Levine, *Rebirth of Feminism,* 85.

39. Interviews, 28 September and 5 October 1979.

40. Cited in Deckard, *Women's Movement,* 337.

41. Quoted in Sara M. Evans, "Tomorrow's Yesterday: Feminist Consciousness and the Future of Women," in Carol Ruth Berkin and Mary Beth Norton, eds., *Women of American: A History* (Boston, 1979), 403.

42. "The Combahee River Collective Statement," in Barbara Smith, ed., *Home Girls: A Black Feminist Anthology* (New York, 1983), 272-82.

43. See Kristin Luker, *Abortion and the Politics of Motherhood* (Berkeley, 1984).

44. See Mayer Zald and Roberta Ash, "Social Movement Organizations: Growth, Decay and Change," *Social Forces* 44 (1966):327-41.

45. Melinda Bart Schlesinger and Pauline Bart, "Collective Work and Self-Identity: The Effect of Working in a Feminist Illegal Abortion Collective," in Richardson and Taylor, *Feminist Frontiers*, 337-44; and Caroline Heyward Sparks, "Program Evaluation of a Community Rape Prevention Program," Ph.D. diss., Ohio State University, 1979.

46. Charlotte Bunch, "Feminism's Future," paper presented at a conference on "Advancing Feminism: Strategies for the '80's," Columbus, 1981.

47. See Susan Schechter, *Women and Male Violence: The Visions and Struggles of the Battered Women's Movement* (Boston, 1982).

48. Freeman, *Social Movements*, xv.

49. Deirdre English, "The War Against Choice," *Mother Jones*, February/March 1981. See also Andrea Dworkin, *Right-Wing Women* (New York, 1983). For a more extended discussion of the relationship between the feminist and antifeminist movements, see Taylor, "Future of Feminism."

50. Linda Charlton, "Sisterhood is Braced for the Reagonauts," *New York Times*, 1 June 1981.

51. From the Yankelovich, Skelly, and White national public opinion poll, reported in Marlene Longenecker, "Abortion: What Do Women Say?" *Sojourner* 9 (December 1981):1-2.

52. Luther P. Gerlach and Virginia H. Hine, *People, Power, Change: Movements of Social Transformation* (Indianapolis, 1970); Cassell, *A Group Called Women*.

53. John D. McCarthy and Mayer N. Zald, *The Trend of Social Movements in America: Professionalization and Resource Mobilization* (Morristown, N.J., 1973).

54. J. Craig Jenkins and Charles Perrow, "Insurgency of the Powerless: Farm Worker Movements, 1946-1972," *American Sociological Review* 42 (1977): 249-58.

55. Freeman, "Resource Mobilization and Strategy."

56. Alma Lutz to Florence Kitchelt, 12 January 1950, Kitchelt papers, box 7 (178), SL.

We are grateful to the following institutions for financial support for the research on which portions of this article are based: the National Endowment for the Humanities for a two-year Basic Research Grant (1981-1983); the Radcliffe Research Scholars Program; the Graduate School of the Ohio State University; the College of Humanities of the Ohio State University; and the College of Social and Behavioral Sciences of the Ohio State University.

Education, Public Policy, and the State

Ronald Lora

Public eduation is one of the pillars of a free people. Without it an educated citizenry is impossible, a sustainable democracy an illusion. Nonetheless, the authors of our republican institutions never envisioned that the national government would try to direct the intellectual and psychological development of our children. Although public education in the United States has long been deeply influenced by political motives, it is guaranteed not by the federal government but by the states, and for most of our history the states restricted themselves to funding, accreditation, and specific requirements such as physical education and American history. Rarely did they do more. Local communities taxed themselves and set policy; teachers selected appropriate textbooks and grouped students as they wished. Neither they nor school administrators anticipated that politicians would one day require compensatory education for low-income students, determine how math and science were to be taught, and stipulate how students were to be tested.

This innocent pattern of local control of schools underwent fundamental change after World War II. Federal involvement in education, propelled by Cold War realities and the educational deficiencies brought to light by the struggle against fascism, grew steadily in the 1950s and exploded in scope and responsibilities during the 1960s, breaking the bonds of custom and prerogative. No issue in precollegiate education was more important than the role of the national government, which became the chief sponsor of change in the nation's elementary and secondary school systems. This essay examines the growing role of the federal government and assesses some of the consequences of that role.[1]

For the first decade and a half after V-J Day, federal education legislation reflected foreign policy concerns and the need to reintegrate millions of war veterans into society. These objectives are explicit in the G.I. Bill, the (federally) Impacted Areas legislation, the National Science Foundation (NSF), and the National Defense Education Act (NDEA). Until the creation of the NSF, federal aid to elementary and secondary education had come in the form of grants for vocational education, school lunches, federal dependents, and Native American children, with annual expenditures amounting to approximately $164,000,000 by 1950. With the advent of the two science programs, however, the United States accredited the instrumentalist views of Vannevar Bush, Admiral Hyman Rickover, and James B. Conant that national survival depended on the successful mobilization of science and technology.[2]

The National Defense Education Act stands alone among major federal education programs in that its sole objective was to improve the quality of public school education. Emphasizing the need for more and better courses in science, mathematics, and foreign languages, it was designed to change public schools throughout the country. That is to say, the federal government did not passively supply money, but attempted to shape the curriculum of the schools. The creation of new curricula for mathematics and the sciences, which were then distributed to the schools, was the salient feature of the NDEA and other government-sponsored programs. Among the better reform curricula were those that emerged from the Biological Sciences Curriculum Study, the Physical Science Study Committee, the School Mathematics Study Group, the Chemical Bond Approach Project, and the Chemical Education Materials Study, all of which date from the 1950s and all of which received financial support from Washington.[3]

It was through these kinds of programs that the federal government attempted to develop a national curriculum. They received much publicity in the national press, including news and opinion magazines like *Time* and *Newsweek*. In retrospect it is remarkable how little objection was raised by professional educators to the new responsibilities being assumed by Washington, but such was the perception of crisis in national security that the new government-education relationship was seen as natural, even desirable.

The government's goal of using the schools to meet crises spawned by the Cold War opened the door to another far-reaching federal campaign—one that mobilized the schools to solve equally pressing domestic problems.[4] With racial friction, poverty, black unemployment, and the rising ethnic consciousness of minority Americans among the social problems facing the activist administrations of John F. Kennedy and Lyndon B. Johnson, equality and aid for the disadvantaged would become the new polestars of federal education policy.[5]

One popular misconception that may be laid to rest at the outset is that federal education policies of the 1960s were primarily concerned about education. They were not. Several of the major acts of the Great Society fairly resonated with noneducational motives: the Economic Opportunity Act (1964) established a war on poverty program that provided funds for Job Corps, Upward Bound, Work-Training for Youth out of school, and community action programs; the Civil Rights Act of 1964 assisted in the desegregation of schools; the Elementary and Secondary Education Act of 1965 (ESEA) provided federal grants of over one billion dollars to states for allocation to school districts with low income families; the Civil Rights Act of 1968 facilitated the desegregation of public education by providing severe penalties for interfering with the exercise of certain rights, such as attending school; the Bilingual Education Act (1968) provided bilingual education programs for (primarily) Spanish-speaking children.

The central agreement among proponents of these programs was that the federal government had responsibilities to Americans suffering economic and cultural privation. Whereas earlier programs under the aegis of the NSF and the NDEA were designed to aid the better students, those of the 1960s and 1970s were meant to help those disadvantaged for reasons of low income, physical disability, and discrimination. Federal policy was reformist not because it sought in the first instance to alter the structure and values of public education (though such was the consequence), but because it sought on a massive scale to aid the underachieving children of minority Americans.

The dream was generous, and often among committed partisans it transcended ulterior political motives. This was especially true of Title I of ESEA, an ambitious effort at compensatory education designed to improve schooling in blighted urban neighborhoods. The inflow from the rural South, often poor and black, had exacerbated the existing problems with underachieving minority children in the larger cities. It was hoped that equal protection before the law, combined with curriculum development and the rebuilding of the inner cities, would improve educational achievement among groups whose life chances were far removed from the hopeful promise of the American dream.

Although the movement for federal aid to education had long existed, it took domestic turmoil in the 1960s to break the logjam against congressional action.[6] Domestic unrest shaped the character of every legislative act passed that can be called an education bill. If *Brown v. Board of Education* created the festering problem of how school desegregation was to be achieved, it was the Civil Rights Act of 1964, the strongest such since Reconstruction, that proved to be a major weapon in the battle. Title VI of this act conferred upon Washington the power to regulate education and to protect civil rights: institutions that denied students the benefits of federal programs on the basis of race, religion, or ethnic composition would be denied federal funds. The import of Title VI was to protect individual rights, to be sure, but of equal importance was the expansion of federal control over education. The traditional relationship between the government and local school districts, in which the government merely appropriated money to be used for specific purposes, gave way to one that required schools to acquiesce in the requirements of all federal programs involving them before funds for any given program could be received. The U. S. Office of Education, once the servant of local and state constituencies, now assumed responsibility for drafting guidelines and enforcing federal law.

This powerful weapon against community control brought the government into every school district in the country. The foremost concern was not education, but, as Senator Humphrey phrased it during the Senate floor debate, racial unrest and segregation in the nation. Segregated education in the South did not end with Title VI and assorted judicial decrees, but the modern integration movement could for the first time envision a day when its objectives might be achieved. By 1972, 36.8 percent of black students were enrolled in majority white schools; the percentage of black pupils attending all-black schools fell to 10.9 percent.[7]

In the midst of this national racial crisis, it was the rediscovery of poverty that permitted the passage of ESEA in 1965. Racial tensions seemed difficult in the extreme to confront directly. The fact that southerners commanded important posts in the House and Senate leadership did not make matters easier. However, if the problems of race could be understood in terms of economic and cultural deprivation, it might still be possible to deal effectively with social conflict in the nation. This intertwining of education with urgent national priorities can be seen in ESEA, an integral part of President Johnson's War on Poverty program.

The philosophical premises of this program emerged from a report prepared by the Council of Economic Advisers (CEA), entitled *The Problem of Poverty in America* (1964). Requested by President Kennedy, but translated into legislative success by his successor, who passionately wanted to help the disadvantaged enter the mainstream of the Great Society, the report reflected the views of Michael Harrington's influential and popular work, *The Other America* (1963). Economic and cultural deprivation resulted from an interdependent set of causal forces, none of which alone was responsible for poverty. A poor education, for example, might initiate a cycle of poverty through low-level jobs, inadequate housing, diet and medical care, resulting in a hopeless attitude that could institutionalize a "culture" of deprivation. Young persons conditioned by such circumstances rarely were able to utilize the educational alternatives, if any, that existed.

The CEA report argued that "equality of opportunity is the American dream, and universal education our noblest pledge to realize it. . . . The incidence of poverty drops as educational attainments rise for non-whites as well as white families at all ages."[8] This belief that educational opportunity could spell the end of poverty lay behind all the war on poverty programs, including the Economic Opportunity Act of 1964, which established the Job Corps, urban and rural community action programs, and Head Start, the latter a broad program designed to succor the children of the poor so that they might enter elementary school able to compete successfully. Medical and dental services were supplemented with social services for the child's home environment, psychological services, and school readiness programs.

Passed in the understanding that racial problems could be understood in terms of economic and cultural deprivation, ESEA and the 1964 Civil Rights Act became the twin agencies whereby the federal government acquired a permanent and growing role in American education. ESEA, the main vehicle of compensatory education, offered financial assistance in the usual categorical form. Title I, funded at approximately 78 percent of the $1.25 billion appropriated under the act, was directed toward school districts in which a minimum of 3 percent of the enrollment (or 100 children) came from families with annual incomes of less than $2,000. Qualifying districts could receive a federal allocation equal to 50 percent of their state's average expenditure per pupil. Impoverished areas, rural and urban, were the main beneficiaries of the new program. State agencies actually allocated the money; however, the guidelines were federal. By 1980 federal expenditures on Title I programs would reach $3 billion per year (Table 1). During the first full year of ESEA, the federal proportion of public elementary and secondary

TABLE 1

U.S. Department of Education Expenditures for Selected Elementary and Secondary Education Programs and Related Activities, Fiscal Years 1960 to 1980 (in thousands of dollars)

Program	1960	1962	1964	1966	1968	1970	1972	1974	1976	1978	1980[1]
Elementary and Secondary Education[2]	63,529	54,821	71,489	915,174	1,436,732	1,467,792	1,869,081	1,766,412	2,166,322	2,848,761	3,548,402
Exceptionally deprived children[3]	—	—	—	746,904	1,049,116	1,170,355	1,570,388	1,460,058	1,760,814	2,346,035	3,005,574
Consolidated programs[4]	63,529	54,821	71,489	168,270	387,616	291,245	272,683	268,000	326,006	395,777	386,428
Bilingual education	—	—	—	—	—	6,192	26,010	38,354	79,549	106,949	156,400
School assistance in federally affected areas	258,176	282,909	334,289	409,593	506,372	656,372	648,608	558,526	598,884	766,349	821,103
Vocational Education[5]	45,179	51,762	54,503	128,468	255,224	283,975	416,945	462,236	590,856	456,438	680,688
Education for the handicapped[6]	72	248	2,516	4,918	16,793	47,846	67,933	89,947	152,050	293,865	734,458
Emergency school aid[7]	—	—	—	5,291	7,437	10,608	92,214	196,045	204,027	259,328	304,497
Follow-Through	—	—	—	—	—	—	2,024	46,595	39,825	52,780	61,400
Indian Education	—	—	—	—	—	—	—	15,694	42,046	58,697	71,226

Source: National Center for Education Statistics, *Digest of Education Statistics, 1982* (Washington D.C., 1982), pp. 173-74.

1. Estimated.

2. Includes amounts distributed under provisions of the Elementary and Secondary Education Act of 1965 (ESEA) and the National Defense Education Act (NDEA). Funds authorized under Title VI of ESEA for education of the handicapped are not included here but under "Education for the Handicapped."

3. Title I of ESEA includes funds for students more than 1 year below grade level, Indian children, migratory children, handicapped children, and delinquent children.

4. Includes amounts authorized under Titles, II, III, and V of ESEA and NDEA Titles III, X, and a portion of V, for guidance, counseling, and testing, and state equalization aid.

5. Amounts for research, innovation, curriculum development, and vocational teacher training excluded.

6. Amounts for teacher training excluded.

7. Also includes Civil Rights services and training, some amounts for education broadcasting facilities, migrant high school equivalency program, youth education, training, and Indochinese refugee children.

school revenues would nearly double, from 4.4 percent to 7.9 percent (Table 2). Other titles offered money for educational research at universities, and, to placate state officials fearful of losing control, money was offered to strengthen state departments of education. Special items such as financial assistance for school resources, texts, instructional materials, and the establishment of educational centers to provide educational innovations at the local level helped to secure the support of private and Catholic groups. Most importantly, however, the new education act utilized the "child-benefit" theory, which held that so long as the primary effect of the aid was for the benefit of the child and the general welfare instead of a religious organization or a particular school, the no-establishment of religion clause of the First Amendment was not violated. The categorical aid, child-benefit approach of 1965 permitted congressmen to avoid the fatal effects of church-state bickering and southern objections to strictly racial policies, both of which had blocked federal aid programs in the past.[9]

The break with tradition that ESEA represented resulted from a happy convergence of circumstances, chief among them an expanding economy, the heady optimism of the early Great Society, and the return to Washington of many intellectuals, confident that they could harness advances in social theory and in technology to social reform. It is not surprising that activists in the Kennedy and Johnson administrations, generous in their technocratic visions but conservative in not wishing to risk defeat through confrontational strategies, placed their reformist hopes around education. ESEA, Head Start, and Project Follow-Through, largely motivated by noneducational concerns, also stand as examples of how practical politicians can deal with explosive issues of fundamental social change. With the sounds of urban riots and massive escalation of the American-Vietnamese War thundering in the background, these social action programs enabled politicians to define racial issues in terms of economic differentials and unequal opportunity, with education the lever to lift the disadvantaged and discontented to middle-class status. The Great Society educational programs thus represented a conservative strategy to maneuver lower-class grievances into manageable channels.

Paralleling and often contradicting the integrated programs of ESEA was the bilingual-bicultural movement of Mexican Americans. Enacted as an amendment (Title VII) of ESEA, the Bilingual Education Act of 1968 provided supplementary funds for school districts with large numbers of limited English-speaking students. (The 1970 census revealed that 8 million Americans spoke a language other than English at

TABLE 2

Revenue receipts of public elementary and secondary schools from Federal, State, and local sources: United States, 1919-1920 to 1979-1980

School Year	Amount in Thousands of Dollars				Percentage Distribution		
	Total	Federal	State	Local (including intermediate)	Federal	State	Local (including intermediate)
1919-20	$ 970,120	$ 2,475	$ 160,085	$ 807,561	0.3	16.5	83.2
1939-40	2,260,527	39,810	684,354	1,536,363	1.8	30.3	68.0
1959-60	14,746,618	651,639	5,768,047	8,326,932	4.4	39.1	56.5
1961-62	17,527,707	760,975	6,789,190	9,977,542	4.3	38.7	56.9
1963-64	20,544,182	896,956	8,078,014	11,569,213	4.4	39.3	56.3
1965-66	25,356,858	1,996,954	9,920,219	13,439,686	7.9	39.1	53.0
1967-68	31,903,064	2,806,469	12,275,536	16,821,063	8.8	38.5	52.7
1969-70	40,266,923	3,219,557	16,062,776	20,984,589	8.0	39.9	52.1
1971-72	50,003,645	4,467,969	19,133,256	26,402,420	8.9	38.3	52.8
1973-74	58,230,892	4,930,351	24,113,409	29,187,132	8.5	41.4	50.1
1975-76	71,206,073	6,318,345	31,776,101	33,111,627	8.9	44.6	46.5
1977-78	81,443,160	7,694,194	35,013,266	38,735,700	9.4	43.0	47.6
1979-80	96,881,165	9,503,537	45,348,814	42,028,813	9.8	46.8	43.4

SOURCE: National Center for Education Statistics, *Digest of Education Statistics, 1983-1984* (Washington, D.C., 1984), 77.

Includes a relatively small amount from nongovernmental sources (gifts and tuition and transportation fees from patrons). These sources accounted for 0.4 percent of total revenue receipts in 1967-68.

home, a number that would rise to 20 million by 1980.) Testimony before the House General Subcommittee on Education brought out that Mexican American adults in the Southwest had completed an average of only 7.1 years of schooling compared to 12.1 years for whites.[10] Although this disparity resulted at least in part from the fact that many Mexican Americans had been born and educated outside the United States, witnesses before the subcommittee tended to blame the American school system.

With the disparity in schooling in mind, Senator Ralph Yarborough of Texas (the initial sponsor of bilingual education) argued that "unless a child becomes very fluent in English he will rarely reach the top in American cultural life. He might as a baseball player, but he could not as a performer on radio; he could not in law; he could not in medicine; he could not in any of the professions or in business."[11] Congress passed the bill in hopes that bilingual education would help Hispanics and other ethnic children of limited English-speaking ability to learn English so that they might enter the mainstream of American life and culture. Special programs were developed to teach Spanish as the native language (with English taught as the second language) and to imbue Spanish-speaking students with knowledge and pride in their culture. When applying for funds, districts were asked to meet a number of criteria beyond that of having a significant number of limited English-speaking students, including the requirement that children must come from low-income families.

The special program for the education of linguistic minorities was a logical extension of the compensatory orientation of other ESEA programs, but it depended, too, on the arrival of hundreds of thousands of refugees from the Cuban revolution and on the growing numbers of limited English-speaking children among Puerto Ricans in New York and Mexican Americans in the Southwest—groups that had been inspired by the successes of the Civil Rights movement to seek protection under equal opportunity laws. The bilingual-bicultural movement also reflected the wave of ethnocentrism in the American social order as minority groups in the 1960s and early 1970s quested for identity within their particular heritages. Not a popular program nationwide, its funding nevertheless grew rapidly from $6.2 million in 1970 to $156.4 million in 1980 (Table 1).

From the beginning tension existed between proponents of two approaches: transitional and maintenance. Congress passed bilingual legislation with the transitional view that after becoming literate in the English language, students would rejoin English-speaking classes.

American culture could more easily assimilate students who had managed that transition. Many ethnic spokesmen, however, defended a maintenance approach, arguing that Mexican Americans should receive an education in their native language, thereby preserving non-English cultures. In practice this contradicted the integrative functions of compensatory education by isolating immigrants and by preserving separate cultural identities.[12] Perhaps inevitably it also alienated some from American mores and customs. If in fact maintenance-oriented bilingual programs discouraged upward mobility, they discriminated, however innocently, against the very groups they were intended to assist.

There have been problems aplenty with bilingual education beyond the isolating effects of ethnic maintenance curricula. The most serious is that the programs have not worked. Such, at least, would seem to be the conclusion of a lengthy study commissioned by the U.S. Office of Education. Less than a third of the Hispanics receiving bilingual education had limited proficiency in English, and most who were proficient remained in bilingual classes despite their achievement. Worst of all, achievement scores in English of bilingual students were lower than those of students who did not participate in bilingual classes; in mathematics the comparative scores were similar. But both groups remained painfully far behind national norms in English and math. In 1980 the dropout rate of Hispanics was double that of whites, suggesting at the very least that Title VII students failed to develop more positive views of schooling.[13]

Power and control at the federal level often grew at the behest of groups that had been energized by civil rights activists and the judicial decisions of the 1960s that promoted black-white integration. The most successful organizations in influencing the schools and in harnessing Washington to their cause were those working to secure the rights of exceptional children, particularly the handicapped. Having concentrated much of their efforts at the state and local levels, the National Association for Retarded Citizens, the Council for Exceptional Children, and numerous smaller organizations understood what ESEA and the 1964 Civil Rights Act had wrought, and shifted their attention toward Washington.

The case for the handicapped was poignant, for their treatment constituted a sorry chapter in the history of American public education. To be sure, some school systems and state legislatures had developed modest special education programs before the 1960s, but abuses abounded toward the handicapped. Schools reflected the attitude of the public, which was apathetic and ignorant of the varieties and complexities of learning disabilities. The few physically and mentally handicapped persons who entered public schools received little or nothing in the way of special education. For the handicapped these circumstances virtually guaranteed failure and frustration.

New hopes that arose during the 1960s with the establishment of the Bureau of Education for the Handicapped were rewarded in the following decade. A significant breakthrough occurred in 1971 when a U. S. district court, shown evidence that education could benefit the retarded, ruled that Pennsylvania school districts must educate all retarded children between the ages of four and twenty-one.[14] Congress responded with several educational acts, the most significant of which was the Education for All Handicapped Children Act (Public Law 94-142) in 1975. The law defined handicapped children as "mentally retarded, hard of hearing, seriously disturbed, orthopedically impaired, or children with specific learning disabilities, who by reason thereof require special education and related services." Those covered by this definition (estimates ranged from four to eight million) were as a matter of national policy to be assured a "free appropriate public education" tailored to meet individual needs.[15]

Except in numbers the impact of PL 94-142 rivaled that of the *Brown* case. Intended only to protect the rights of the handicapped, the act in fact carefully prescribed the duties of states and schools and mandated complex due process procedures that, if disregarded, would result in a cut-off of all federal funds. Insofar as possible, handicapped children were to be mainstreamed—integrated into regular classrooms or the least restrictive environment—with only the most profoundly handicapped segregated in special learning centers.[16] Because this mandate affected every school district and teacher in the United States, PL 94-142 was unrivaled among 1970s legislation in its importance to the growth of federal authority in education.

Criticism was immediate and sharp.[17] The costs and paperwork generated by the congressional mandate were substantial. Though Congress established elaborate procedures and regulations and rapidly increased its appropriations to the handicapped (Table 1), it failed to deliver the dollars promised, never funding more than an eighth of school district costs. It resembled "a regulation by the city council that you take your next-door neighbor to dinner twice a week and pay for it out of your own pocket," wrote one critic.[18] However small the financial support, federal standards remained intact. With the states largely ignored, it fell to school districts to hire special educationists, eliminate architectural barriers to the handicapped, arrange for transportation, and provide appropriate developmental, corrective, and supportive services, "including speech pathology and audiology, psychological services, physical and occupational therapy, recreation, and medical and counseling services."[19]

The statute also mandated that each child receive an "individualized education program," defined as:

> a written statement for each handicapped child . . . which statement shall include (A) a statement of the present levels of educational performance of such child, (B) a statement of annual goals, including short-term instructional objectives, (C) a statement of the specific educational services to be provided to such child, and the extent to which such child will be able to participate in regular educational programs, (D) the projected date for initiation and anticipated duration of such services, and (E) appropriate objective criteria and evaluation procedures and schedules for determining, on at least an annual basis, whether instructional objectives are being achieved.[20]

Numberous court cases followed upon parental dissatisfaction over classification procedures and the quality of services provided.

The Handicapped Children Act represented a culmination of two decades of federal curriculum activity during which federal dollars and directives introduced and supported controversial programs ranging from compensatory education to school integration, bilingual education, and sexual parity in school athletics. Critics found the new role of the federal government oppressive, particularly in the heavy obligations imposed on the schools. Teachers felt that their professional autonomy was violated. Many doubted their ability to handle the special needs of the handicapped or worried that nonhandicapped students would suffer undue neglect. By 1980 approximately 70 percent of the four million children in special education programs had been placed in regular classes, requiring from the teaching and professional staff an enormous commitment in time.[21]

The extent to which the federal government has augmented its power vis-a-vis lower levels of educational authority is clearly reflected in the changed role of its judicial branch. In the quest for equality of educational opportunity, the Supreme Court of the United States often has led the way for American minorities. Although critics were wont to call the Supreme Court "the national school board," federal judicial power is not unlimited. Its authority is confined by the separation of powers doctrine, the nature of the cases brought before it, and by the doctrine of federalism which, under the Tenth Amendment, acknowledges educational policy making to be a state and local power. In practice, however, since mid-century the judiciary has exerted enormous influence on the

American school system, becoming one of the chief federal instruments of social reform.

The struggle of blacks to win decent schools for their children is a poignant story, long and painful. Progress was granted grudgingly by white Americans. Ramshackle schools or shanties, poorly educated teachers, insufficient money, lack of adequate plumbing and electrical facilities in places, and few if any buses were the heritage of racism—and that heritage extended well into the latter half of the twentieth century.

One of the century's rare moments of conscience came in 1954 with reference to Topeka, Kansas. Topeka was a Jim Crow city in which virtually 100 percent of the important jobs were held by whites. The situation in the black schools was hardly better, and it, along with similar cases from Delaware, Virginia, and South Carolina, led to *Brown v. Board of Education of Topeka.* Relying on the equal protection clause of the Fourteenth Amendment in order to overturn the "separate but equal" doctrine established half-a-century earlier, Chief Justice Earl Warren read the Court's decision that segregated schools were "inherently unequal" and in violation of the Fourteenth Amendment. Quoting sociological and psychological evidence recently presented to the Court, the Chief Justice stated:

> Segregation of white and colored children in public schools has a detrimental effect upon the colored children. The impact is greater when it has the sanction of law; for the policy of separating the races is usually interpreted as denoting the inferiority of the Negro group. A sense of inferiority affects the motivation of the child to learn. Segregation with the sanction of law, therefore, has a tendency to retard the educational and mental development of Negro children and to deprive them of some of the benefits they would receive in a racially integrated school system.[22]

This sweeping indictment of segregated schools left open the question of when desegregation must begin. In 1955 the *Brown* case was remanded to the Court, which ruled that the difficulties of eliminating dual school systems notwithstanding, public school districts must make "prompt and reasonable" efforts to comply with *Brown I.* District courts were to order local school officials to admit students to public schools "on a racially nondiscriminatory basis with all deliberate speed."[23]

The *Brown* decision marked the beginning of a concerted movement for civil rights and racial integration, even though at the time it left ambiguous whether all school segregation was harmful or just "state-imposed discrimination," whether states should be neutral only or whether they should undertake affirmative action to integrate school systems. This was perhaps the key moment in regard to the growth of federal power in the nation's schools. And the decision was clear enough to spark immediate and fierce resistance in the South. Several southern states countered with "interposition" and "nullification" resolutions calling for public defiance of the high Court. A remarkable defense of southern custom came in the "Southern Manifesto," authored by Senator Sam J. Ervin of North Carolina and signed by nineteen senators and seventy-seven representatives. It decried the Court's exercise of "naked judicial power" and pledged to use all lawful means to block the implementation of *Brown*.[24] With resistance spreading through the South, President Eisenhower, during the most serious domestic crisis of his administration, was compelled to dispatch troops to Little Rock, Arkansas, to assert the supremacy of federal over state authority and to protect the lives of black children who had chosen to attend all-white schools.

Nearly a decade passed before the Supreme Court acted to force the implementation of *Brown*. The board of supervisors of Prince Edward County, Virginia, resisted desegregation by closing the public schools for the 1959-60 school year. White citizens immediately established all-white private schools, financed in part by the Virginia legislature. The Court decided in *Griffin v. County School Board of Prince Edward County* (1964) that the public school closing had violated the equal protection of the laws guaranteed by the Fourteenth Amendment and took the opportunity to explain the meaning of "all deliberate speed": "The time for mere 'deliberate speed' has run out, and that phrase can no longer justify denying these Prince Edward County school children their constitutional rights to an education equal to that afforded by the public schools in other parts of Virginia."[25] In the following year, the Court ruled that deliberate speed required efforts more expeditious than the one-grade-a-year plan adopted in Fort Smith, Arkansas.

Two decisions of 1968, *Green v. County School Board of New Kent County* and *Monroe v. Board of Commissioners*, added significantly to federal authority. The Court moved beyond *Brown* by ruling unconstitutional local efforts to avoid integration by adopting "freedom of choice" plans that permitted pupils to choose the public school they wished to attend. Had such plans resulted in integrated schools, the Court would not have spoken as to possible modes of integration, but in New Kent County, Virginia, where freedom of choice was to replace a dual school system with racial assignment, no whites had chosen the black school and only a few blacks had opted to attend white schools. In a footnote the Court suggested how integration might be achieved, a noteworthy item in that previous decisions had followed the American tradition of relying completely on local authorities to determine an appropriate mode of action. Thus the Court for the first time assumed the obligation to determine whether school boards were in fact moving toward "a unitary system in which racial discrimination would be eliminated root and branch."[26] The *Green* decision was doubly controversial because it dealt only with *de jure* segregation in the South, leaving intact school systems of northern and western cities where racial segregation was *de facto*, based on residential housing patterns rather than law.

In a Mississippi case, *Alexander v. Holmes County Board of Education* (1969), the Court reversed a lower court decision allowing thirty-three school districts more time to desegregate (a decision acceptable to the Justice Department) by enunciating a definition of all deliberate speed that blacks had awaited since 1954: " 'All deliberate speed' for desegregation is no longer constitutionally permissible. . . . The obligation of every school district is to terminate dual systems at once." To which Justice Black added these forceful words: "There is no longer any excuse for permitting the 'all deliberate speed' phrase to delay the time when Negro children and white children will sit together and learn together in the same public schools. . . . There is no reason why such a wholesale deprivation of constitutional rights should be tolerated another minute."[27]

This highlighted the interplay among federal branches of government relative to ending racial discrimination in the schools. Heretofore, the Court had deferred to the Office of Education for guidelines on correcting racial imbalance. Now the Court moved openly toward affirmative action to achieve a unitary school system, leaving Nixon administration officials wondering how they might counter the emerging Court strategy.

Early in the Nixon presidency, court attention shifted to the issue of whether forced busing was an appropriate vehicle of integration. Nothing in school desegregation efforts was more controversial. In *Swann v. Charlotte-Mecklenburg Board of Education* (1971), one of the first major cases of the Burger Court, the Court's unanimous opinion on several cases involving southern schools argued that school districts in which *de jure* segregation existed must do everything possible to achieve racial balance, including busing when necessary. Moreover, it consented to desegregation plans that included gerrymandering to achieve an equitable racial mix, and it declared that racial assignment to achieve integration is constitutionally acceptable.[28] The response in Congress, in the states, and in the Nixon administration was often angry, and various efforts, legislative and administrative, were made to circumvent the ruling. President Nixon in a 1972 special message to Congress asked for a moratorium on busing. The dual school system of the South had been largely dismantled, he argued, which fulfilled the purpose of *Brown*. Because so many plans had resulted in violence and "community disruption," it was time that states and local school boards resumed their rights and responsibilities.

Despite President Nixon's attempt to derail busing—an attempt that would ultimately fail—the action in *Swann* inspired district courts to attack segregation in northern and western urban areas such as Las Vegas, Denver, Detroit, Los Angeles, and Boston, with heavy concentrations of blacks and sometimes Hispanics. In Las Vegas, Nevada, west side elementary enrollment was 97 percent black; of the 102 blacks among the city's 1,359 teachers, 83 were assigned to west side schools. The school board, while building new school buildings in both the black and white neighborhoods, had closed schools in the border areas that contained a racially mixed population. The Supreme Court held in *Kelly v. Guinn* (1972) that the board had thus promoted segregation and ordered it to integrate both students and faculty. The deliberately segregative practices in the Denver, Colorado, school system led to *Keyes v. School District No. 1* (1973), in which the Supreme Court held that schools that were predominantly black and Hispanic could not be considered integrated, as the local district court had found.[29] Hispanics constituted an identifiable class for purposes of the Fourteenth Amendment.

The *Keyes* decision elicited an important dissent from Justice Powell who, expressing reservations about compulsory busing solely to maximize integration, argued that "the rights and interests of children affected by a desegregation program also are entitled to consideration." Court remedies, too vigorously imposed, might risk a deterioration of community support for public schools: "No one can estimate the extent to which dismantling neighborhood education will hasten an exodus to private schools, leaving public school systems the preserve of the disadvantaged of both races."[30] Powell's dissent, far from rejecting the busing remedy, was a plea for a more balanced consideration of the legitimate and competing interests within communities.

As the Court grew more conservative, due to internal changes and perhaps due also to increased public and political pressures against busing, it refused to grant busing consistent and unqualified support. With respect to Detroit, where whites had for many years left the inner city in large numbers so that by 1970 it was predominantly black, the Court agreed that unconstitutional segregation within a single school district existed, but when considering all the school districts of the metropolitan area as a unit, it could not find that the "differing racial composition between schools in the city and in the outlying suburbs was caused by official activity of any sort."[31] Thus, in *Milliken v. Bradley* (1974), the Court rejected interdistrict busing.

The *Milliken* ruling suggested that the Court sought a resting period after years of intensive activity. *Brown* had called for the elimination of segregated schools with all deliberate speed, *Green* had insisted on immediate compliance, *Swann* had ordered district-wide busing, and *Keyes* had extended the foregoing to northern cities, adding that racial segregation in a significant portion of a school district called for remedial action throughout the entire district. *Milliken*, however, suggested that despite *Swann* and *Keyes*, under certain circumstances all-black schools may be constitutionally permissible.

After *Milliken*, the record of the Court has been mixed. It upheld busing in some cases (*Dayton Board of Education v. Brinkman*, 1979), while either rejecting it or refusing to overturn lower court rulings in others (*Evans v. Buchanon*, 1977).[32] After the election of Ronald Reagan in 1980, the Supreme Court was reluctant to hear new major desegregation cases, leaving matters in a state of uncertainty. There was some feeling on the Court that the burden of desegregation had fallen disproportionately upon the children of America, on the innocent instead of those responsible for the nation's racial inequalities.

Busing has never been popular. Presidents from Nixon to Reagan have either opposed it or distanced themselves from it and a number of influential intellectuals came to see it as an unsound educational practice.[33] There had seldom been much doubt about the views of the American people. As horror stories came to them of young children being bused through alien and violent neighborhoods to integrate schools far away, they opposed the practice by heavy majorities. In the midst of the busing controversy, the Gallup Poll in August 1971 asked Americans: "In general, do you favor or oppose the busing of Negro and white children from one school district to another?" Only 18 percent favored busing, leaving 82 percent opposed or with no opinion.[34] The scare in any case was much overdone. When the busing controversy reached its height during the early 1970s, few pupils were being bused to achieve integration (only 3 percent throughout the nation). As desegregation efforts multiplied, busing mileage in some states actually decreased, for segregation itself had required extensive busing. It soon became clear that the issue was not busing per se, since nearly half of the nation's children rode buses to school. Instead, it was over the concept of neighborhood schools, which often was the conventional euphemism for racially segregated or unbalanced schools.

The government and the courts had made significant, if wavering, efforts to integrate the schools after 1964, but the ambiguities of discrimination and federal objectives have resulted in confusion. Unless a consensus is reached on the mixing of educational and social objectives, it is likely that desegregation issues will continue to fester so long as population movements continue, discrimination in jobs and housing exists, and social discrimination remains prevalent—all problems of the broader body politic and more difficult to control than administrative practices in the schools. Meanwhile, the public has seemed content to rest on such achievements as had been made, particularly in the South. At the time of the Civil Rights Act of 1964, only 2 percent of southern black students attended schools with whites; in less than a decade, 91 percent did so, though not all in majority-white schools. In 1972, 46 percent of southern blacks attended majority-white schools.[35]

The foregoing decisions have had a decided impact on education and have resulted in a growing body of legal requirements with which school districts and other educational institutions must comply. It is clear that dual school systems and *de jure* racial segregation are unconstitutional, and the courts have repeatedly demonstrated that they will redress grievances that come from racially motivated assignments of students, construction of facilities, and teacher assignments that maintain segregated patterns of schooling. Busing is employed to achieve racial balance, but its use is more limited than its supporters envisioned fifteen years ago. The vast outcry over the "intrusion" of courts into educational disputes that in fact were over other matters has forced a cooling of the reform possibilities of judicial action.

After two decades of compensatory education and billions of dollars spent, what has been accomplished? How effective was the attempt to improve the learning skills of the disadvantaged? How does one assess the federal role? Were there clear benefits for society as a whole?

Samuel Halperin, assistant U.S. commissioner of education in the

U.S. Office of Education (1964-66) and deputy assistant secretary for legislation in the Department of Health, Education, and Welfare (1966-69), has drawn attention to the achievements of ESEA. He cites breaking the barriers of federal aid to education, focusing attention on the needs of children (particularly those in some way disadvantaged), and fueling other movements in search of equality of opportunity in education. Compensatory education under ESEA titles, he argues, promoted parental and community involvement in the schools, more evaluation and accountability, and led to the recruitment of quality personnel.[36] Those are significant achievements. After decades of struggle on behalf of major federal bills to support education, ESEA did break the impasse to become an "enduring political fact." Most will agree that ESEA reflected a positive commitment to aid the disadvantaged. Whether the subject is migrant workers, bilingual education programs, congressional interest in Head Start, or expansion of school lunch programs, it seems clear that ESEA aided by establishing the "principle that underachieving children are entitled to above-average educational expenditures."[37]

Yet when all this is granted, much remains to be said. Several years after the establishment of the ESEA program, Alice Rivlin concluded in a study for the Brookings Institution that these compensatory services were natural experiments undertaken in the belief that federal resources "spent to compensate for lack of intellectual stimulation at home would improve the performance of poor children in school and break the cycle of poverty. . . . The decision was to provide funds to local education systems for programs for poor children. The educators hoped for significant improvements in the average performance of poor children. The analyst hoped that something would be learned from the experience. Both have been largely disappointed."[38]

Nearly a decade and a half later, Rivlin's assessment remains valid. Much attention has been given to ESEA Title I, the main pillar of the federal role in education. From the beginning it was never clear whether Title I was designed primarily for economically or for educationally disadvantaged students. By the late 1970s, Title I served about one in six elementary school children, many of whom were neither poor nor low achievers. Approximately half of those in the program were low achievers; only 40 percent were poor. In practice the program served both the economically and educationally disadvantaged, but less than one-third of either group nationwide. The failure to reach two-thirds of the poor and the educationally disadvantaged was due in part to the manner in which funds were allocated—first to states, then to districts that qualified under the poverty criteria, and finally to schools that met both the poverty and low achievement criteria. Disadvantaged children attending schools not receiving Title I funds could not participate.[39]

There is some evidence that the pull-out programs are counter productive. Under government regulations Title I teachers are to serve only eligible students, but they may not be the only teachers of such students. Thus for a portion of each day or week, students must be removed from ("pulled out" of) their regular classrooms to form special classes in reading or arithmetic. One study of this practice uncovered significant evidence of negative effects that can occur when students are pulled from regular classes and segregated into others according to income and achievement categories. The stigma can be psychologically harmful, and this already poignant situation is made worse by the fact that pull-out programs have not led to improved academic achievement.[40]

Literally thousands of impressionistic reports exist claiming that government initiatives often seemed out of touch with local realities, ranging from the statement that perhaps a majority of local and state administrators never accepted the broader goals of compensatory education to examples of parents seeking funds for school clothing rather than for better instructional materials.[41] A more serious problem was that not all regular teachers were ready to focus on the 30 to 40 percent not going to college compared to the majority who were. In practice federal actions seemed to bypass the local teachers, who had interests and theories of their own about the purposes and techniques of learning. Teachers and aides (themselves all too often poorly educated and poorly trained in the tasks they were asked to perform) were assigned to schools without consultation, without preparation, and without plans to integrate them into the ongoing education programs. For these and other reasons, cooperation between regular and extra-classroom teachers was difficult to achieve. It was only natural for regular teachers to resent the intrusion of well-paid specialists, funded by programs conceived of far away, to pursue objectives that were, at the least, controversial. The symbolic and invidious distinction between regular teachers and federally-funded personnel came with federally financed projects to reshape the schools' curriculum by designing "teacher proof" materials that would work, in Charles Silberman's words, "whether teachers liked the materials or not or taught them well or badly."[42] Working at salaries higher than they could have earned in teaching, graduate students and spouses of professors and friends produced packages of learning that could be installed painlessly and inexpensively. Most would only gather dust.

But did Johnny learn to read? Because the major effort of Title I is geared toward improving reading and mathematics skills, evaluation might seem to be a simple process. Such is not the case, however. Little is known about how compensatory education is best provided. In part because program guidelines were often ambiguous, even contradictory, it was difficult to tell when the guidelines had been met, let alone when they measured educational outcomes. A nationwide study of Title I project reports concludes that most of them "continue to resemble educational travel brochures, with extensive anecdotes and little objective data to support claims of 'success.' " They are self-serving, designed to meet federal reporting requirements. "I want information to justify expansion of the program. I'm not interested in information showing students are behind national norms," said one school superintendent.[43]

It has been virtually impossible to establish situations in which a clearly defined group of Title I students can be compared with a nonparticipatory group over a significant period of time. But two independent evaluations have attempted to do so. The Educational Testing Service tested more than forty thousand students who had participated in compensatory education programs and compared the results with those obtained from a control group. The study found no significant differences, concluding weakly that "compensatory students tend not to fall further behind noncompensatory students during the academic year." Another detailed study completed for Systems Development Corporation reported that compensatory education "has had consistently positive effects on achievement growth," but that these effects are small.[44] These are the most optimistic assessments that measurement will permit. They stand in mute testimony against the confident claims of educational renewal voiced twenty years ago.

Recent years have brought a flood of commissions, studies, and reports on American education. "A Nation at Risk," an appraisal by the National Commission on Excellence in Education, warns of "a rising tide of mediocrity that threatens our very future as a nation and a people."[45] For years school officials have reported more vandalism and greater absenteeism, less serious reading and fewer completed homework assignments. One index of academic achievement, the Scholastic Aptitude Test, which measures the verbal and mathematical skills of high school seniors, has declined steadily for nearly two decades (Table 3).

TABLE 3

SCHOLASTIC APTITUDE TEST SCORE AVERAGES FOR
COLLEGE-BOUND HIGH-SCHOOL SENIORS, BY SEX:
UNITED STATES, 1966-1967 TO 1980-1981

	SCHOOL YEAR			
SCORES	1966-1967	1970-1971	1975-1976	1980-1981
Verbal				
Male	463	454	433	430
Female	468	457	430	418
Total	466	455	431	424
Mathematical				
Male	514	507	497	492
Female	467	466	446	443
Total	492	488	472	466

SOURCE: Report of the Twentieth Century Fund Task Force on Federal Elementary and Secondary Education Policy, *Making the Grade* (New York, 1983), p. 54.

The overwhelming consensus among public school teachers is that the level of learning has fallen since the mid-1960s.

It cannot be said that the federal government is responsible in any large measure for the trouble in the nation's schools. It is coincidental that the decline in standards and achievement occurred during the waxing of federal power in education. However, the irony does serve to throw into sharp relief the major thrust of federal programs. Washington has pursued a course leading to greater equality of opportunity in the schools, as its programs of compensatory education indicate. In many cases it acted responsibly as states and local communities remained largely indifferent to the aspirations of their underprivileged constituents. While forging new roles for itself in the educational arena, however, Washington policy-makers reached a silent, largely unconscious, decision that they could not pursue simultaneously programs that guaranteed both equal opportunity and academic excellence.

An evaluation of the federal role in education gains cogency as political rather than strictly educational objectives are kept in mind. Despite its great importance to democracy, education has never been the highest priority in the United States, and it could hardly be expected that the federal government would make it so. Since World War II, Washington has turned to the educational system only as threats to the total social system developed. In the immediate postwar years the threat came from abroad. After 1960 it came from within. Political pressure from those who remained largely outside the framework of influence and privilege, often expressing itself in tensions over race and poverty, forced Washington to expand the areas of opportunity for citizens. Public education became an important government vehicle on the road to equal opportunity. But it was a vehicle, not a destination. (The Supreme Court's intervention against segregation was not based on educational principles primarily.) From the vantage point of twenty years, we have learned that compensatory education programs, however unsuccessful educationally, were successful politically. The programs helped to stabilize the social system by creating hope for the disadvantaged and by buying time as revolt that threatened in the ghettos and in the streets burned itself out.

The political needs of the federal government have altered the balance of power in the American political system. For example, the U.S. Constitution omits any mention of education, thus delegating responsibility to the states. Yet it is no longer true that in public education the states are sovereign. Their policies are in vital ways subject to the authority of Congress and the Supreme Court. The courts decide what laws that pertain to education mean. Congressional involvement, as we have seen, has grown in response to national crises and controversies. The enlarged federal presence is often felt in indirect ways, as when the granting of financial aid is made contingent upon acceptance of federal guidelines and regulations on curriculum and civil rights policies. "With Title VI as the stick and federal funds as the carrot," writes Diane Ravitch, "the federal government became a significant factor in setting rules for the nation's schools, colleges, and universities. A school system whose budget relied on federal funds for almost 10 percent of its revenues or a major university that received several millions for research programs and fellowships was not in a strong position to oppose federal directives."[46]

The authority of the federal government is due to much more than its share of education expenditures in the nation, which is relatively small. The categorical aid approach permits it largely to preclude states and local communities from determining the disposition of federal funds. The decision-making power remains with Congress, the Department of Education, and other federal agencies, for with categorical aid come guidelines, regulations, and requirements of regular reports. Federal standards become the norm. Thus a new partnership between the states and Washington has developed. It is often not an equal one. Programs for handicapped children, for example, are centralized in the Bureau of Education for the Handicapped, making them a federal and not a state responsibility.

The new importance of education in national politics was highlighted during the 1976 presidential campaign when Jimmy Carter, seeking the support of educational organizations, promised to establish a separate Department of Education (DOE). After fulfilling that promise, he received the strong endorsement of the National Education Association in 1980; however, the Republican candidate Ronald Reagan called for the abolition of the department. The fact that President Carter lost the election does not obscure the fact that education had become an important national issue. It seems improbable that the DOE and the federal government will much enlarge their roles in the immediate future. Yet if recent history is an accurate guide, the government, when responding to a crisis, will again turn to the educational system. At that time all the precedents for a still larger federal role will already be in place.

1. This paper is limited to a discussion of the growth of federal power in elementary and secondary education, but much of its argument is applicable to higher education as well, including funding for research and development, affirmative action under Title IX of the Education Amendments of 1972, and programs of student aid. A vigorous critique of federal involvement in the internal processes of universities can be found in Daniel Patrick Moynihan, "State vs. Academe," *Harper's* 261 (December 1980):31-40.

2. The impact of the early cold war on American education is discussed in Ronald Lora, "Education: Schools as Crucible in Cold War America," in Robert H. Bremner and Gary W. Reichard, eds., *Reshaping America: Society and Institutions, 1945-1960* (Columbus, 1982), 223-60.

3. Paul E. Marsh and Ross A. Gortner, *Federal Aid to Education: Two Programs*, The Economics and Politics of Public Education 6 (Syracuse, N.Y., 1963); John Goodlad, *School Curriculum Reform* (New York, 1964); Robert W. Heath, ed., *New Curricula* (New York, 1964); and William Wooton, *SMSG: The Making of a Curriculum* (New Haven, Conn., 1965).

4. Helpful in this regard is J. Myron Atkin, "The Government in the Classroom," *Daedalus* 109 (Summer 1980):85-97.

5. President Johnson's deep faith in education as a ticket to a better life is examined in Philip R. Rulon, *The Compassionate Samaritan* (Chicago, 1981). A superb study of the domestic policy process in education during the Kennedy and Johnson administrations is Hugh D. Graham, *The Uncertain Triumph: Federal Education Policy in the Kennedy and Johnson Years* (Chapel Hill, N.C.: 1984).

6. For historical studies of the efforts to obtain federal aid, see especially Gordon Canfield Lee, *The Struggle for Federal Aid—First Phase: A History of the Attempts to obtain Federal Aid for the Common Schools, 1870-1890* (New York, 1949); Frank J. Munger and Richard F. Fenno, Jr., *National Politics and Federal Aid to Education*, The Economics and Politics of Public Education 3 (Syracuse, N. Y., 1962); and Sidney W. Tiedt, *The Role of the Federal Govern-*

ment in Education (New York, 1966). See also Charles A. Quattlebaum, *Federal Aid to Elementary Education: An Analytic Study of the Issue, Its Background and Relevant Legislative Proposals, with a Compilation of Arguments Pro and Con* (Washington, D.C., 1948); and Harry Zeitlin, "Efforts to Achieve Federal Aid to Education: Developments During the New Deal," *Teachers College Record* 61 (January 1960):195-202.

7. Norman C. Thomas, *Education in National Politics* (New York, 1975), 50-51. Gary Orfield, *The Reconstruction of Southern Education: The Schools and the 1964 Civil Rights Act* (New York, 1969), is illuminating on desegregation efforts in the South.

8. Quoted in Joel Spring, *American Education* (New York, 1982), 181. Also useful on the civil rights movement and the war on poverty as they relate to education is Joel Spring, *The Sorting Machine: National Educational Policy Since 1945* (New York, 1976).

9. Stephen K. Bailey and Edith K. Mosher, *ESEA: The Office of Education Administers a Law* (Syracuse, N.Y., 1968). Two articles useful on the passage of ESEA and the management of Title I are James W. Guthrie, "A Political Case History: Passage of the ESEA," *Phi Delta Kappan* 49 (February 1968):302-6; and Jerome T. Murphy, "Title I of ESEA: The Politics of Implementing Federal Education Reform," *Harvard Educational Review* 41 (February 1971):35-63.

10. U.S., Congress, House, Committee on Education and Labor, General Subcommittee on Education, *Bilingual Education Programs*, Hearings, 90th Cong., 1st sess., H. R. 9840 and H.R. 10224, 1967, p. 141.

11. U.S., Congress, Senate, Committee on Labor and Public Welfare, Special Subcommittee on Bilingual Education, *Bilingual Education*, 90th Cong., 1st sess., 1967, p. 43.

12. Cf. Abigail M. Thernstrom on the cultural maintenance thrust of bilingual instruction: "We once believed that the nation represented values to which immigrants could subscribe—values which transcended ethnic lines. And we believed in the role of schools in transmitting those values. The advent of bilingual education did not, of course, single-handedly strip us of our faith in an American culture of sufficiently universal appeal to cross ethnic lines. But in promoting the notion that the process of Americanization was hopelessly ethnocentric, and in robbing the schools of their traditional integrative function, it has certainly played an important part": "E Pluribus Plura—Congress and Bilingual Education," *Public Interest* 60 (Summer 1980):22.

13. Malcolm N. Danoff, "Evaluation of the Impact of ESEA Title VII Spanish/English Bilingual Education Programs" (Palo Alto, Calif., 1978). An exploration of various developments in bilingual-bicultural education after 1968 is Susan Gilbert Schneider, *Revolution, Reaction or Reform: The 1974 Bilingual Education Act* (New York, 1976). Iris C. Rotberg discusses the evolving federal role in bilingual education and its impact upon legislation, court decisions, and regulations in "Some Legal and Research Considerations in Establishing Federal Policy in Bilingual Education," *Harvard Educational Review* 52 (May 1982):49-68.

14. *Pennsylvania Association for Retarded Children v. Commonwealth of Pennsylvania*, 334 F. Supp. 1257 (E. D. Pa. 1971).

15. Erwin L. Levine and Elizabeth M. Wexler, *PL 94-142: An Act of Congress* (New York, 1981), 32, 193, 198. *An Act of Congress* reprints Public Law 94-142 and discusses the process of its enactment.

16. The possibilities and problems of mainstreaming are discussed in J. W. Birch, *Mainstreaming: Educable Mentally Retarded Children in Regular Classes* (Reston, Va., 1974); R. A. Jones, ed., *Mainstreaming: The Minority Child in Regular Classes* (Reston, Va., 1976); and M. C. Reynolds, ed., *Mainstreaming: Origins and Implications* (Reston, Va., 1976).

17. Many of the major criticisms are expressed in John C. Pittenger and Peter Kuriloff, "Educating the Handicapped: Reforming a Radical Law," *Public Interest* 66 (Winter 1982):72-96.

18. Quoted in Diane Ravitch, *The Troubled Crusade: American Education, 1945-1980* (New York, 1983), 309.

19. Levine and Wexler, *PL 94-142*, 193.

20. Ibid., 194.

21. National Center for Education Statistics, *The Condition of Education, 1981* (Washington, D.C., 1981), 266.

22. *Brown v. Board of Education of Topeka*, 347 U.S. 483 (1954), 494-95.

23. *Brown v. Board of Education of Topeka*, 349 U.S. 295 (1955), 301. A useful study of the ramifications of *Brown* as the Supreme Court moved from color blindness to the color consciousness of affirmative action, is Raymond Wolters, *The Burden of Brown: Thirty Years of School Desegregation* (Knoxville, Tenn., 1984).

24. Laughlin McDonald, "The Legal Barriers Crumble," *Southern Exposure* 7 (May 1979):25.

25. *Griffin v. County School Board of Prince Edward County*, 377 U.S. 218 (1964), 234.

26. *Green v. County School Board of New Kent County*, 391 U.S. 430 (1968), 442, 438; *Monroe v. Board of Commissioners of the City of Jackson*, 391 U.S. 450 (1968).

27. *Alexander v. Holmes County Board of Education*, 396 U.S. 19 (1969), 20, 1220, 1222.

28. *Swann v. Charlotte-Mecklenburg Board of Education*, 402 U.S. 1, (1970), 25-31.

29. *Kelly v. Guinn*, 456 F.2d 100 (9th Cir. 1972); *Keyes v. District No. 1*, 413 U.S. 189 (1973).

30. *Keyes v. School District No. 1*, 247, 250.

31. *Milliken v. Bradley*, 418 U.S. 717 (1974), 757.

32. *Dayton Board of Education v. Brinkman*, 433 U.S. 406 (1977); *Evans v. Buchanon*, 555 F. 2d 373 (3d Cir. 1977).

33. Two articles that highlight criticisms made of busing as a means to achieve school desegregation are Nathan Glazer, "Is Busing Necessary?", *Commentary* 53 (March 1972):39-52; and David J. Armor, "The Evidence on Busing," *Public Interest* 28 (Summer 1972):90-126. A vigorous critique of Armor's article is Thomas F. Pettigrew, Elizabeth L. Useem, Clarence Normand, and

Marshall S. Smith, "Busing: A Review of 'The Evidence'," *Public Interest* 30 (Winter 1973):88-118. Nicolaus Mills, ed., *Busing U.S.A.* (New York, 1979), is an excellent anthology on busing, desegregation, and the "white flight" controversy.

34. George H. Gallup, *The Gallup Poll—American Public Opinion*, 1935-1971: Vol. 3, 1959-1971 (New York, 1972), 2,323.

35. U.S. Commission on Civil Rights, *Twenty Years After Brown: Equality of Educational Opportunity* (Washington, D.C., 1975), 47; *Statistical Abstract of the United States* (1976), 127.

36. Samuel Halperin, "The Positive Side," *Phi Delta Kappan* 57 (November 1975):147-51.

37. Ibid., 149.

38. Quoted in Mary Frase Williams, *Government in the Classroom: Dollars and Power in Education* (New York, 1979), 111.

39. William W. Cooley, "Effectiveness of Compensatory Education," *Educational Leadership* 38 (January 1981):298-301.

40. Report of the Twentieth Century Fund Task Force on Federal Elementary and Secondary Education Policy, *Making the Grade* (New York, 1983), 101-3; G. V. Glass and M. L. Smith, *"Pull Out" in Compensatory Education* (Boulder, Colo., 1977).

41. William Wayson, "The Negative Side," *Phi Delta Kappan* 57 (November 1975):151-56.

42. Charles Silberman, *Crisis in the Classroom* (New York, 1970), 181.

43. *Making the Grade*, 97, 98. The quotations are from Jane L. David, *Local Uses of Title I Evaluations* (Menlo Park, Calif., 1978), 3, 17.

44. *Making the Grade*, 99-100.

45. National Commission on Excellence in Education, "A Nation at Risk: The Imperative for Educational Reform," *Chronicle of Higher Education* 26 (4 May 1983):11. Other reports on the state of American education include Ernest L. Boyer, *High School: A Report on Secondary Education in America*, The Carnegie Foundation for the Advancement of Teaching (New York, 1983); Task Force on Education for Economic Growth, Education Commission of the States, *Action For Excellence: A Comprehensive Plan to Improve Our Nation's Schools* (Denver, Colo, 1983); National Association of High School Principals and the National Association of Independent Schools, *Horace's Compromise: The Dilemma of the American High School* (New York, 1984); *Making the Grade*; and National Coalition of Advocates for Students, *Barriers to Excellence: Our Children at Risk* (Boston, 1985).

46. Ravitch, *The Troubled Crusade*, 268.

The Nuclear Question

Allan M. Winkler

I would like to thank Barbara Clarke Mossberg, Glenn A. May, and Steve Johnson for their thoughtful comments on an earlier draft of this essay—A.M.W.

Since 1945, when the United States dropped two atomic bombs on Japan, Americans have grappled with the dilemmas of the nuclear age. Throughout the postwar period, they have been torn between their hopes for the promise of the potent new force and their fears for the cataclysmic destruction it could bring. Initially they believed that nuclear weapons provided security in the aftermath of World War II. They believed, too, that nuclear energy offered an inexpensive and accessible source of power to all people on earth. Those hopes proved short-lived.

Americans became increasingly concerned as they began to understand the practical effects of this technological change. They found that atomic development, once started, could not be checked. They discovered that nuclear concerns intertwined with virtually all compelling national issues. In foreign affairs Americans debated how best to control a terrifying arms race against the backdrop of the Cold War. At home they weighed the costs of nuclear energy against other economic needs. In every area atomic arguments helped shape public mood. Sometimes proponents of nuclear expansion predominated; at other times critics had the upper hand. Whatever their conflicts with each other, scientists and businessmen, government officials and concerned citizens all agreed that nuclear issues were among the most pressing—and most difficult to resolve—in the United States.

NUCLEAR WEAPONRY AND DEFENSE

Technological development shaped nuclear strategy from the dawn of the atomic age. The United States embarked upon the Manhattan Project to create a bomb with the intention of using that weapon in the Second World War. Between 1942 and 1945 the effort cost the enormous sum of $2 billion, required installations in nineteen states and Canada, and absorbed much of the nation's scientific expertise. Buoyed by the successful Trinity test at Alamogordo, New Mexico, on 16 July 1945, the United States detonated its only two functional bombs over Hiroshima and Nagasaki and brought the Pacific war to an end.[1]

After World War II, the nation began to stockpile more powerful weapons. With the Soviet Union's explosion of its own atomic device in 1949, the United States decided to embark upon the creation of a different kind of bomb. The early atomic weapons worked on the principle of fission—splitting the atom apart. Now a new effort, spearheaded by physicist Edward Teller, sought to create a larger explosion through the process of fusion—driving atomic particles together to produce an even more destructive effect. In the early 1950s, both Americans and Russians experimented with hydrogen devices. On 1 March 1954, at the Bikini Atoll in the Pacific, the United States successfully tested a weapon one thousand times more powerful than either of the bombs dropped on Japan. A year and a half later the Soviet Union detonated a comparable hydrogen bomb.[2]

New weapons demanded more sophisticated delivery systems. The United States relied on the B-52 jet bomber to carry its bombs. Based at home, it was intercontinental in range and could penetrate deep into Soviet territory. Then in 1957 the Soviet Union shocked the United States, first by flight testing an intercontinental ballistic missile, then by launching Sputnik, a small satellite that went into orbit in space. Assuming that the Russians now possessed a superior delivery capability, Americans suddenly felt vulnerable to attack. In response to the Soviet achievement, the United States sped up its own missile program, both to avoid being left behind in the orbiting race and to ensure that it could deliver hydrogen bombs.[3]

From the mid-1950s on, hydrogen bombs and intercontinental ballistic missiles were the basic military components of the nuclear age. Improvements occurred all the time, but the major elements remained the same. Stockpiles increased as the United States came to rely on a combination of B-52s, land-based missiles, and submarine-based missiles for its defense. Both the Soviet Union and the United States began to develop antiballistic missile systems. And in 1970 the United States, then the Soviet Union, developed Multiple Independently Targetable Reentry Vehicle (MIRV) technology to allow a missile to contain several warheads that could go off in different directions in the course of an attack.[4]

In the early days of the atomic age, American policy makers viewed the bomb as a lever in growing confrontations with the Russians. Although Secretary of War Henry L. Stimson warned of trying to negotiate with this new weapon "ostentatiously on our hip," he thought it could be used to extract concessions from the Soviets in eastern Europe. Secretary of State James F. Byrnes found that mere American possession of the bomb did not make the Russians easier to handle. They proved unwilling to capitulate or to back away from their own perceived interests, even though the United States had sole possession of the new weapon. President Harry S Truman became increasingly aware of the constraints surrounding the bomb. "I am not sure it can ever be used," he acknowledged privately in October 1945.[5]

Despite a growing recognition that the bomb did not create diplomatic omnipotence. American military planners began to plan for its possible strategic use. While still in possession of an atomic monopoly, the United States anticipated using the bomb against Russian cities in any future war. The atomic bomb was "primarily an offensive weapon for use against large urban and industrial targets," declared an Air Force report in the fall of 1945. The assumption was that such bombing was the best way to undermine Soviet military might, as it was believed it had helped undermine German and Japanese resistance in the last war. Targets were assigned, even though American capabilities remained severely limited in the first postwar years.[6]

When planners concluded in 1949 that the planned offensive against urban and industrial targets would not guarantee victory in a war against the Soviet Union, they broadened strategy to include military forces and nuclear installations as targets in the early 1950s. American leaders intended "counterforce" targeting to limit damage to the United States.[7]

During the administration of Dwight D. Eisenhower, the United States began to rely even more heavily on atomic weapons for purposes of defense. Seriously concerned about keeping the budget under control, Eisenhower declared in his State of the Union message on 7 January 1954 that the United States would deter aggression by maintaining "a massive capability to strike back." New weapons necessary to implement the policy would reduce manpower needs and save money in the end. Five days later, in a speech to the Council on Foreign Relations, Secretary of State John Foster Dulles outlined even more explicitly the doctrine that came to be known as "massive retaliation." The United States, Dulles announced, would "depend primarily upon a great capacity to retaliate, instantly, by means and at places of our choosing," to counter aggression anywhere in the world.[8]

Despite the ominous nature of the "massive retaliation" slogan, the Eisenhower administration remained vague about how the atomic arsenal might be used and proceeded with restraint. The United States threatened the Chinese with nuclear weapons if they did not agree to end the Korean War. Dulles, according to some accounts, offered the French atomic bombs in their campaign against the Vietnamese. Still, the weapons remained unused. Eisenhower wanted to control the arms race and insisted on sufficiency rather than superiority in the process of preparing for attack.[9]

Nonetheless, planning continued. A Strategic Air Command document in 1954 envisioned a tightly-coordinated operation against the Soviet Union that could, according to a Navy observer, leave that nation "a smoking, radiating ruin at the end of two hours." Before Eisenhower left office, military officials from the various services produced the first Single Integrated Operational Plan (SIOP) for fighting a nuclear war. That scheme provided an "optimum mix" of military, industrial, and government targets for destruction in a single, coordinated attack. Eisenhower himself was frightened at the enormous number of targets and at the anticipated overkill.[10]

John F. Kennedy's administration carried the planning process a step further. In June 1962, in a commencement address at the University of Michigan, Secretary of Defense Robert S. McNamara emphasized that in any future war the United States sought "the destruction of the enemy's military forces, not of his civilian population." In that speech and others, he stressed the need to survive a surprise attack and to respond with a successful second strike. "Massive retaliation" gave way to a new policy of "flexible response" aimed at countering the objections of critics who claimed that the Eisenhower approach left no alternatives between capitulation and all-out war.[11]

In the mid-1960s, McNamara became concerned about the large-scale spending on strategic systems, particularly as the Soviet nuclear capability expanded. His response was to shift course, to speak of an "assured destruction" strategy, in which much of the Soviet Union's industrial power and population would be destroyed in a retaliatory strike. No longer could the United States hope to survive only by eliminating the enemy's strategic reserves. The nation's forces were intended to deter the other side from using its might in what would be an unwinnable conflict for both. "Mutual assured destruction" (MAD) became the slogan of the day.[12]

The next shift came as the administration of Richard M. Nixon began to seek ways of enhancing the flexibility of nuclear war plans. Secretary of Defense James R. Schlesinger was concerned that the goal of massive counterattack might lead to unstoppable escalation if nuclear war occurred. He also understood that technological developments made more accurate targeting and retargeting possible. In early 1974 he announced a policy of measured response to aggression in which the United States would try to control escalation before a full-scale war broke out. Damage limitation, possibly through the use of focused and precise nuclear action, became the policy of the United States.[13]

When the Democrats regained power in the election of 1976, they began another reexamination of American strategic goals. As relations with the Russians deteriorated, Presidential Directive-59 (PD-59), signed by President Jimmy Carter on 25 July 1980, called for increased targeting of Soviet military and political resources. It improved the nuclear command and control structure. It also committed the United States to fight a prolonged nuclear war that could last months, and not simply hours or days.[14]

The administration of Ronald Reagan took that approach one step further in National Security Division Directive 13 (NSDD-13), signed in October 1981. Although the document remained secret, a classified five-year defense guidance leaked to the press provided the essentials. It stated that "should deterrence fail and strategic nuclear war with the USSR occur, the United States must prevail and be able to force the Soviet Union to seek earliest termination of hostilities on terms favorable to the United States." Building on the blocks of the past, the nation now seemed committed to winning a nuclear war.[15]

As American strategists drafted military plans for the nation's defense, they also considered the protection of the homefront population in case of attack. Civil defense was an issue of major concern in the first decades of the atomic age. From time to time Americans embarked upon drives to provide shelters, above and below the ground, to counter enemy bombs that might get through. But large-scale funding proved hard to get, and civil defense campaigns enjoyed only mixed success.[16]

Civil defense planning in the early postwar years led to the establishment of a Federal Civil Defense Administration in January 1951. The costs of blast-proof shelters proved prohibitive, however, and so the government tried, through propaganda campaigns, to cajole the public into taking the steps that could lead to safety in case of attack. "Duck and Cover" was the slogan of the early 1950s. A film of that name introducing "Bert the Turtle" underscored the need to seek protection from flying glass and debris in a raid. Twenty million copies of a cartoon booklet told the same story. One frame declared that in the face of danger, "BERT DUCKS AND COVERS. HE'S SMART, BUT *HE* HAS HIS SHELTER ON HIS BACK. YOU MUST LEARN TO FIND SHELTER." A final one concluded: "DON'T STAND AND LOOK. DUCK AND COVER!"[17]

The power of the new thermonulcear bomb led to a change of policy. Shelters no longer seemed effective, and so, for a time, the Eisenhower administration encouraged evacuation in case of attack. The Interstate Highway Act of 1956, providing easier access to the suburbs in the automobile age, also established an expeditious means of exit from the cities in an atomic war. The orientation, according to the *Bulletin of the Atomic Scientists*, changed "from 'Duck and Cover' to 'Run Like Hell.' "[18]

The orientation shifted again with the growing awareness of nuclear fallout. Protection from blast might be impossible, but shelter could be provided from the radioactive particles that followed. A National Shelter Policy in 1958 left every citizen responsible for his own protection while giving the government the authority to provide leadership, direction, and advice.[19]

The popular press seized on the shelter issue. *Life* magazine featured an "H-Bomb Hideaway" for $3,000 in 1955. *Good Housekeeping* carried a full-page editorial in November 1958 urging the building of family shelters. By the end of 1960, the government estimated that there were one million family fallout shelters in the United States.[20]

The real boom in shelter building, however, came with John Kennedy's encouragement. Troubled by his confrontation with Soviet Premier Nikita Khrushchev in Vienna in July 1961, he called for and received $207.6 million from Congress for a fallout shelter program. Later that year he embarked on a five-year shelter-building program to protect the entire population. The government printed 25 million copies of a small booklet entitled *Fallout Protection: What to Know and Do about Nuclear Attack*, to be distributed through post offices and offices of civil defense.

The public was concerned. "At cocktail parties and P.T.A. meetings and family dinners, on buses and commuter trains and around office watercoolers," *Time* magazine noted, "talk turns to shelters." Opponents claimed that shelters would do little good in a nuclear holocaust, yet might encourage a false security or a willingness to take military chances that could have fatal results. In time the administration began to retreat, particularly after the signing of the Limited Test Ban Treaty of 1963. A once-heated issue began to cool down.[21]

In the years that followed, various leaders continued to assert the importance of civil defense. Lyndon B. Johnson called it "an important element of our total defense effort." Gerald Ford asserted that "our civil defense program continues to be an essential element of the nation's deterrent posture." The program in the early 1970s came to embrace potential peacetime disasters as well as those possible in time of nuclear war. A number of new agencies began to take responsibility for handling the disasters that could occur. In 1978 Jimmy Carter authorized an even stronger civil defense effort, and in 1979 Congress pulled together all functions into a single organization, the Federal Emergency Management Agency (FEMA).[22]

The Republican administration that came to power in 1981 moved the process even further along. Deputy Under Secretary of Defense T. K. Jones argued in an interview with *Los Angeles Times* reporter Robert Scheer that the American people could survive a nuclear attack. "Dig a hole, cover it with a couple of doors and then throw three feet of dirt on top," he said. "It's the dirt that does it. . . . If there are enough shovels to go around, everybody's going to make it." To that end, the administration decided to fund a major civil defense program, despite the reservations of the Joint Chiefs of Staff and the Office of Management and Budget. In the 1983 fiscal year it requested $252 million for civil defense, more than twice the amount of the preceding year. FEMA began work on a seven-year plan estimated to cost $4.2 billion. Critics in the 1980s were even more vocal than they had been in the past. They argued, as they had for years, that civil defense could not provide adequate protection from the perils of nuclear war, and that the administration was engaging in a naive and futile exercise. Nonetheless, proponents of the program had the upper hand once more.[23]

NUCLEAR POWER

As the debate over defense unfolded, Americans contemplated possible peaceful uses of atomic energy. Soon after the explosion of the Hiroshima bomb, the *New York Times* speculated about civilian applications, even about an atomic plane. "Release of atomic energy," one article concluded, "promises to widen and broaden the application of air transport to the world's extension of communication and business, and cannot be limited merely to destructiveness." Robert M. Hutchins, chancellor of the University of Chicago, predicted that "a very few individuals working a few hours a day at very easy tasks in the central atomic power plant will provide all the heat, light, and power required by the community, and these utilities will be so cheap that their cost can hardly be reckoned." Power "too cheap to meter" became the dream of the day. Americans believed, as Walt Disney argued in *Our Friend the Atom*, that atomic energy could "be put to use for creation, for the welfare of all mankind."[24]

According to the terms of the Atomic Energy Act of 1946, responsibility for the nuclear power program lay squarely with the government. After serious consideration of who should be in charge of atomic development in the post-Manhattan Project period, the nation decided on civilian control. A new Atomic Energy Commission (AEC) held a monopoly over all nuclear materials and facilities, and over all developmental projects. Military uses of atomic energy were most important, with peaceful applications something of an afterthought, useful largely to provide the AEC with a softer image. Nonetheless, a foundation for a nuclear power industry had been laid.[25]

Progress on the power program was slow. Physicist J. Robert Oppenheimer, one of the leading figures in the development of the bomb, predicted that although nuclear reactors might create usable energy within five years, it would be thirty to fifty years before such energy became a major power source. There were, according to David Lilienthal, first chairman of the AEC, "a whole mass of involved, difficult, scientific, technical, and industrial engineering problems" that had to be overcome. Many of the nation's most prominent scientists, however, were not eager to work on reactor questions. They preferred to devote their attention to more exciting nuclear projects.[26]

A breakthrough came when Admiral Hyman Rickover began to direct work on a nuclear-powered submarine. He envisioned a reactor containing a small core of uranium fuel that would generate heat to boil water and create steam as it fissioned. The steam would drive a turbine connected to the submarine's propeller shaft. Rickover's close relationship with the Westinghouse Electric Corporation resulted in the successful launch of the *Nautilus* in 1954, and provided a model of a workable means of creating power on land.[27]

In the early 1950s, as basic research continued on a number of experimental reactors, the AEC tried to promote the involvement of American industry in the nuclear process. An Industrial Participation Program offered companies not previously involved access to research in progress and encouraged them to examine questions of economy and design. The Atomic Energy Act of 1954, amending the 1946 measure, permitted private firms to build and operate reactors on their own, with licensing and regulation to be provided by the AEC. The government retained control of nuclear fuel, but the AEC would make fissionable material available to licensed plants. The act further encouraged industrial involvement in research activity and wider dissemination of atomic information. With the creation of a new legal basis for development, the nuclear industry was on its way.[28]

A wave of optimism about the possibilities of power prevailed in the mid-1950s. AEC Chairman Lewis Strauss professed "faith in the atomic future" as he asserted that "our knowledge of the atom is intended by the Creator for the service and not the destruction of mankind." Strauss and others in the agency believed that only technical and organizational details remained to be worked out. The power industry launched a public relations campaign to persuade the public that a new age lay ahead.[29]

In September 1954 work began on a nuclear power plant at Shippingport, Pennsylvania. The Dusquesne Light Company offered to provide the site and to build and operate the generating facility. Westinghouse, along with General Electric a leader in the nuclear field, designed and constructed the plant's reactor. "It is not expected that this first plant will produce electric power at costs competitive with power from conventional fuels," the AEC noted. Nonetheless, the plant, which began operation in 1957, was a technical success.[30]

Some plants in the 1950s were built by private funds, but the AEC proved willing to finance contruction when necessary. The Power Demonstration Reactor Program authorized government funding for plants to be built and operated by private companies that would have the option of buying the steam the reactors produced. The program allowed for experimentation with different forms of reactors and encouraged hope in the ultimate feasibility of inexpensive nuclear power. In early 1961, however, only two reactors were operational. By the end of the next year, four were working, with twelve more small plants under construction. Still, the AEC remained hopeful. A 1962 report to President John F. Kennedy asserted that nuclear power was "on the threshold of economic competitiveness." With but a little government encouragement, that goal could be reached.[31]

The early 1960s showed a continued effort to demonstrate that nuclear power could be competitive. In 1963 General Electric and Westinghouse launched a series of "turnkey" projects, in which they assumed all risks in building plants that utilities could simply take over. The Oyster Creek generating facility built by General Electric for the Jersey Central Power and Light Company was the first and best known of those plants. Jersey Central, which gambled that a nuclear plant could produce electricity more cheaply than a fossil unit, was to pay $66 million, an estimated $30 million less than it cost to build. General Electric was willing to let the plant serve as a "loss leader" to demonstrate the feasibility of nuclear power to other customers.[32]

The program was a success. By 1964 a number of utility companies had begun to examine bids from the manufacturers of reactors. The next year, some of the firms were beginning to talk terms. Over the next few years, the AEC issued construction permits for several dozen plants near the nation's major cities. In 1966 and 1967 alone, utilities ordered about fifty plants, which accounted for half the new power generating capacity planned during that time. The public seemed receptive to nuclear development. As costs rose at the end of the decade, the process slowed, but in the early 1970s, another surge of orders occurred, now for larger plants. Between 1970 and 1974, more than a hundred reactors were ordered. Then the process slowed again and finally came to a halt.[33]

Problems had been evident for some time, and many of those revolved around the question of safety. In 1957 the AEC issued a report based on research done at the Brookhaven National Laboratory. Known by its AEC number—WASH-740—and by its title—"Theoretical Possibilities and Consequences of Major Accidents in Large Nuclear Plants"—the report was a worst-case study. It predicted that an accident at a typical reactor could cause thirty-four hundred deaths and forty-three thousand serious injuries. Property damage could range from $500,000 to $7 billion. To ease the fears of financial ruin, the Price-Anderson Act of 1957 established that accident compensation would come from a reactor operator's private insurance, plus $500 million from the government, with neither operator nor government liable for damages over that amount.[34]

The act, however, failed to address the human consequences of a nuclear accident. The dangers remained, and public concern mounted. The AEC, responsible both for promoting and for regulating atomic energy, required only that licensees "provide reasonable assurance" that their reactors would be safe. With those loose guidelines, controversy was inevitable. Trouble arose in Michigan in 1956, when the Power Reactor Development Company sought to build a fast-breeder reactor in Monroe, near Detroit. The legal battle initiated by local interests ultimately went all the way to the U.S. Supreme Court, which ruled in 1961 that the Enrico Fermi plant was acceptable as long as the AEC followed procedures that had already been laid down and acted fairly within the framework of its own regulations.[35]

Spokesmen for the nuclear industry sought to persuade the public that nuclear power posed no appreciable risks. In 1965 Chauncy Starr, a leading industrialist, declared before the American Nuclear Society, "Safety is a relative matter and I believe we have reached a point in the demonstrated safety of nuclear power to say nuclear power is safe, period."[36]

Not everyone agreed. Fears became more pronounced as accidents occurred at a number of plants. In January 1961, at Stationary Low-Power Reactor No. 1 in Idaho, the core went supercritical when a control rod was pulled out. A steam explosion resulted, and two servicemen were killed instantly. A third died on the way to the hospital. All three bodies remained so radioactive that burial had to wait for three weeks.[37]

The Fermi plant, after years of trouble, suffered a similar problem in 1966. In October, as control rods were being withdrawn from the core to allow a nuclear reaction to take place, radiation levels suddenly rose precipitously. Alarms went off and the plant was shut down. A small piece of zirconium had broken off, stopped the flow of coolant, and caused the partial melting of the core. The process was halted, but for a time there was concern that evacuation of Detroit might be necessary.[38]

In the mid-1960s there was talk about the "China Syndrome"—a sequence of events in which the mass of radioactive material could overheat and begin to melt. In that scenario the molten core would sear its way through the reactor floor, into the ground beneath, and on toward the general direction of China. Explosions might occur. At the very least, radioactivity would contaminate the surroundings. The larger the reactors, the greater the meltdown fears.[39]

As concern grew the government recognized the need to reassess safety risks. In March 1972 work on a new study began. Led by Norman C. Rasmussen, a nuclear physicist at the Massachusetts Institute of Technology, the effort concentrated on examining the probability of a nuclear accident, and the consequences if one occurred. In the summer of 1974, the first draft of the "Reactor Safety Study: An Assessment of Accident Risks in U.S. Commercial Nuclear Plants"—or WASH-1400 —appeared. It was published in final form in October 1975.[40]

Several thousand pages long, the study found the risks of a reactor accident much smaller than those to which people were normally exposed. The likelihood of a reactor accident causing 1000 or more fatalities was "one in 1 million or once in a million years . . . just the probability that a meteor would strike a U.S. population center and cause 1000 fatalities." In a worst-case scenario, the Rasmussen report said, thirty-three hundred people might die.[41]

Criticism came soon after publication of the draft. The American Physical Society pointed out that the report had neglected the cumulative death toll from cancer and leukemia caused by the release of radioactivity. The Environmental Protection Agency also found the estimates too low. A critique provided by the Union of Concerned Scientists and the Sierra Club argued that the chances of a major accident taking place were far greater than the report indicated. Though some of the figures were changed in the final version, the basic conclusions remained. The AEC was pleased with the report; other observers remained unconvinced.[42]

The critics were vindicated as accidents continued to occur. A terrible fire swept through the Brown's Ferry Nuclear Plant in Alabama in March 1972 and left one reactor in a dangerous state. But the most dramatic accident unfolded at the Three Mile Island plant in Pennsylvania in March 1979. Operator error and system malfunction led the reactor to heat up dramatically and come close to a meltdown. Hydrogen gas began to build up in the reactor chamber, and serious consequences seemed possible.[43]

The accident at Three Mile Island had a major impact both on residents of the area and on the nuclear industry as a whole. Nearly 150,000 people fled their homes. Reporters flocked to the region and covered the lead story day after day. In time it became clear that the basic nuclear safety-monitoring system itself was at fault. The Nuclear Regulatory Commission, formed in 1974 when the AEC split into two parts—the NRC to deal with regulation and the Energy Research and Development Agency to promote atomic progress—had never fully come to terms with safety questions that were becoming increasingly complex.[44]

The nuclear power industry now found itself under fire. Environmental groups intervened in the licensing process and demanded that changes be made. Expensive safety features, some of them poorly planned, were added to plants already under construction. Huge cost overruns resulted, and plants took far longer to complete than builders expected. As predictions of future energy needs were scaled down, plants being built seemed less necessary than before. In the summer of

1983 the Washington Public Power Supply System suffered a serious financial shock. Several reactors under construction were declared superfluous and building stopped. Without plants to generate electricity, there was no way to make payments on bonds sold to pay for construction. The system defaulted in the largest municipal bond default in history.[45]

Throughout the country the future of nuclear power remained unclear. Antinuclear demonstrations, aimed at focusing opposition to reactors, occurred around the country. Growth ceased, as no orders for new plants were placed after 1978. The fate of fifty-seven units underway in early 1984, two-thirds of them more than half-completed, was uncertain. In Ohio, Cincinnati Gas & Electric announced that it planned to convert the 97%-finished William H. Zimmer plant into a coal-burning facility to cut down costs. Everywhere the vision of a cheap and inexhaustible power supply seemed distant indeed.[46]

PROTEST AND ARMS CONTROL

Throughout the postwar period, Americans engaged in nuclear development programs sought to control the destructive consequences of the atom before it was too late. Watching the Trinity test at Alamogordo, Robert Oppenheimer was reminded of the words of the Hindu holy book, the Bhagavad Gita: "I am become Death, The shatterer of worlds." Niels Bohr, Leo Szilard, and other scientists feared an arms race that could not be checked. Policy makers realized that something had to be done.[47]

The first efforts at international control came in 1946. Harry Truman and his advisers decided to see if regulation might be possible through the newly-created United Nations. A plan, drafted by Under Secretary of State Dean Acheson and TVA head David E. Lilienthal, provided for a series of steps through which the United States would relinquish its monopoly while still retaining its advantage until the very end. Bernard Baruch, the new ambassador to the UN Atomic Energy Commission, modified the plan to allow for international inspection and elimination of the veto in the Security Council in discussions of nuclear controls. The Russians, concerned about external interference in their affairs, balked and offered a plan of their own that called first for destruction of all atomic weapons, then discussions about controls. Negotiations bogged down and all plans died.[48]

As testing increased in the 1950s, Americans became aware of the effects of fallout on the world at large. The BRAVO test in 1954 showered radioactive particles on crewmen of the Japanese fishing boat *Fukuryu Maru* or *Lucky Dragon*. They became sick with various forms of radiation sickness, and several months later one of them died. More and more in the next few years, people around the world came to fear the tiny particles in the atmosphere that could have such a potent effect.[49]

Popular literature and film seized upon the catastrophic consequences of nuclear war. One of the best-known accounts was Australian Nevil Shute's novel *On the Beach*. Published in 1957 and made into an American film two years later, it described a war that released so much radioactive waste that all life in the northern hemisphere was destroyed, while the southern hemisphere could do little more than wait for the residue to come and bring the same deadly end. Though not particularly distinguished, the film upset members of the Eisenhower administration who insisted that what appeared on the screen was not necessarily an accurate picture of what would happen in the event of war.[50]

At about the same time, Walter M. Miller, Jr., took an equally discouraging view in his book *A Canticle for Leibowitz*, a minor classic that told the tale of the rise and fall of civilization as humans failed to learn the lessons of their deeds. After "the Flame Deluge," cities "had become puddles of glass, surrounded by vast acreages of broken stone." The cycle of revival and descent into oblivion occurred time and again. "Have we no choice but to play the Phoenix in an unending sequence of rise and fall?" one of Miller's characters asked. The answer seemed to be no.[51]

Some Americans began to work actively toward an end to the nuclear threat. The National Committee for a Sane Nuclear Policy, established in 1957 and better known simply as SANE, sought an end to the nuclear testing that was poisoning the atmosphere and risking the destruction of the earth. Made up of such people as *Saturday Review* editor Norman Cousins, American Friends Service Committee official Clarence S. Pickett, and entertainer Steve Allen, SANE sponsored newspaper advertisements, organized rallies, and printed materials aimed at getting its point across. In 1958 the United States and the Soviet Union embarked upon a voluntary moratorium on testing. Several years later, as East-West tensions became more severe, the moratorium ended. The Soviets resumed testing in September 1961, the Americans the following March.[52]

Efforts to limit nuclear testing through a treaty finally succeeded in 1963. Chastened by the frightening confrontation in the Cuban missile crisis, the United States and the Soviet Union began to talk about some kind of accommodation at last. The major point of disagreement dealt with the number of on-site inspections to be allowed each year on Soviet soil. In late 1962 Russian Prime Minister Nikita Khrushchev was prepared to allow two or three. John Kennedy wanted eight or ten.[53]

Kennedy broke the deadlock in June 1963 with a commencement speech at American University. In the nuclear age, he said, "total war makes no sense," and he called for an attainable peace. The United States, he announced, would again refrain from atmospheric testing as long as other nations similarly abstained. To move the process still further, he sent W. Averell Harriman, an effective negotiator with experience in Russian affairs, to work out the details in Moscow.[54]

Though Kennedy hoped for a comprehensive test-ban agreement, he was prepared to take what he could get. The treaty negotiated sought "the speediest possible achievement of an agreement on general and complete disarmament," but banned only nuclear tests in the atmosphere. Underground tests were still permitted by its terms. Nonetheless, it was a major step forward in the effort to control arms.[55]

The Limited Test Ban Treaty was signed by Great Britain, the Soviet Union, and the United States. It still had to be ratified by the American Senate, and Kennedy worked hard to ensure the necessary support. In the end he had far more votes than he needed, and the treaty went into effect. Though testing continued underground and led to the development of antiballistic missile systems and multiple warheads, the treaty provided a model for future agreements.[56]

Richard Nixon took the next step. Suspicious at first of accommodation, he came to favor Strategic Arms Limitation Talks (SALT) as he became convinced that a nuclear accord could rest at the center of a web of contacts with the Soviet Union. He and national security adviser Henry Kissinger saw arms control as part of the "linkage" that tied all areas of foreign policy together. The SALT I agreement, signed in 1972 after three years of negotiation and then ratified, was the result.[57]

The SALT I treaty included an "interim agreement" on offensive forces that was to last for five years. It set ceilings on intercontinental and other ballistic missiles in an effort to find a point where the two nations were relatively evenly matched. More important was the antiballistic missile treaty that was part of the larger accord. ABM systems were expensive and threatened to destabilize the strategic balance by undermining the assumption that it was impossible to find a way of limiting damage in a nuclear exchange. If protection was possible, a nation might be more ready to engage in nuclear war. The ABM treaty restricted each nation to the development and deployment of two anti-ballistic missile systems. In 1974 another agreement reduced the number to one.[58]

Under Jimmy Carter the arms limitation process continued. Well aware of the way the arms race was escalating in spite of the earlier agreements, he was determined to draw the line. The SALT II talks, which began even before Carter took office, concluded in 1979 with the signing of a new treaty. The complex SALT II agreement capped the number of warheads that could be placed on missiles, limited the number of multiple-warhead missiles, and froze the number of delivery mechanisms permitted.[59]

The treaty, however, met with a cool response in the United States. Hawks and doves alike were disappointed with its provisions. Opposition in the Senate was intense. By one count only twelve votes were uncertain, and Carter needed nine of them to win. Carter did all he could, but after initial gains, support began to erode. The Soviet invasion of Afghanistan in December 1979 killed any possibility of ratification. The Reagan administration, unwilling to pursue the SALT II approach, announced Strategic Arms Reduction Talks (START), but all efforts to reach agreement with the Soviet Union ended in failure. Arms control would have to wait.[60]

Arms control activism was closely related to the negotiations that occurred after 1963. For a time following the Limited Test Ban Treaty, activism began to decline. Americans who had been worried about fallout and cataclysmic war seemed less concerned now that positive steps were being taken to ease the threat. Hiroshima and Nagasaki faded into the past. More attention focused on the Vietnam War. Then, toward the end of the 1970s, a new concern began to appear. Some people were worried about the safety of nuclear reactors. More were troubled by the failure of the arms control process, the buildup of atomic arsenals, and the apparent inclination of top officials to prevail in a nuclear war. Activists who had found protest dormant earlier seized upon the nuclear issue that now struck a resonant chord.[61]

Once again anxieties were reflected in the literature of the day, as authors explored the nuclear threat just as they had two decades before. In 1975 Robert C. O'Brien, winner of the Newberry Prize, told the story of the last two survivors of an atomic war in his novel *Z for Zachariah*. Ann Burden, lacking any of the conveniences she had known earlier, had to make her own way in the face of almost impossible odds. In 1982 Bernard Malamud, one of the nation's best-known authors, published *God's Grace*, in which he described Calvin Cohn, a paleologist who happened to be at the bottom of the sea during a nuclear war. Cohn had to recreate the essentials of human experience in a world inhabited only by apes and chimpanzees. William Prochnau's *Trinity's Child* the next year described a nuclear war in progress. Whitley Strieber and James W. Kunetka's *Warday*, a Book-of-the-Month Club main selection in 1984, pictured in vivid detail the effects of limited nuclear war.[62]

As literature reflected and helped define the popular mood, a series of organizations mobilized to check the growing nuclear threat. Physicians for Social Responsibility, in hibernation after the 1963 Test Ban Treaty, revived in March 1979. Dr. Bernard Lown, the founder, had a hand in the revival. In early 1980 the group organized a symposium on "The Medical Consequences of Nuclear Weapons and Nuclear War" that spelled out the possible effects of military action more explicitly than ever before. Dr. Helen Caldicott, an Australian-born pediatrician, became president and toured the country spreading the message. As a result of her efforts, the organization grew from three thousand in 1981 to sixteen thousand in 1982.[63]

The Union of Concerned Scientists likewise seized upon the nuclear threat. Henry W. Kendall, an MIT physicist, had founded the organization in 1969 to oppose the drift toward antiballistic missile systems. In the 1970s the group had shifted focus to the issue of nuclear power, but then in 1980 returned to its original weapons-oriented approach. Kendall observed that Ronald Reagan's hard-line stance on issues of war and peace brought out a "latent anxiety" and "started to really scare people." It also led opponents to act. The Union of Concerned Scientists planned a series of teach-ins at colleges on Veterans Day, 1981. Two dozen such assemblies were expected; 150 were held. The media proved interested, and the attention received from newspapers and television helped the movement along.[64]

Meanwhile Randall Forsberg, first a staffer at the Stockholm International Peace Research Institute, then head of her own Institute for Defense and Disarmament Studies in Brookline, Massachusetts, came up with a new idea for arms control: a nuclear freeze. She argued that after the Test Ban Treaty of 1963, the experts had given up on the idea of comprehensive disarmament and come to accept the notion of a permanent arms race. "The buzz word," she said, "was stability." But then as Reagan launched a massive military buildup, complete with new missile systems and submarines, the United States seemed to reject even that limited goal.[65]

Forsberg wanted a mutual and verifiable freeze. In early 1980 the Fellowship of Reconciliation organized a meeting of several dozen peace groups to consider the proposal. Word reached Vermont, and as a result of the efforts of the American Friends Service Committee, the Forsberg proposal received a favorable hearing at town meetings throughout the state. Such discussions spread elsewhere and were soon occurring around the country.[66]

Other efforts fueled the protest movement. Ground Zero week in the spring of 1982 dramatized the devastating effects of a nuclear war. In 150 cities and 500 communities, people showed the destruction that would occur within two miles of a blast. Veteran activists participating in those programs and others found themselves supported by a host of people who had never before been so involved, but whose long-dormant fears were coming alive.[67]

As Americans became attuned to nuclear questions, they found ample support for their fears. Jonathan Schell's eloquent series of articles in the *New Yorker*, published in book form in 1982 as *The Fate of the Earth*, had an enormous impact. He portrayed more vividly than anyone else the "republic of insects and grass" that could result from a nuclear war. In a sequel series of articles in early 1984, Schell came back "to the fantastic, horrifying, brutal, and absurd fact that we human beings have actually gone ahead and wired our planet for its and our destruction." The 1983 ABC television special *The Day After* reached an audience estimated at 100 million as it showed people vaporizing on screen and survivors facing a world so chaotic that the future was uncertain at best. It led to sober discussions about whether the scenario was realistic and whether children should be exposed to anything so devastating. Not long thereafter Americans became aware of the possibility of a "nuclear winter" as a result of dust and smoke in the atmosphere in the aftermath of an atomic war. Cornell University astronomer Carl Sagan and others presented their findings at a conference in Washington, D.C., published them in *Science*, and made them even more public with an article in *Parade* magazine.[68]

Publicity fueled a movement that already had a life of its own. Americans had verbalized their fears in the 1950s, suppressed them for the next decade and a half, then found themselves in the late 1970s and early 1980s unable to ignore the horrifying possibilities of nuclear catastrophe any longer. Wherever they looked, they saw a specter that would not disappear.

The question of how to cope with the nuclear threat, ever-present in the years since 1945, was pressing once again. In the recent period, as before, it intersected with public policy and public mood, as Americans struggled with problems of economy and stability, with issues of survival and defense. People who expected nuclear progress to bring stability and security discovered that atomic energy only created new problems they could not avoid. Whether dealing with weapons or reactors, they found their early hopes giving way to deeper fears. They were now more aware than ever that nuclear science, by releasing a terrible secret in 1945, had provided the world with a puzzling and potentially shattering gift.

1. Martin L. Sherwin, *A World Destroyed: The Atomic Bomb and the Grand Alliance* (New York, 1975); Barton J. Bernstein, "Roosevelt, Truman, and the Atomic Bomb, 1941-1945: A Reinterpretation," *Political Science Quarterly* 90 (Spring 1975):23-69.

2. "Science and the Citizen," *Scientific American*, March 1950, 24-26; Louis N. Ridenour, "The Hydrogen Bomb," *Scientific American*, March 1950, 11-15; Herbert F. York, "The Debate over the Hydrogen Bomb," *Scientific American*, October 1975, 106-13; David Alan Rosenberg, "American Atomic Strategy and the Hydrogen Bomb Decision," *Journal of American History* 66 (June 1979): 62-87; McGeorge Bundy, "The Missed Chance to Stop the H-Bomb," *New York Review of Books*, 13 May 1982, 13-14, 16-19; Richard G. Hewlett and Francis Duncan, *Atomic Shield, 1947-1952, Vol. II: A History of the United States Atomic Energy Commission* (Springfield, Virginia, 1972), 521-45, 590-93.

3. The Harvard Nuclear Study Group (Albert Carnesale, Paul Doty, Stanley Hoffmann, Samuel P. Huntington, Joseph S. Nye, Jr., Scott D. Sagan), *Living with Nuclear Weapons* (New York, 1983), 79, 82-83; Townsend Hoopes, *The Devil and John Foster Dulles* (Boston, 1973), 424-26.

4. Harvard Nuclear Study Group, 84, 90-93.

5. Gar Alperovitz, *Atomic Diplomacy: Hiroshima and Potsdam* (New York, 1965), 235; Sherwin, *A World Destroyed*, 198; Barton J. Bernstein, "The Challenges and Dangers of Nuclear Weapons: American Foreign Policy and Strategy, 1941-1961," *Foreign Service Journal*, September 1978, 10; Gregg Herken, *The Winning Weapon: The Atomic Bomb in the Cold War, 1945-1950* (New York, 1980), 43-68.

6. Aaron L. Friedberg, "A History of the U.S. Strategic 'Doctrine'—1945 to 1980," *Journal of Strategic Studies* 3 (December 1980):40, 45.

7. Herbert Y. Schandler, "U. S. Policy on the Use of Nuclear Weapons, 1945-1975," Congressional Research Service, 1975, 17; Friedberg, "A History of the U.S. Strategic 'Doctrine,' "40-41, 46-47; David Alan Rosenberg, "The Origins of Overkill: Nuclear Weapons and American Strategy, 1945-1960," *International Security* 7 (Spring 1983):25.

8. Dwight D. Eisenhower, "Annual Message to the Congress on the State of the Union," 7 January 1954, *Public Papers of the Presidents of the United States: Dwight D. Eisenhower, 1954* (Washington, D.C., 1960), 10; John Foster Dulles, "The Evolution of Foreign Policy," *Department of State Bulletin* 30 (25 January 1954):108; Samuel F. Wells, Jr., "The Origins of Massive Retaliation," *Political Science Quarterly* 96 (Spring 1981):33-34.

9. Schandler, "U.S. Policy on the Use of Nuclear Weapons," 11-12; Bernstein, "Challenges and Dangers," 14-15; David Alan Rosenberg, " 'A Smoking Radiating Ruin at the End Of Two Hours': Documents on American Plans for Nuclear War with the Soviet Union, 1954-1955," *International Security* 6 (Winter 1981-1982):14.

10. Rosenberg, " 'Smoking Radiating Ruin,' " 11; Friedberg, "A History of the U.S. Strategic 'Doctrine,' " 42, 47; Rosenberg, "Origins of Overkill," 8.

11. Robert S. McNamara, "Defense Arrangements of the North Atlantic Community," *Department of State Bulletin* 47 (9 July 1962):67; Schandler, "U.S. Policy on the Use of Nuclear Weapons," 19; Friedberg, "A History of the U.S. Strategic Doctrine," 47-49; Harvard Nuclear Study Group, 84.

12. Friedberg, "A History of the U.S. Strategic 'Doctrine,' " 50-51; Harvard Nuclear Study Group, 88-89.

13. James R. Schlesinger, *Annual Defense Department Report, Fiscal Year 1975* (Washington, D.C., 1974), 38; Friedberg, "A History of the U.S. Strategic 'Doctrine,' " 55-58.

14. Jeffrey Richelson, "PD-59, NSDD-13 and the Reagan Strategic Modernization Program," *Journal of Strategic Studies* 6 (June 1983):125, 129.

15. *Washington Post*, 10 November 1982; Richelson, "PD-59, NSDD-13" p. 131.

16. Allan M. Winkler, "Civil Defense in the Atomic Age," *Bulletin of the Atomic Scientists* 40 (June 1984).

17. *Bert the Turtle Says Duck and Cover*, Spencer R. Quick Files, Box 1, Harry S Truman Papers, Harry S Truman Library, Independence, Missouri.

18. Mary M. Simpson, "A Long Hard Look at Civil Defense," *Bulletin of the Atomic Scientists* 12 (November 1956):346.

19. Robert A. Divine, *Blowing on the Wind: The Nuclear Test Ban Debate, 1954-1960* (New York, 1978), 36-57; Address by Leo A. Hoegh, 2 December 1958, White House Office, Staff Research Group Series, Box 15, Dwight D. Eisenhower Papers, Dwight D. Eisenhower Library, Abilene, Kansas.

20. "H-Bomb Hideaway," *Life*, 23 May 1955, 169-70; "A Frightening Message for a Thanksgiving Issue," *Good Housekeeping*, November 1958, 61; *Information Bulletin*, No. 270, 10 January 1961, Secretariat Collection, Box 1433, Folder—S & I 16—Civil Defense, Records of the US Atomic Energy Commission (RG 326), in U.S. Department of Energy Archives, Germantown, Maryland.

21. Steuart L. Pittman, "Government and Civil Defense," in *Who Speaks for Civil Defense?*, ed. Eugene P. Wigner (New York, 1968), 54-55, 61-62, 68-70; "All Out Against Fallout," *Time*, 4 August 1961, 11; "Survival: Are Shelters the Answer?" *Newsweek*, 6 November 1961, 19, 21; *Fallout Protection: What to Know and Do About Nuclear Attack*, Box 75, Sidney R. Yates Papers, Harry S Truman Library; "Civil Defense: The Sheltered Life," *Time*, 20 October 1961, 21.

22. Fred M. Kaplan, "The Soviet Civil Defense Myth, Part 2," *Bulletin of the Atomic Scientists* 34 (April 1978):45; Michael Riordan, ed., *The Day After Midnight: The Effects of Nuclear War* (Palo Alto, California, 1982), 75; *Signifi-*

cant Events in United States Civil Defense History (Washington, D.C., n.d.); "Significant Events in U.S. Civil Defense History," (updated typescript).

23. Robert Scheer, *With Enough Shovels: Reagan, Bush, and Nuclear War* (New York, 1982), 18, 21; Thomas J. Kerr, *Civil Defense in the U.S.: Bandaid for a Holocaust?* (Boulder, Colorado, 1983), 165-67; Jennifer Leaning, *Civil Defense in the Nuclear Age: What Purpose Does It Serve and What Survival Does It Promise?* (Cambridge, Mass., 1982), 1-13; "Fallout Shelters: Making a Comeback," *Newsweek*, 22 February 1982, 10; "Does Civil Defense Make Sense?" *Newsweek*, 26 April 1982, 31.

24. *New York Times*, 8 August 1945; Joseph C. Goulden, *The Best Years, 1945-1950* (New York, 1976), 262; "Pulling the Nuclear Plug," *Time*, 13 February 1984, 34; Heinz Haber, *The Walt Disney Story of Our Friend the Atom* (New York, 1956), 13.

25. Steven L. Del Sesto, *Science, Politics, and Controversy: Civilian Nuclear Power in the United States, 1946-1974* (Boulder, Colorado, 1979), 17-24; George T. Mazuzan and Roger Trask, "An Outline History of Nuclear Regulation and Licensing, 1946-1979," April 1979, 8, in Historical Office, Office of the Secretary, Nuclear Regulatory Commission, Washington, D.C.; Michael J. Brenner, *Nuclear Power and Non-Proliferation: The Remaking of U.S. Policy* (New York, 1981), 3-4; Hewlett and Duncan, *Atomic Shield*, 96; For the fullest treatment of the nuclear power industry, see George T. Mazuzan and J. Samuel Walker, *Controlling the Atom: The Beginnings of Nuclear Regulation, 1946-1962* (Berkeley, Calif., 1984).

26. Mazuzan and Trask, "An Outline History of Nuclear Regulation and Licensing," 9; Del Sesto, *Science, Politics, and Controversy*, 40.

27. Daniel Ford, "The Cult of the Atom—1," *New Yorker*, 25 October 1982, 115-18; Report to the National Security Council on the Status of Nuclear Power Programs, by the Chairman, Atomic Energy Commission, 24 March 1955, 6, White House Office, OSANSA Series, Box 1, Eisenhower Papers; Richard G. Hewlett and Francis Duncan, *Nuclear Navy, 1946-1962* (Chicago, 1974), 15-224.

28. Mazuzan and Trask, "An Outline History of Nuclear Regulation and Licensing," 14-17; Fritz F. Heimann, "How Can We Get the Nuclear Job Done?" in *The Nuclear Power Controversy*, ed. Arthur W. Murphy (Englewood Cliffs, New Jersey, 1976), 91-92; Arthur W. Murphy, "Nuclear Power Plant Regulation," in Murphy, *The Nuclear Power Controversy*, 109; Del Sesto, *Science, Politics, and Controversy*, 53-54.

29. Lewis Strauss, "My Faith in the Atomic Future," *Reader's Digest*, August 1955, 17; Lewis Strauss, "Atomic Power at the New Year," 8 January 1958, OF, Central File, Box 253, Eisenhower Papers; Electric Companies Public Information Program, Special PIP Study of Information Aspects of Nuclear Energy Development, 20 October 1953, OF, Central File, Box 523, Eisenhower Papers.

30. Mazuzan and Trask, "An Outline History of Nuclear Regulation and Licensing," 18.

31. Del Sesto, *Science, Politics, and Controversy*, 56-57; Mazuzan and Trask, "An Outline History of Nuclear Regulation and Licensing," 43; George

T. Mazuzan and J. Samuel Walker, "The Safety Goal Issue in Historical Perspective," December 1980, 6, in Historical Office, Office of the Secretary, Nuclear Regulatory Commission, Washington, D.C.; Ford, "Cult of the Atom—I," 133.

32. Heimann, "How Can We Get the Nuclear Job Done?", 93-94; Ford, "Cult of the Atom—I," 134; Del Sesto, *Science, Politics, and Controversy*, 85.

33. Ford, "Cult of the Atom—I," 134; Del Sesto, *Science, Politics, and Controversy*, 91; Heimann, "How Can We Get the Nuclear Job Done?", 95-96; Irvin C. Bupp and Jean-Claude Derian, *Light Water: How the Nuclear Dream Dissolved* (New York, 1978), 49-50.

34. U.S. Atomic Energy Commission, *Theoretical Possibilities and Consequences of Major Accidents in Large Nuclear Power Plants*, WASH-740, March 1957 (Washington, D.C., 1957); Sheldon Novick, *The Careless Atom* (Boston, 1969), 62-63, 71; Gene Bryerton, *Nuclear Dilemma* (New York, 1970), 28-29; David Bodansky and Fred H. Schmidt, "Safety Aspects of Nuclear Energy," in Murphy, *The Nuclear Power Controversy*, 36; McKinley C. Olson, *Unacceptable Risk: The Nuclear Power Controversy* (New York, 1976), 54-55.

35. Mazuzan and Walker, "Safety Goal Issue," 1-2.

36. Ibid., 10.

37. Dwight A. Ink to Christopher H. Russell, 10 January 1961, White House Office, Staff Research Group, Box 2, Eisenhower Papers; Walter C. Patterson, *Nuclear Power* (New York, 1976), 175-76.

38. Novick, *The Careless Atom*, pp. 156-60; Patterson, *Nuclear Power*, 180-82; Olson, *Unacceptable Risk*, 21, 62-64; John G. Fuller, "We Almost Lost Detroit," in *The Silent Bomb: A Guide to the Nuclear Energy Controversy*, ed. Peter Faulkner (New York, 1977), 45-59.

39. Ford, "Cult of the Atom—I," pp. 136-37; Patterson, *Nuclear Power*, 183.

40. *Reactor Safety Study: An Assessment of Risks in U.S. Commercial Nuclear Power Plants*, WASH-1400 (NUREG-75/014), October 1975 (Springfield, Virginia, n.d.); Bodansky and Schmidt, "Safety Aspects of Nuclear Energy," 37; California Assembly, Committee on Resources, Land Use and Energy, "Reactor Safety," in Faulkner, *The Silent Bomb*, 145; *New York Times*, 21 August 1974, Ford, "The Cult of the Atom—II," *New Yorker* 1 November 1982, 47-49.

41. Bodansky and Schmidt, "Safety Aspects of Nuclear Energy," 37-39; California Assembly, Committee on Resources, Land Use and Energy, "Reactor Safety," 145-50; Olson, *Unacceptable Risk*, 22-24; Ford, "Cult of the Atom—II," 49-52.

42. Ford, "Cult of the Atom—II," 57-62; "Rasmussen Issues Revised Odds on a Nuclear Catastrophe," *Science* 190 (14 November 1975):640; "Nuclear Reactor Safety—The APS Submits Its Report," *Physics Today* 28 (July 1975):38-43, 80; Norman C. Rasmussen, "The Safety Study and its Feedback," *Bulletin of the Atomic Scientists* 31 (September 1975):25-28.

43. "A Nuclear Nightmare," *Time*, 9 April 1979, 8, 11-12, 15-19; "Nuclear Accident," *Newsweek*, 9 April 1979, 24-28, 30, 33; *Report of the President's Commission on the Accident at Three Mile Island—The Need for Change: The Legacy of TMI* (Washington, D.C., 1979), 10, 27, 101-61; U.S. Senate, *Nuclear*

Accident and Recovery at Three Mile Island: A Report Prepared by the Sub-committee on Nuclear Regulation for the Committee on Environment and Public Works, 96th Congress, 2d Session, Serial No. 96-14, June 1980 (Washington, D.C., 1980), 9-40, 89-160; Charles Perrow, "The President's Commission and the Normal Accident," in *Accident at Three Mile Island: The Human Dimensions*, eds. David L. Sills, C. P. Wolf, and Vivien B. Shelanski (Boulder, Colorado, 1982), 173-83.

44. Cynthia Bullock Flynn, "Reactions of Local Residents to the Accident at Three Mile Island," in Sills, Wolf, and Shelanski, *Accident at Three Mile Island*, 49-56; Ford, "Cult of the Atom—II," 97-100.

45. "Whoops! A \$2 Billion Blunder," *Time*, 8 August 1983, 50-52; *New York Times*, 14 August 1983; "Pulling the Nuclear Plug," *Time*, 13 February 1984, 34.

46. "Pulling the Nuclear Plug," *Time*, 35; "A Meltdown for Nuclear Power," *Business Week*, 30 January 1984, 18; *New York Times*, 22 January 1984.

47. Nicholas Humphrey, "Four Minutes to Midnight," (The Bronowski Memorial Lecture), *Listener*, 29 October 1981, 498; Sherwin, *A World Destroyed*, 91-108; 116-18; 201-2.

48. Barton J. Bernstein, "American Foreign Policy and the Origins of the Cold War," in *Politics and Policies of the Truman Administration*, ed. Barton J. Bernstein, (Chicago, 1970), 46-49.

49. "Radiation: 'Glimpse Into Hell,' " *Newsweek*, 13 January 1958, 78; *Fallout*, Box 20, Records of the Committee for a Sane Nuclear Policy, Swarthmore College Library, Swarthmore, Pennsylvania; Divine, *Blowing on the Wind*, 4-5, 7, 29-30; George H. Gallup, *The Gallup Poll: Public Opinion, 1935-1971*, vol. 2 (New York, 1972), 1,322, 1,488.

50. Nevil Shute, *On the Beach* (New York, 1957); Joseph Keyerleber, "On the Beach," in *Nuclear War Films*, ed. Jack G. Shaheen (Carbondale and Edwardsville, Illinois, 1978), 31-38; Minutes of Cabinet Meeting, 11 December 1959, Whitman Cabinet Series, Box 15, Eisenhower Papers; Possible Questions and Suggested Answers on the Film "On the Beach," 8 December 1959, Whitman Cabinet Series, Box 15, Eisenhower Papers.

51. Walter M. Miller, Jr., *A Canticle for Leibowitz* (New York, 1980), 58, 245.

52. A Short History of SANE (typescript, n.d.), Box B-24, Records of the Committee for a Sane Nuclear Policy; Lawrence S. Wittner, *Rebels against War: The American Peace Movement, 1941-1960* (New York, 1969), 242-45.

53. Michael Mandelbaum, *The Nuclear Question: The United States and Nuclear Weapons, 1946-1976* (New York, 1979), 159-71; Edgar M. Bottome, *The Balance of Terror: A Guide to the Arms Race* (Boston, 1971), 96; Glenn T. Seaborg, *Kennedy, Khrushchev, and the Test Ban* (Berkeley, Calif., 1981), 172-85.

54. John F. Kennedy, "Commencement Address at American University in Washington," 10 June 1963, *Public Papers of the Presidents of the United States: John F. Kennedy: 1963* (Washington, D.C., 1964), 460-64; Mandelbaum, *Nuclear Question*, 172-76.

55. "Treaty Banning Nuclear Weapon Tests in the Atmosphere, in Outer

Space and Under Water," in Seaborg, *Kennedy, Khruschev and the Test Ban,* pp. 302-5.

56. Mandelbaum, *Nuclear Question,* 179-81; Bottome, *The Balance of Terror,* 97.

57. Michael Mandelbaum, *The Nuclear Revolution: International Politics before and after Hiroshima* (New York, 1981), 194; Mandelbaum, *Nuclear Question,* 199; Stanford Arms Control Group, *International Arms Control: Issues and Agreements,* ed. Coit D. Blacker and Gloria Duffy (Stanford, Calif., 1984), 225-29, 245-49.

58. "SALT I Accords, 1972," in Stanford Arms Control Group, 413-33; Stanford Arms Control Group, 229-45, 249-54; Harvard Nuclear Study Group, 92-95.

59. Stanford Arms Control Group, 260-67; "SALT II Treaty, 1979," in Stanford Arms Control Group, 446-77; Mandelbaum, *Nuclear Revolution,* 194; Mandelbaum, *Nuclear Question,* 207, Harvard Nuclear Study Group, 97-99; Nigel Calder, *Nuclear Nightmares: An Investigation into Possible Wars* (New York, 1981), 120.

60. Stanford Arms Control Group, 267-76; "SALT II: Sealed with a Kiss," *Newsweek,* 9 July 1979, 25; Harvard Nuclear Study Group, 98-99, 196, 206, 211.

61. Paul Boyer, "From Activism to Apathy: The American People and Nuclear Weapons, 1963-1980," *Journal of American History* 70 (March 1984): 821-44.

62. Robert C. O'Brien, *Z for Zachariah* (New York, 1975); Bernard Malamud, *God's Grace* (New York, 1982); William Prochnau, *Trinity's Child* (New York, 1983); Whitley Strieber and James W. Kunetka, *Warday* (New York, 1984).

63. Jonathon A. Leonard, "Danger: Nuclear War," *Harvard Magazine,* November-December 1980, 21-24; Fox Butterfield, "Anatomy of the Nuclear Protest," *New York Times Magazine,* 11 July 1982, p. 17.

64. Butterfield, "Anatomy of the Nuclear Protest," 17.

65. Ibid., 32, 34.

66. "A Matter of Life and Death," *Newsweek,* 26 April 1982, 21-22.

67. Ibid., p. 21.

68. Jonathon Schell, *The Fate of the Earth* (New York, 1982); Jonathon Schell, "Reflections: The Abolition: I—Defining the Great Predicament," *New Yorker,* 2 January 1984, 58; Jonathon Schell, "Reflections: The Abolition: II—A Deliberate Policy," *New Yorker,* 9 January 1984. "TV's Nuclear Nightmare," *Newsweek,* 21 November 1983; *New York Times,* 13 November 1983; *Register-Guard* (Eugene, Oregon), 15 November 1983, 21 November 1983, 23 November 1983; Summary of Conference Findings, The World After Nuclear War, 1735 New York Avenue, N.W., Suite 400, Washington, D.C. 20006, R. P. Turco, D. B. Toon, T. P. Ackerman, J. B. Pollack, Carl Sagan, "Nuclear Winter: Global Consequences of Multiple Nuclear Explosions," *Science* 222 (23 December 1983):1,283-90; Carl Sagan, "The Nuclear Winter," *Parade,* 30 October 1983, 1, 4-5, 7; Janet Raloff, "Beyond Armageddon," *Science News* 124 (12 November 1983):314-17.

PART TWO

POLITICS AND THE ECONOMY

Challenges to the Mixed Economy:
The State and Private Enterprise

Ellis W. Hawley

As Americans entered the 1960s, they brought with them a political economy usually described as "mixed." It was in major respects a market economy, one in which judgments rendered by commercial markets played a major role in allocating resources and product shares. Yet it had also developed important elements of nonmarket coordination through an expanded government, "private governments" exercising various forms of private power, and organizational "intersects" featuring interpenetrations of the public and private sectors. And although this developing mix had once been decried as combining the worst of two worlds, as impairing "the efficiency of the competitive system without the compensating benefits of rationalized collective action,"[1] the kind of economic growth that had taken place in the 1940s and 1950s had stilled most critics. American neocapitalism, so celebrants were proclaiming, had become a superlative blend of the best in individualism and collectivism and by doing so had become the world's most successful economic order.[2]

A major development since 1960 has been the growth of challenges to a mix once seen as achieving such beneficial results. As new problems and demands arose, the claims of effectiveness lost much of their credence, and from a variety of quarters came new critiques challenging the assumptions of the 1950s and new efforts seeking, with varying degrees of success, to change the mix or add new ingredients to it. The years since 1960 have seen a "regulatory revolution" followed by a deregulatory one, a new debate over national planning versus market freedom, a new clash between statists and antistatists, and new warnings that Americans must make hard choices and quit seeking syntheses that by their very nature are impossible to achieve. To a degree unparalleled since the debates preceding and following World War II, the roles of the market, the state, and the syndicate in America's political economy again became open questions to which competing answers were being offered.

This essay presents a survey and analysis of these developments. Beginning with the early 1960s, it seeks to reconstruct and understand the emergence of the new critiques and initiatives, the contexts in which they gained and lost strength, their effects on the mix being criticized, and the choices Americans have made and postponed. An understanding of these forces, it is hoped, will both illuminate current policy debates and provide an altered perspective from which to view the period's history.

Viewed in retrospect, the critiques of America's political economy in the early 1960s seem weak, ineffectual, and lacking in staying power. Yet if the resulting debate was a passing phenomenon, it was not without importance. It not only opened the way to developments eventually productive of more powerful critiques but also offered brief glimpses of the competing designs for reconstruction that would dominate subsequent debate.

At the heart of the debate was the contention that the system was not achieving its full potential for economic growth and that its failures in this regard were hampering America's capacity to realize such national goals as full employment, a progressive social order, and victory in the Cold War. Speedier growth, so liberals had argued in the late 1950s, could provide the means for dealing with the nation's remaining social ills and enhancing its capacity for world leadership. And such growth, they insisted, could be achieved without impairing the basic economic mix that had given America both freedom and affluence. There was no good reason why Americans should tolerate the chronic economic slack, unpredictable slowdowns, and unsatisfied social needs that had been characteristic of the Eisenhower years. Nor was there any reason they should endure the humiliations that had come following the Communist successes in space, technology, and the Third World.[3]

The way to have speedier growth, such critics believed, was through proper application of the "new economics" of John Maynard Keynes. It would require, in other words, the generation and implementation of Keynesian packages of fiscal and monetary policy designed to keep aggregate demand at levels conducive to full utilization of resources, which in turn would require educating the President and overcoming the obduracy of unenlightened politicians elsewhere in the government. This was the project upon which such Keynesian economic advisers as Walter Heller and Kermit Gordon embarked after Kennedy's inaugural, and eventually they succeeded in devising and implementing a policy package applying the new economics prescriptions that seemed suited to the situation. They resisted talk of new taxes to pay for an enlarged defense budget and, accepting the constraints imposed by Kennedy's international economic policy and political resistance to domestic spending, they designed a stimulative tax cut, won support for it from corporate leaders and a number of political conservatives, and saw it become law in February 1964. In the boom that followed, they claimed full vindication for all they had been saying, ignoring those who attributed the boom to other factors and who claimed that such a "reactionary" form of Keynesian stimulus could not have the contemplated social benefits.[4]

For much of America, too, the experience of 1964 seemed to vindicate what celebrants had been saying about the nation's mix of market and nonmarket institutions.[5] The public and quasi-public institutions, it could be argued, had proved responsive to enlightened leadership, producing the policy decisions needed for superior economic performance; and the private sector had reacted in the ways expected. Both had shown that there was no need for institutional reform. Yet in the years between 1961 and 1964, as unemployment remained higher than seemed necessary, cost-push inflation offset much of the effort made to reduce it, and the unenlightened kept resisting Keynesian prescriptions, there were foreshadowings of later challenges to the established mix. There was talk at times of a stronger institutional base for the new economics, one in which the Council of Economic Advisers might wield budgetary powers similar to the monetary powers of the Federal Reserve Board. There was talk also of regulatory reform as an alternative route to better economic performance, of institutional reforms that could reduce burdensome international constraints, and of debureaucratization to release new social and individual energies.[6] And there was not only talk but some action aimed at reducing structural impediments to full resource utilization and at building forms of corporatist collaboration that could turn the generators of cost-push inflation into more responsible social partners.

Both before and after Kennedy's inauguration, the problem of structural impediments had been stressed by some analysts, especially those associated with the Federal Reserve Board and the Labor Department. Among some Keynesians, too, structural action was regarded as a desirable complement to fiscal and monetary action, something that in technical terms could shift the Phillips curve leftward and thus reduce the amount of unemployment needed to maintain price stability.[7] In particular, it was argued, a progressive economy needed jobs programs targeted toward overcoming the lack of technical skills and pockets of areal underdevelopment that accounted for a substantial portion of the unemployment problem. And when joined with efforts to secure new kinds of federal relief, such arguments did lead to new action agencies engaged in new forms of market intervention. In 1961 Congress authorized an Area Redevelopment Agency, thus beginning a program of aid to depressed areas that would grow much larger under successor agencies; and in 1962 it approved a manpower development and training program, tiny at first but eventually growing into a major component of the subsequent War on Poverty. In operation both programs tended to become dispensers of relief rather than dissolvers of structural impediments, but they were launched with hopes of becoming an important new ingredient in America's superior mix of market and nonmarket coordination.[8]

Structural impediments of another sort were also stressed by analysts worried about the growth of monopoly power and its ability to block needed adjustments and negate Keynesian leverage. The portion of the mix needing expansion and revitalization, as they saw it, was that committed to maintaining competitive markets. And at times during the Kennedy administration, particularly during quarrels with business representatives or when its Antitrust Division under Lee Loevinger made antibigness gestures, it seemed that an antitrust revival might be in the offing. Such, however, did not prove to be the case. Antitrust activities failed to break out of the cautious, system-maintenance pattern of the Eisenhower years; and the administration's failure to support the "antimonopoly" positions of congressional leaders such as Estes Kefauver and Emanuel Celler indicated a general unwillingness to embrace antitrust thinking.[9] Indeed, insofar as the Kennedy administration acted on the "monopoly problem" at all, it tended to embrace the solution that had produced new mechanisms of corporatist collaboration in Europe and Japan, a solution that sought to equip modern concentrations of private economic power with a system-conscious higher rationality and make them partners in the management of national progress.

The most fully developed manifestation of such thinking was in the fascination of some Kennedyites with French "indicative" planning. In France, a study group reported in 1962, business and government had fashioned mechanisms of joint forecasting and consultation that kept both committed to designs for national progress and led to superior economic performance.[10] But the major American innovation to come from such thought was the wage-price guidelines announced in January 1962 and defended in the subsequent presidential actions forcing a steel price rollback.[11] These were supposed to rally responsible elements of business, government, and labor around formulas that would keep wage settlements noninflationary by limiting raises to productivity increases. The guidelines were also seen by some as preliminary to a more extensive kind of cooperative planning, but those trying to develop the envisioned consultation and liaison mechanisms had little success. They were hampered initially by Commerce Secretary Luther Hodges' efforts to reform his Business Advisory Council—efforts that led the agency to secede from the department and become the independent Business Council[12]—and subsequently by the bitterness of the steel episode and the recriminatory rhetoric that accompanied the stock market declines and political campaigning of 1962. Despite the cooperation that developed on the tax cut, a sense of guarded antagonism between business and governmental leaders persisted; and among business leaders talk of emulating the French model, particularly after the role of investment controls in it became clearer, aroused little enthusiasm. Most of them seemed relieved when the idea was shelved and ceased to be discussed.[13]

As of 1964, then, there had been some foreshadowing of later critiques and challenges. But this had produced only minor institutional innovations that showed little promise of becoming anything more. The system, it could be convincingly argued, had again vindicated itself, showing that its nonmarket components could work effectively without damaging what was valuable about its market aspects. Moreover, it was also being argued, the system was now providing the means for discharging America's responsibilities abroad and making social improvements at home. Working through existing institutions, Americans had been successful not only in laying the basis for an ever larger national product but in altering its consumption in ways that would mean an ever growing national security and an ever more satisfying collective life. Having achieved the world's most successful economic order, they were now on their way to implementing a "pax Americana" and building a "great society."[14]

During the early years of the Johnson administration, as Congress responded to the President's calls for new or expanded social programs, the controlling assumptions remained largely unchanged. By 1966 Johnson had not only made important new commitments abroad but had secured major laws in the areas of social security, housing, education, poor relief, and cultural uplift. Not since the Roosevelt era had there been similar expansions in both the welfare and national security states.[15] Yet unlike the previous expansions, these were rarely offered as ways to correct economic malperformance. Nor were they widely condemned as being destructive of the mainsprings that made the economy work. The assumptions were that the institutional mix providing an ever larger national product would remain undisturbed, that the increment in the product would more than pay for the new commitments and programs, and that public expenditures so circumscribed could speed social progress without endangering that in the economic sphere.[16]

In part the willingness to act on such assumptions stemmed from the impotence of congressional conservatism in the wake of the election of 1964. But also involved was Johnson's success in persuading leading businessmen that they had nothing to fear from statist expansion of this sort. Early in his administration, he had set out to make them "partners" in the enterprise, moving particularly to build on the cordiality developed during the implementation of the tax cut. There followed a series of meetings and other social exchanges, at which members of the Business Council and other business groups were given the "Johnson treatment" and came away agreeing that he was a friend of free enterprise. In addition there were efforts to develop more effective consensus-building machinery, particularly through new leadership for the Commerce and Treasury departments and rejuvenated liaison committees linking the Business Council to both the White House and the executive departments.[17] And helping further to ease business fears was an accelerated tendency toward interpenetrations of the public and private sectors, enlarging what analysts were calling the "new public sector" of quasi-private organizations, administrative "partnerships," and "government-oriented corporations."[18] Some called it "arsenalization" of the entrepreneurial spirit[19]; and in the eyes of others, such coziness signified "sell-out" or "capture." But initially, such criticisms had little impact on either legislative or administrative action.

What seemed more threatening to the economic order was the emergence of new movements to expand regulatory activity—movements that were intent upon exposing failures of the economy in regard to safety, opportunity, and the environment. "Regulationist" remedies were beginning to find their way into law, producing such Great Society measures as those imposing new standards of motor vehicle safety, new responsibilities in hiring and promotion practices, and new regulations to improve water and air quality.[20] Yet, as of 1966, even this development had produced relatively little alarm among business leaders and economic analysts. The results could still be seen as only another form of social improvement or public goods to be purchased with a portion of the growth increment. And though such "regulationists" as Ralph Nader were in some ways challenging basic institutional premises, the responsible politicians seemed to have them contained well short of where they could damage economic performance. Their activity could be tolerated as not much more than an innocuous fad.[21]

By 1967, however, a variety of developments made it increasingly difficult to accept the existing assumptions and by doing so created openings for new critiques of the economic order. The escalation in Vietnam was now producing military budgets that could not be paid for with the growth increment, at least not without major cutbacks in the new social programs. The new economics was also proving far less capable of producing sound policy advice than it was supposed to be. Those applying it were being forced to admit serious miscalculations in their projections concerning military expenditures, investment behavior, and monetary growth. In addition there was much evidence that even sound advice could still get bogged down in political squabbling. Finally, economic indicators were now telling a story of increasing malperformance—of steadily worsening inflation interspersed with "credit crunches," "mini-recessions," "dollar crises," and recriminatory finger-pointing by politicians, businessmen, and labor leaders.[22]

The proper response should probably have been war taxes and war controls. But calling for these was sure to strengthen both the opponents of the war and those questioning the value of the social programs. Johnson chose instead to ask for a temporary income tax surcharge of 10 percent, hoping this would curb inflation without forcing him to sacrifice either "guns" or "butter"; but with this reasoning the Democratic leadership in Congress no longer agreed. To secure such a tax, he was finally forced, after lengthy delays, to accept a $6 billion cut in his social budget. When this failed to curb inflation, those applying the new economics were further discredited.[23] Indeed, as his adminstration drew to a close, Johnson could be and was being charged with a triple failure. The Vietnam gamble had been a losing one, and had also cost him the opportunity to realize his social goals and inflicted substantial damage on the economic system he was committed to preserve.

These perceptions of failure opened the door not only to advocates of alternative foreign and social policies but also to challengers of the economic mix once hailed as superior to any other in the world. On the political right there was growing support for reducing the roles of public regulators, managers, and compensators, the assumption being that they rather than the market sector were the source of economic instability and malperformance. This was the prescription, for example, offered by the increasingly influential Milton Friedman, whose monetarist theories were now doing a better job of predicting economic behavior than were their Keynesian rivals.[24] And on the political left there was a marked revival of Marxist and populist analyses, indicting corporate institutions for their "administered prices," their misuse of economic resources, and their dehumanization of social processes. America still had no major socialist or labor party. But in 1967 and 1968 it had a New Left, capturing the headlines and providing newly mobilized discontented groups with an anti-establishment demonology. Those who had once proclaimed an "end to ideology" in the economic sphere, seeing it in the future as the sphere of technicians rather than ideologues, had been proven wrong.[25]

In this context, too, the movements for expanding the system's regulatory, antitrust, and planning components were all taking on new life and becoming more difficult to contain. Ralph Nader's one-man crusade for automobile safety was now on the verge of becoming a "public-interest conglomerate" devoted to developing in consumers a new consciousness of corporate abuses.[26] A more radical strain was now entering the environmental protection movement, one that saw growth as an evil and insisted that the new public goods be paid for by reducing "swollen profits" and "wasteful consumption."[27] New inquiries into the "monopoly problem," among them a White House study headed by Phil C. Neal of the University of Chicago, found hidden taxes being exacted through monopoly power and recommended action to halt conglomerate mergers and restructure oligopolistic industries. The real threat to America's mixed economy, such reformers said, was that coming from a new wave of "trust building."[28] And in conjunction with mounting critiques of Keynesianism, guidelinery, and pluralistic interest-group models came a revival of interest in more direct forms of economic planning.[29] The nation, it was again being argued, needed new institutional machinery for coordinating its fragmented economic policy-making, rebuilding a national consensus, and reorienting interest-group energies into constructive channels. It needed, in other words, a system of national planning through which to devise and manage appropriate market interventions; and, as in the past, the designs for such a system came both in statist and corporatist forms.[30]

One unintended consequence, then, of Johnson's military and social programs was economic misbehavior that undercut established beliefs about the American system and inaugurated new economic debates rivaling those of the 1930s. For a generation most Americans had believed that the mixture created by New Deal reform and the maturation of modern organizational institutions had produced a "new capitalism" capable of outperforming any other system, a capitalism that had remained "free" yet was no longer plagued by the instabilities, disorders, and excesses once thought to be the price of freedom. But as the decade of the 1960s ended, a growing number of critics were discovering again the monopoly problem, the statist encroachment, the institutional and knowledge gaps, and the areas of American backwardness that had been featured in earlier debates. They were ready to reconsider the respective roles assigned to market and nonmarket coordination, the mechanisms of public-private interaction, and the wisdom of what was being done abroad. And though some would soon be arguing that the illusion of a "new capitalism" had really rested on a temporary confluence of energy surpluses with American leadership in mass production technology, a state of affairs that could not have lasted much longer anyway, it was the failures and frustrations of the late 1960s that began the process of disillusionment and left a political order ill equipped to cope with what was to follow.

The Nixon administration's first plan for dealing with the worsening economic situation was the strategy of "gradualism". This Friedman-esque policy called for restoring price stability through control of the monetary growth rate, on the hope that this could be done gradually so as to keep the "slowing pains" bearable and the increase in unemployment minimal. In operation, however, the money controllers failed to show the steadiness and patience that Friedman had counselled, and to the surprise of most of those involved, the impact of slowed monetary growth fell mostly on output rather than prices. By mid-1970 the economy was undergoing a severe recession, marked by rising unemployment, stagnating production, mounting deficits, bearish stock market behavior, and highly publicized business bankruptcies. Yet the rate of inflation was now higher than it had been when Nixon took over and seemed to be accelerating.[31] The political costs of this "stagflation" were made all too apparent in the November elections.

The difficulty, Nixon's advisors told him, lay in inflationary expectations that were shaping wage and price decisions in ways forcing monetary authorities either to validate the expectations or cause a slump. Such was the view of Arthur F. Burns, who had become chairman of the Federal Reserve Board; John Connally, who in late 1970 became Secretary of the Treasury; corporate liberal groups like the Business Council and the Committee for Economic Development; and self-proclaimed responsible labor leaders. For those accepting this analysis, the remedy was a supplementary incomes policy controlling wage and profit income so as to change expectations, discipline the irresponsible, and allow the slump to be cured without making the inflationary situation worse. By mid-1971 such thinking had already produced a Productivity Commission, a Construction Industry Stabilization Committee, a series of "inflation alerts," and a rollback in projected price increases for structural steel; and on August 15 it led to action under an Economic Stabilization Act that Democratic congressmen had forced on the President in an effort to embarrass him. Announcing a New Economic Policy, Nixon offered an extraordinary package that included a 90-day wage-price freeze, new tax incentives and spending cuts, a suspension of the dollar's convertibility to gold, and a 10 percent surcharge on imported goods. Together, he argued, these measures could simultaneously curb inflation, reduce unemployment, and shrink balance-of-payments deficits.[32]

Initially, Nixon could hail the results as a "remarkable success." In the international arena, the tariff surcharge became a weapon for securing currency realignment. And during Phases I and II (the freeze followed by controlled price and wage increases supposed to keep inflation to a 2 to 3 percent range), economic performance as measured by the inflation, unemployment, and growth indexes showed the kind of improvement that paid political dividends in the election of 1972.[33] This very success, however, made it difficult to shelve the new tool when the administration concluded that it was no longer needed. Phase III, beginning in January 1973, was supposed to be a transition to decontrol, one marked by more voluntarism and self-administration. But an unexpected new surge of inflation, one powered by world food shortages, more expensive oil imports, tighter raw materials markets, and monetary misjudgments, produced strong criticism of the Phase III apparatus. This led in June to another freeze and then to a stricter Phase IV system that became discredited when it could not duplicate the successes of Phases I and II. By 1974 both the administration and Congress had concluded that such controls were doing more harm than good; and the result, despite the nation's first taste of double-digit inflation, was decontrol measures that had freed much of the economy even before the April expiration of presidential control authority.[34] Only oil, the price of which was being pushed upward by the shock of the Arab embargo and the new foreign cartel operations, remained subject to control, the authority for this coming from a special Emergency Petroleum Allocation Act.[35]

Contrary to the expectations of some commentators, the Nixon experiment did not lead to permanent machinery for defining and administering an incomes policy. Yet if it did not leave much of an institutional legacy, differing aspects of it provided intellectual ammunition for the movements that were now seeking to change the mix that had established itself in post-World War II America. The "new libertarians," citing the maxims of "Chicago school" economics and laissez-faire fundamentalism, could point to the experiences of 1973 and 1974 as evidence for their indictment of almost all interventionism. They argued that it was time to recognize that stability could come only by shrinking the state and letting the market operate.[36] The "new corporatists," less enthralled by the free-market models, could point to the experiment's multipartite boards and advisory committees as the kind of agencies through which a badly needed "social partnership" might materialize and operate.[37] And those again advocating national planning could view the Phase II mechanisms as a workable component in a larger planning complex, one that would also include new machinery for growth planning, social assessment, manpower development, and better fiscal and monetary management. Only through such machinery, the planners argued, could America cope with the systemic failures reflected in persisting "stagflation," declining productivity, and loss of international competitiveness. As one design for doing so, they offered the Humphrey-Javits Balanced Growth and Economic Planning Bill of 1975, generally acknowledged to be the handiwork of the Initiatives Committee for National Economic Planning co-chaired by economist Wassily Leontieff and labor leader Leonard Woodcock and including such prominent businessmen as Robert Roosa, Michael Blumenthal, Irwin Miller, and John R. Bunting, Jr. The bill would have established an Economic Planning Board in the Executive Office of the President and authorized it to prepare national plans for submission to Congress.[38]

The period of Nixon's experimentation was also a period during which the "new regulationists" active in the environmental, safety, consumer, women's, and minority rights movements made substantial progress toward creating a new regulatory component. Growing rapidly after legislation passed in the early 1970s were such regulatory agencies as the Occupational Safety and Health Administration, the Consumer Product Safety Commission, and the Environmental Protection Agency. Expanding as well were the controls over personnel practices administered by the Equal Employment Opportunity Commission.[39] And infusing the whole was a new anticorporate outlook uncharacteristic of either the older, more industry-specific regulation or the "responsible" regulatory initiatives associated with Johnson's Great Society. To the consternation of an administration that had hoped to reap political benefits from "sound" additions to such public goods, the rule-making processes seemed to have fallen into the hands of movement activists, who had become increasingly effective at group mobilization and the use of sophisticated lobbying, litigation, and publicity techniques. The New Left of the late 1960s had now largely disappeared, but a "new politics" was at work, particularly in the regulatory arena. And in the eyes of some observers, its output was tantamount to a second managerial revolution, shifting power from professional business managers to a new class of anticorporate bureaucrats and in the process destroying workable mechanisms of public-private cooperation, aggravating the problems faced by the nation's economic managers, and forcing Americans to pay exorbitant costs for their social gains. Such was the view, in particular, of establishment economists, business educators, and the new business organizations formed to contain and roll back the new regulation.[40]

As the new regulation grew, the old also came under attack as having been captured by regulated industries and used by them to sustain antisocial and exploitative practices. Exposés by Nader's "raiders" and other groups offered documentation for such charges, and as remedies movement activists proceeded both to develop new consumer watchdogs and advocates in the older regulated areas and to urge various kinds of deregulation and "market restoration." In doing the latter, their arguments often sounded much like those of the new libertarians or those made in a growing body of studies of regulatory costs inspired by Chicago-school economics.[41] And the result, as the decade of the 1970s progressed, was a curious alliance of the new politics with the new libertarianism and a market-oriented, marginal-costs-conscious "regulatory reformism," all seeking to dismantle older regulatory mechanisms that many in the affected industries were still defending. It was a development that led the Nixon administration to begin studies of potential deregulation in the transportation field and one that by the mid-1970s was producing a variety of bills and plans for deregulating the airlines, the railroad and trucking industries, the communications and banking fields, and various other areas where commission regulation of the industry-specific type had once been seen as the way to protect and advance the public interest.[42]

Nor did the antitrust component in the American mix escape notice. On the contrary the system-maintenance activity that had become the chief purpose and preoccupation of the antitrust agencies in the 1950s and 1960s was under strong attack as having contributed to systemic failures. It had become the subject of intense debate, and in this context three streams of antitrust revisionism were emerging and offering designs for a new type of antitrust activity. From the neolibertarian, Chicago-school-economics quarter came studies purporting to show that antitrust had served primarily to protect the backward and inefficient and to perpetuate "populist nonsense." It needed a drastic overhaul that would make it more efficiency- and performance-minded and keep it from doing further economic damage.[43] From the neopopulist quarter, where elements of the consumer movement had now coalesced with longtime critics of oligopolistic behavior, came exposés of antitrust's failure to deal with antisocial and antidemocratic corporate power, coupled with proposals for industrial restructuring and deconcentration that were now being given serious consideration by congressional committees.[44] And from those charged with antitrust enforcement, caught now between these conflicting critiques,[45] came proposals for improved procedures and enhanced authority, their argument being that these would equip the antitrust agencies to play an important role in remedying the nation's economic maladies. By 1975 this kind of revisionism had produced a new Antitrust Procedures and Penalties Act, launched its own studies of the concentration and inefficiency problems, and begun suggesting ways to turn the neopopulist proposals into "reasonable" legislation.[46]

By the mid 1970s, then, as Americans prepared to celebrate their bicentennial, the system through which they conducted economic affairs seemed in a state of greater flux than at any time since the era of Franklin D. Roosevelt. The governmental part of the system seemed again to be changing, acquiring a new regulatory component, getting rid of some of its earlier regulatory machinery, overhauling its antitrust component, and showing signs of adding new planning and coordinating mechanisms. The private portion appeared to be in a similar state of transition, with the line between regulated and unregulated industries changing, the legitimacy of the corporate revolution again in question, long-established protective mechanisms in jeopardy, and the first managerial revolution allegedly in the process of being superseded by a second. And the portion of the system having both governmental and private characteristics seemed particularly unstable. For some critics its enlargement was the answer to systemic ills, but others questioned its basic legitimacy, attributing to it such evils as the military-industrial complex, corporate subversion of popular sovereignty, and "arsenalization" of the entrepreneurial spirit.

Just what new mix would emerge from this state of flux, however, was not clear. Nor was it clear which agencies would play the major role in the process of change. Uncertain as well, in the wake of the Watergate scandals, Nixon's resignation, and the congressional elections of 1974, was the capacity of the political order, thus unsettled, to make the decisions and choices that would shape the outcome of the intensifying economic debate.

As Jimmy Carter entered the White House in January 1977, the nation's economic maladies seemed to be growing worse. Unemployment had reached 9 percent in 1975, had receded slightly in the wake of new tax cuts and jobs programs, and was climbing again as the election was held. Inflation had not been cured by idling men and resources. Having reached 12 percent in 1974, it was still at 7 percent and seemed ready to move upward again if measures were taken to reduce unemployment. Productivity figures were increasingly discouraging, and interest grew in systems with strikingly better records, especially that of the Japanese. Adding to the sense of malaise, humiliation, and uncertainty were the ongoing and still inconclusive battles over regulation, antitrust, planning, and national energy policy. On these matters the Ford administration and the post-Watergate Congress had been at odds, and the result, for the most part, had been frustration and stalemate for all concerned. New regulationist initiatives had been largely blocked by vetoes and threatened vetoes; deregulationists had to settle for a limited railroad revitalization measure; antitrust revision, despite extensive hearings on "industrial reorganization" and near passage of an oil companies divestiture bill, had produced only another establishment-oriented improvements act strengthening investigatory powers and facilitating remedial litigation; and from a protracted debate over how to enhance energy independence had come an incoherent and largely ineffective combination of extended price controls, fuel efficiency standards, standby emergency powers, and special subsidies.[47]

Carter, some hoped, might bring "new forces" to bear on such problems, forces that would have healing, unifying, and inspirational effects, would overcome the fragmentation of the political order and the loss of faith in the presidency, and would thus unleash a new burst of institutional creativity. But the hope was never realized; and the performance of the economy kept worsening, reaching crisis proportions again under the impact of the second oil "shock" in 1979. Mixed packages of stimulants and restraints, medicine that was supposed to bring down both the unemployment rate and the rate of inflation, seemed only to aggravate the problems of stagflation, instability, and declining productivity. A new set of wage-price guidelines, established in late 1978, had little or no impact. They could not keep unemployment from rising to nearly 8 percent and inflation for a time in 1979 to 18 percent. National energy plans were torn to shreds in the intensified warfare of conflicting interests, the outcome being further frustration on the part of planners, resource managers, and decontrollers alike. And internationally the competitiveness of American industry kept declining, aggravating the balance-of-payments situation, weakening such basic industries as steel and automobiles, and producing such industrial relief measures as the $1.5 billion bail-out loan to the Chrysler Corporation.[48]

Debates over the appropriateness of the American institutional mix also kept intensifying. Arguments over the antitrust and regulatory components reached a crescendo in a new wave of congressional hearings, executive inquiries, and scholarly polemics. These raised hopes in a variety of reformist quarters and there followed, depending on one's perspective, such victories or defeats as the strip mining and clean air acts of 1977, the airlines deregulation act of 1978, the curbing of Federal Trade Commission powers in 1979, and the trucking, railroad, and banking deregulation measures of 1980.[49] The debate over planning versus "market restoration" swirled not only around the proposed energy plans but also around the new incomes guidelines, proposed revisions of the manpower and area redevelopment programs, suggestions for an industrial policy resembling that of the Japanese, and the push for employment planning targets that led to the Humphrey-Hawkins Act of 1978.[50] And the dispute over the burdens and benefits of "public goods" reached a new intensity as efforts were made to impose cost-benefit analysis on the new regulation and as mobilizers of a taxpayer revolt won victories in California and other states.[51]

What the outcome would be was difficult to discern at the time, particularly in view of the efforts of planners and deconcentrationists to take advantage of the crisis of 1979. But, as various commentators noted, the initiative seemed to be passing to those who would shrink the role of the state, not only in the older areas of regulation but also in its newly developed regulatory, social, and managerial components. Another major change in the public mood seemed underway, one comparable to that following New Deal reformism. But of major importance, too, was the emergence and increasing effectiveness of a more highly organized and energetic political activism in the business community. Operating through the recently formed Business Roundtable, beefed-up versions of older business organizations, and a variety of newly organized political action committees, this business counteroffensive was now proving that it could block targeted proposals, particularly the bills for a new consumer agency and pro-labor revision of the collective bargaining law. It was also turning pro-business lobbying and public relations work into one of the few growth industries of the late 1970s. And through its support of the neolibertarian and neoconservative movements in the intellectual community, it had helped to make statist solutions and anticorporate critiques less respectable.[52]

What was less clear, as the decade drew to a close, was whether this business power would continue to be linked to the objective of market restoration or would associate itself instead with new managerial and planning mechanisms. Another major development of the period was the appearance and growth of the so-called "reindustrialization" movement, envisioning another industrial frontier created by research and development, and arguing that if America was to remain a leading industrial power it must forge new planning and developmental institutions comparable to those through which its international rivals, particularly the Japanese, had been able to pick and support industrial winners. In the movement were a number of liberal academics, politicians, and labor leaders, some of whom had been involved in the earlier calls for national planning, and several of whom had links to the Carter administration, particularly to the White House staff, a special task force on economic renewal, and an Economic Revitalization Board appointed in September 1980.[53] In it, too, were groups trying to save jobs in the failing industries of the northern and eastern states. But it also had a strong business wing, exemplified by such figures as Henry Ford II, investment banker Felix Rohatyn, management consultant Peter Drucker, and B. F. Goodrich chairman John D. Ong. The movement was publicized and promoted through organs like *Business Week* and conferences like the one held at the Harvard Business School. And it seemed to offer the possibility of a business-supported "planning" with business leaders becoming influential members of the teams that were to negotiate and implement the plans.[54]

Indeed, in another new economic program of tax, aid, and planning proposals, set forth in September 1980, Carter seemed to offer organized business groups just such a role. The objective, said *Newsweek*, appeared to be "a smallish made-in-America version of the government-business partnership in productive Japan."[55] But the reaction was not enthusiastic, and most businessmen and business groups ended up supporting the Republicans, led now by Ronald Reagan and offering, along with traditional critiques of the regulatory and welfare state, a new "supply-side economics." The latter explained how permanent tax cuts could not only provide the capital and incentives for economic "revitalization" but also reduce the state's capacity for destabilizing and wasteful interventions. It was an economics that claimed to have rediscovered the truths of the classical system, including Say's Law and the relation of growth to incentives. It claimed, in addition, to have discovered truly workable models of prosperity-building in the tax cuts of the 1920s and early 1960s; and from 1975 on, it had been acquiring new converts and centers of propagation, most notably in conservative "think tanks" and departments of economics, in congressional offices like those of Jack Kemp and William Roth, in the editorial staff of the *Wall Street Journal*, and in the headquarters of groups spawned by the so-called taxpayer revolt. The solution favored by those embracing these rediscoveries was the Kemp-Roth Tax Reduction Bill; in 1980 this bill became a major part of the economic prescription in Reagan's campaign addresses.[56]

To the support of business groups, conservative intellectuals, and party regulars, Reagan was also able to add several other relatively new political forces. One was a New Right concerned with social issues and the deterioration of traditional mores, family structures, and religious piety. Another was a revived quasi-militarism anxious about the deterioration of America's defense establishment and international position, and a third was a kind of working-class rightism responsive to the conservative symbolism associated with patriotism, striving, hard work, and self help. By 1980, moreover, Carter's popularity and political ratings had sunk to the lowest of any president, leading many traditional Democrats to abandon what had been a winning coalition in 1976. The result was a solid triumph for the Republicans, opening up real opportunities for implementing the new economics of the right and in the process changing drastically the institutional mix upon which Americans would rest their hopes for the nation's economic future.[57]

In the months following Reagan's inaugural, much of the program that he had advocated in 1980 was translated into major changes in public policy. A tax reduction measure resembling the Kemp-Roth proposal was passed in July 1981. By its terms personal income tax rates were to be cut some 23 percent over a three-year period, substantial reductions were to be made in estate, gift, and capital gains taxes, and a wide variety of new allowances and other incentives were to become part of the tax code. At the same time, a new budget was devised and put through, featuring major cuts in nondefense spending coupled with increases for the defense budget. And in line with the prescriptions coming from Reagan's monetarist and deregulationist supporters, there were actions slowing the monetary growth rate and relaxing the kinds of regulatory rules that had generated most of the business complaints. Some talked of a "Reagan Revolution"; and although such talk seemed to exaggerate what was happening, the changes clearly added up to a new departure unexplainable by theories of political incrementalism and capable, if sustained, of substantially altering the existing balance of market and nonmarket coordination.[58]

By 1982, however, it seemed clear that the Reagan administration had erred in thinking that its economic goals could be achieved with only trivial costs. In theory monetarist prescriptions were supposed to conquer inflation while "supply-side" and deregulationist prescriptions produced a robust growth, thus making either a recession or continuing budgetary deficits unnecessary. But in practice the "monetary shock" produced a severe recession marked by unemployment rates of nearly 11 percent, credit stringency that drove many farmers, builders, and small businessmen into bankruptcy, and mounting deficits. Fighting inflation was proving to be a costly business, and throughout the year political commentators expressed doubts about the capacity of the conservative coalition to carry the costs of such an enterprise. Not until 1983, when the extent of the recession's impact on inflation became clear and signs of recovery began to appear, did such doubts give way to somewhat grudging admiration for Reagan's success in maintaining his political base, convincing those who were bearing the costs that they must "stay the course," and sustaining his broad design for economic improvement through retrenchment in government. A little of the tax and spending cuts had been taken back, but "Reaganomics" had not been abandoned in the way that Nixon's gradualism had been. Although some credited the recovery to a kind of military Keynesianism operating through the expanded defense budget, the Reaganites pointed to it as vindication for the new economics of the right.[59]

Reagan's success in surviving the recession and limiting its political damage also appeared to strengthen the likelihood of his reelection and the capacity of his political coalition to continue its reshaping of the economic and social arms of the American state. As of 1983 the kind of demand management machinery that had seemed so effective in the mid-1960s was falling into disuse, stabilization having now become a goal to be sought by "hemming in" the state rather than assigning it a managerial role. Regulatory missions also continued to shrink, both in the newer regulatory component and in the older one. Social entitlements and safety nets were condemned as impediments to, rather than facilitators of, social progress. And antitrust activity, as administered by a restaffed Antitrust Division and reinterpreted in new court rulings, was stripped of its "populist" dimension and reoriented along the lines previously urged by neolibertarians, Chicago-school economists, and chroniclers of big business achievements. With corporate efficiency and dynamism now regarded as evidence of competition, monopoly power cases were being dropped or settled, antimerger barriers relaxed, and rules for preserving small business abandoned.[60]

In all of these respects, the balance between market and nonmarket coordination was being further altered in favor of the former. One must hasten to add, however, that some of the reshaping was of the government-expanding rather than government-shrinking variety. The defense establishment, with its peculiar interpenetrations of the public and private sector, was again growing. The commerce secretariat, still much concerned about trade deficits and international competitiveness, showed signs of becoming another growth sector. And in some parts of the Reagan coalition, the push was on for a rightist version of social regulation, one that in theory would use the state to uphold and revitalize the traditional institutions and outlooks that had once helped the invisible hand of the marketplace to achieve such beneficial results.[61]

How stable such an altered mix would be, however, remained an open question. It was possible, so some commentators noted, that recovery would reignite inflationary processes, reawaken concerns about the quality of American life, or put currently subordinated social policy questions back on the political agenda, all of which could bring renewed pressures for regulatory, managerial, and support machinery. It was possible also that a change in the political climate or in the capacity to project a favorable public image would make the coalition's work more vulnerable to the charges of inequity, hard-heartedness, and antidemocratic depoliticization that were being leveled against it. And it was possible as well that a realization of how little "Reaganomics" was doing to improve the nation's international competitiveness, defense posture, and social disharmonies would open the way to a new push for consensus-building, targeting, and harmonizing mechanisms. Waiting in the wings, as the Reaganites persisted with their project, were the heirs of the "limits to growth" and "small is beautiful" thinking once associated with the new politics, the heirs of a liberalism that hoped to reestablish and build upon the mixed economy of the mid-1960s, and the post-1980 extensions of the reindustrialization movement, manifested now in a variety of proposals for an "industrial policy" and offered both as a neoliberal alternative to "Reaganomics" and as a logical supplement to the administration's supply-side measures.[62]

In the eyes of some observers, a major nation in the 1980s could have no weakness "more devastating" than "the inability to define the role of the government in the economy."[63] But seemingly, the United States was now among the nations unable to do so. As Americans had entered the 1960s, it had seemed a settled question; but in the 1980s a debate that had been reopened in the late 1960s had apparently not yet been closed. There were choices still to be made.

Thus, in the history of relations between the American state and private enterprise, the period since 1960 has been one of supreme confidence in the institutional heritage followed by developments that severely shook such confidence, produced new critiques of and challenges to established relationships, and again brought into question what historians had once thought to be settled. The debates over growth, structural defects, and public goods in the early 1960s proved to be preludes for what was to follow. But in the boom of the mid-1960s, with its seeming vindication of the existing institutional structure and its growth increments for improving the social and international orders, these debates had all but faded away. The beginning of the unsettlement still in evidence in 1983 came at the end of the 1960s, when assumptions about what could be done with the growth increment proved exceedingly faulty, when the establishment methods for enhancing it began to encounter unexpected obstacles or to produce intolerable side effects, and when a political establishment discredited by military and economic failure could no longer contain the forces associated with a new politics practiced by a new set of political entrepreneurs. A situation developed where it was possible to add a new regulatory component to the American state while dismantling a part of the old one, although as a result a countermovement for deregulation was also begun and would eventually develop into a formidable political force. And as efforts to deal with the worsening economic situation failed, the nation considered and heatedly debated a series of proposals for a "new antitrust," new forms of "capitalist planning," and new ways of releasing entrepreneurial energy and enhancing worker effort.

By the late 1970s, the degree of unsettlement approached that of the 1930s. America, it seemed at the time, might again take up the kind of corporatist institutional development it had attempted under the early New Deal; it might embark on massive corporate restructuring of the kind carried out under the Public Utilities Holding Company Act of 1935; it might seek to complete the second managerial revolution that was allegedly the goal of the new regulation; or it might embrace the prescriptions for state-shrinking and greater business freedom offered by the political and intellectual right. But for Ronald Reagan the choice seemed relatively clear. With his elevation to power in 1981, followed by his demonstration that he could "stay the course" despite high unemployment rates and severe "slowing pains," the first three options seemed at least temporarily closed off. How long they would continue to be so remained to be seen.

1. Paul T. Homan, "The Pattern of the New Deal," *Political Science Quarterly* 51 (June 1936):181.

2. See, for example, Frederick L. Allen, *The Big Change* (New York, 1952); Adolf A. Berle, *Twentieth Century Capitalist Revolution* (New York, 1954); John K. Galbraith, *American Capitalism* (Boston, 1952); David Lilienthal, *Big Business* (New York, 1953); John D. Hicks, "The Third American Revolution," *Nebraska History* 36 (1955):227-45. In general the formula being celebrated assigned the state a stabilizing role to be achieved by a proper mix of monetary and fiscal policies together with some regulations to alleviate negative externalities, such protectionist mechanisms as were needed to maintain political stability, and the provision of appropriate quantities of public goods.

3. See Allen J. Matusow, *The Unraveling of America* (New York, 1984), 8-13, 42-51. See also Leon Keyserling, "Eggheads and Politics," *New Republic* 139 (27 October 1958):13-17; James Tobin, "Defense, Dollars, and Doctrines," *Yale Review* 47 (March 1958):321-24; and Council of Economic Advisers, *Annual Report* (1962).

4. See especially Matusow, *Unraveling of America*, 42-59; Robert M. Collins, *The Business Response to Keynes, 1929-1964* (New York, 1981), 177-95; Walter Heller, *New Dimensions of Political Economy* (Cambridge, 1966), 1-82; Theodore Sorenson, *Kennedy* (New York, 1965), 393-433; Jim Heath, *John F. Kennedy and the Business Community* (Chicago, 1969), 22-47, 114-22; Herbert Stein, *The Fiscal Revolution in America* (Chicago, 1969), 373-453; and E. Ray Canterbury, *Economics on a New Frontier* (Belmont, California, 1968), 13-37, 73-105. For dissents concerning the measure's effects, see Michael Harrington, "Reactionary Keynesianism," *Encounter* 26 (March 1966):50-52, and Milton Friedman, *Dollars and Deficits* (Englewood Cliffs, N.J., 1968), 126-52. The claims of the Keynesians were spelled out in Arthur M. Okum, "Measuring the Impact of the 1964 Tax Reduction," in Walter W. Heller, ed., *Perspectives on Economic Growth* (New York, 1968), 27-49.

5. See "We Are All Keynesians Now," *Time* 86 (31 December 1965):64.

6. See, for example, the proposal for a presidential power to adjust tax rates in U.S., President, *Economic Report of the President* (1962), 18-22; the proposals for improving the international monetary system in Robert Triffin, *Gold and*

the Dollar Crisis (New Haven, 1961); the discussions of regulatory reform efforts in Heath, *Kennedy, and the Business Community*, 78-80, and Thomas K. McCraw, *Prophets of Regulation* (Cambridge, 1984), 219-21; and the early New Left critique in James Weinstein and David Eakins, "The Ultra-Right and Cold War Liberalism," *Studies on the Left* 3 (1962):3-8.

7. The Phillips curve, named after the British economist A. W. Phillips, measures the trade-off between inflation and unemployment because of frictions in the system. Shifting it leftward reduces the size of the trade-off. See A. W. Phillips, "The Relation Between Unemployment and the Rate of Change of Money Wage Rates in the United Kingdom," *Economica* 25 (1958):283-99.

8. Matusow, *Unraveling of America*, 100-105; Canterbury, *Economics on a New Frontier*, 30-37, 73-76; Conley H. Dillon, *The Area Redevelopment Administration* (College Park, Maryland, 1964); Sar A. Levitan, *Federal Manpower Policies* (Kalamazoo, 1964).

9. Lee Loevinger, "Antitrust in 1961 and 1962," *Antitrust Bulletin* 8 (May-June 1963); 349-79; Matusow, *Unraveling of America*, 34-39; Hobart Rowen, *The Free Enterprisers* (New York, 1964), 81-83; Heath, *Kennedy and the Business Community* 48-55.

10. James Tobin, *National Economic Policy* (New Haven, 1966), 11-13; Otis L. Graham, Jr., *Toward a Planned Society* (New York, 1976), 136-37; Arthur M. Schlesinger, Jr., *A Thousand Days* (Boston, 1965), 540-41; Walter F. Blass, "Economic Planning European Style," *Harvard Business Review* 41 (Sept.-Oct. 1963):109-20.

11. On the guidelines, see Council of Economic Advisers, *Annual Report* (1962), 185-90; John Sheahan, *The Wage-Price Guideposts* (Washington, 1967); and William J. Barber, "The Kennedy Years: Purposeful Pedagogy," in Craufurd D. Goodwin, ed., *Exhortation and Controls* (Washington, 1975). On the steel episode, see Heath, *Kennedy and the Business Community*, 66-74; Grant McConnell, *Steel and the Presidency—1962* (New York, 1963); and Roy Hoopes, *The Steel Crisis* (New York, 1963).

12. The best accounts of this are in Rowen, *Free Enterprisers*, 61-79, and Kim McQuaid, *Big Business and Presidential Power* (New York, 1982), 199-205.

13. McQuaid, *Big Business*, 219-22; Rowen, *Free Enterprisers*, 285-87.

14. See, for example, James Tobin, "The New Era of Good Feeling between Business and Government," *Challenge* (June 1965):23-26; and "We Are All Keynesians Now," *Time* 86 (31 December 1965):64.

15. See Matusow, *Unraveling of America*, 217-42; Sar Levitan and Robert Taggart, *The Promise of Greatness* (Cambridge, 1976); Vaughn D. Bornet, *The Presidency of Lyndon B. Johnson* (Lawrence, Kans., 1983), 219-51; Rowland Evans and Robert Novak, *Lyndon B. Johnson: The Exercise of Power* (New York, 1966), 491-500. For an account of the euphoria prevailing at the end of the "Congress of fulfillment," plus a detailed discussion of the roots and nature of key measures, see James L. Sundquist, *Politics and Policy* (Washington, 1968).

16. Tobin, *National Economic Policy*, 41-42; McQuaid, *Big Business*, 236-37; Doris Kearns, *Lyndon Johnson and the American Dream* (New York, 1976), 189-91, 210-13, 295-99.

17. Theodore Levitt, "The Johnson Treatment," *Harvard Business Review* 45 (Jan.-Feb. 1967):114-28; McQuaid, *Big Business*, 223-40.

18. Murray Weidenbaum, *The Modern Public Sector* (New York, 1969), 3-23, 31-58, 93-113; Alan Pifer, "The Quasi-Nongovernmental Organization," in Carnegie Corporation, *Annual Report* (New York, 1967).

19. Weidenbaum, *Modern Public Sector*, 34, 60-61.

20. Included here would be the Water Quality Act of 1965, the Clean Water Restoration Act of 1966, the Clean Air and Solid Waste Disposal Act of 1965, the Air Quality Act of 1967, the National Traffic and Motor Vehicle Safety Act of 1966, and the new guidelines developed under the Civil Rights Act of 1964. On the legislation involved, see Sundquist, *Politics and Policy*, 363-71; Richard Vietor, *Environmental Politics and the Coal Coalition* (College Station, Texas, 1980), 143-50; and Michael Pertschuk, *Revolt against Regulation* (Berkeley, 1982), 30-33.

21. Pertschuk, *Revolt Against Regulation*, 51-52; McQuaid, *Big Business*, 288.

22. One of the best accounts of the coming of economic difficulties and the accompanying setbacks for the new economics is in Matusow, *Unraveling of America*, 155-79. See also James L. Cochrane, "The Johnson Administration: Moral Suasion Goes to War," in Goodwin, ed., *Exhortation and Controls*, 193-293; Charles E. McLure, Jr., *Fiscal Failure: Lessons of the Sixties* (Washington, 1972), 2-45; James Tobin, *The New Economics One Decade Older* (Princeton, 1972), 34-39; McQuaid, *Big Business*, 238-42.

23. McQuaid, *Big Business*, 242-54; Matusow, *Unraveling of America*, 170-74; McLure, *Fiscal Failure*, 43-45.

24. See Matusow, *Unraveling of America*, 162-69. For Friedman's analysis and prescriptions, see his *Dollars and Deficits* and his "The Role of Monetary Policy," *American Economic Review* 58 (March 1968):1-17. For other aspects of the rightist revival, see Jonathan M. Kolkey, *The New Right* (Washington, 1983), 261-62, 269-73, and George H. Nash, *The Conservative Intellectual Movement in America since 1945* (New York, 1976), 293-94, 334-42.

25. See Matusow, *Unraveling of America*, 308-44; Irwin Unger, *The Movement* (New York, 1974), 51-148; and Edward J. Bacciocco, Jr., *The New Left in America* (Stanford, 1974), 109-220. On the "end of ideology" writers and their critics, see Chaim I. Waxman, ed., *The End of Ideology Debate* (New York, 1968).

26. Susan Gross, "The Nader Network," *Business and Society Review* 13 (Spring 1975):5-6.

27. Vietor, *Environmental Politics*, 156-57; Samuel P. Hays, "From Conservation to Environment," *Environmental Review* 6 (Fall 1982):15-26.

28. "Foreword" and "Report of the White House Task Force on Antitrust Policy," *Antitrust Law and Economics Review* 2 (Winter 1968-69):1-9, 11-76.

29. Leading the critique of pluralism were such works as Grant McConnell's *Private Power and American Democracy* (New York, 1966), Theodore Lowi's *The End of Liberalism* (New York, 1969), and G. William Domhoff's *Who Rules America?* (Englewood Cliffs, 1967).

30. See, for example, Allan G. Gruchy, "Neoinstitutionalism and the Economics of Dissent," *Journal of Economic Issues* 3 (March 1969):14-17; Wallace Peterson, "Planning and the Market Economy," *Journal of Economic Issues* 3 (March 1969):126-43; Gerhard Colm and Luther Gulick, *Program Planning for National Goals* (Washington, 1968); and Carlton E. Spitzer, "Wanted: A Business-Government Partnership," *Public Relations Journal* 24 (December 1968):27-29.

31. McLure, *Fiscal Failure*, 47-54; Leonard Silk, *Nixonomics* (New York, 1972), 3-13; Rodney J. Morrison, *Expectations and Inflation* (Lexington, 1973), 26-30, 88-100.

32. Marvin H. Kosters, *Controls and Inflation* (Washington, 1975), 5-7; Roger Miller and R. M. Williams, *The New Economics of Richard Nixon* (New York, 1972); Silk, *Nixonomics*, 13-19, 42, 53-80; McQuaid, *Big Business*, 266-72.

33. Robert F. Lanzillotti *et al.*, *Phase II in Review* (Washington, 1975); Kosters, *Controls and Inflation*, 19-21, 30-32; McQuaid, *Big Business*, 272-81; David P. Calleo, *The Imperious Economy* (Cambridge, 1982), 62-64.

34. Kosters, *Controls and Inflation*, 21-39, 111-15; Lanzillotti *et al.*, *Phase II*, 198-99; McQuaid, *Big Business*, 281-82.

35. Richard Vietor, *Energy Policy in America since 1945* (New York, 1984), 243-46.

36. Kolkey, *New Right*, 304-9; George J. Stigler, *The Citizen and the State* (Chicago, 1975).

37. See, for example, Kosters, *Controls and Inflation*, 104-5.

38. Otis L. Graham, Jr., "The National Imperative to Plan," *Nation* 223 (6 Nov. 1976):463-66, 477; Graham, *Toward a Planned Society*, 277-79; Leonard Silk and David Vogel, *Ethics and Profits* (New York, 1976), 81-88.

39. See David Vogel, "The New Social Regulation in Historical and Comparative Perspective," in Thomas McCraw, ed., *Regulation in Perspective* (Cambridge, 1981), 155-75; Murray L. Weidenbaum, "The New Wave of Government Regulation of Business," *Business and Society Review* 15 (Fall 1975):81-86; and the discussion of the "regulatory revolution" in McQuaid, *Big Business*, 286-89. Key measures in the coming of the "new regulation" were the Magnuson-Moss FTC Act Amendments (1969), the National Environmental Policy Act (1969), the Water Quality Improvement Act (1970), the Clean Air Act Amendments (1970), the Occupational Safety and Health Act (1970), and the Consumer Product Safety Act (1972). Also of major importance was the ruling in *Sierra Club vs. Ruckelshaus*, holding that acceptable clean air plans must allow no significant deterioration in existing air quality. On this see Vietor, *Environmental Politics*, 194-208.

40. Weidenbaum, "New Wave of Government Regulation," *Business and Society Review* 15 (Fall 1975):83-86; Vogel, "New Social Regulation," in McCraw, ed., *Regulation in Perspective*, 169-79; Pertschuk, *Revolt against Regulation*, 52-59; Vietor, *Energy Policy*, 256-58, 270-71; "Business and the New Class," in Irving Kristol, *Two Cheers for Capitalism* (New York, 1977).

41. The "capture" theory became a staple both with the New Left and the new politics and with the Chicago-school "free marketeers." See, in particular, Gabriel Kolko, *The Triumph of Conservatism* (New York, 1963) and *Railroads and Regulation* (Princeton, 1965); Edward F. Cox, et al., *The Nader Report on the Federal Trade Commission* (New York, 1969); Robert Fellmeth, *The Interstate Commerce Omission* (New York, 1970); Mark J. Green, *The Closed Enterprise System* (New York, 1972); Thomas G. Moore, *Freight Transportation Regulation* (Washington, 1972); George J. Stigler, "The Theory of Economic Regulation," *Bell Journal of Economics and Management Science* 2 (Spring 1971):3-21. Also feeding into the growing stream of criticism was an older critique that had stressed the inability of the methods being used to achieve the goals desired. On this see Paul W. MacAvoy, ed., *The Crisis of the Regulatory Commissions* (New York, 1970).

42. One of the leading advocates of marginal-costs reformism was Alfred E. Kahn. See McCraw, *Prophets of Regulation*, 230-59, and Kahn, *The Economics of Regulation*, 2 vols. (New York, 1970, 1971). On the Nixon administration response, see Silk, *Nixonomics*, 37-41. On the deregulation initiatives of the mid-1970s, see McCraw, *Prophets of Regulation*, 266-68; John R. Meyer and Alexander Morton, "A Better Way to Run the Railroads," *Harvard Business Review* 52 (July-August 1974); U. S. House of Representatives, Committee on Interstate and Foreign Commerce, *Regulatory Reform* (94 Cong., 1st sess., 1976); Paul W. MacAvoy, *The Regulated Industries and the Economy* (New York, 1979), 15-17, 129-30.

43. "Report of the Task Force on Productivity and Competition," *Antitrust Law and Economics Review* 2 (Spring 1969):13-40; D. T. Armentano, *The Myths of Anti-Trust* (New York, 1972).

44. Green, *Closed Enterprise System*; "The Industrial Reorganization Act," *Columbia Law Review* 73 (1973):635-75; Thomas Goho and David Smith, "The Hart Bill," *Arkansas Business and Economic Review* 8 (Spring 1974):32-37; U.S. Senate, Committee on the Judiciary, Subcommittee on Antitrust and Monopoly, *The Industrial Reorganization Act* (93 Cong., 1st sess, 1974); Fred R. Harris, "The New Populism and Industrial Reform," *Antitrust Law and Economics Review* 4 (Summer 1971):9-46.

45. The conflicting pressures were particularly apparent during the early years of the Nixon administration, when Richard W. McLaren headed the Antitrust Division. He began cases aimed at curbing the conglomerate merger movement, came under severe criticism from those who saw this as populistic nonsense, and decided to resign in December 1971. See "The Sharp New Line on Antitrust," *Business Week* (21 June 1969):120-22; Ralph Jensen, *Let Me Say This About That* (New York, 1972), 43-47; Willard Mueller, "The Anti-Antitrust Movement," *Antitrust Law and Economics Review* 13 (3 November 1981):59-91.

46. "Antitrust Developments," *American Bar Association Antitrust Law Journal* 46 (1977):749-814; *Congressional Quarterly Almanac* (1974), 291-92; Joe Sims, "A Critical Profile of the National Antitrust Commission," *Washington and Lee Law Review* 37 (Winter 1980):1-23.

47. On the economy in 1977, see James Tobin, "Full Recovery or Stagna-

tion?" in Werner Sichel, ed., *Economic Advice and Executive Policy* (New York, 1978), 97-109; Otto Eckstein, *The Great Recession* (Amsterdam, 1978); and Calleo, *Imperious Economy*, 138-41. Reflecting the increased interest in the Japanese system were such works as Hugh Patrick and Henry Rosovsky, eds., *Asia's New Giant* (Washington, 1976); Albert M. Craig, ed., *Japan: A Comparative View* (Princeton, 1979); and Ezra F. Vogel, *Japan as Number One* (Cambridge, 1979). On regulatory, antitrust, and energy developments, see *Congressional Quarterly Almanac* (1975), 12, 586, 729; (1976), 6, 10, 19; U.S. Senate, Committee on the Judiciary, Subcommittee on Antitrust and Monopoly, *The Antitrust Improvements Act of 1975* (94 Cong., 1st sess., 1976); Vietor, *Energy Policy in America since 1945*, 219-24, 249-58; Vietor, *Environmental Politics*, 109-18, 207-20.

48. Calleo, *Imperious Economy*, 141-50; McQuaid, *Big Business*, 298-304; Vietor, *Energy Policy in America since 1945*, 259-70; Herbert Stein, "The Failure of Carter's Anti-Inflation Policy," *Fortune* 101 (24 March 1980):50-52; Charles Shami and Edward Knight, "The Anti-Inflation Program of the Carter Administration," in Fund for Public Policy Research, *Studies in Taxation, Public Finance, and Related Subjects* 3 (1979):115-37; *Congressional Quarterly Weekly Report* 37 (22 December 1979):2871-72; 38 (19 January 1980):137-38; 38 (17 May 1980):1,311.

49. *Congressional Quarterly Almanac* (1978), 27-28; (1979), 14, 20-21; (1980), 13-14, 19-22; Sims, "Critical Profile of National Antitrust Commission," *Washington and Lee Law Review* 37 (Winter 1980):1-23; Alfred Regnery, "Antitrust Reform," *Trial* 15 (April 1979):26-29; A. F. Ehrbar, "Bigness Becomes the Target of the Trustbusters," *Fortune* 99 (26 March 1979):34-38; Vietor, *Environmental Politics*, 118-25, 220-26; Pertschuk, *Revolt against Regulation*, 105-16; Walter Guzzardi, Jr., "A Search for Sanity in Antitrust," *Fortune* 97 (30 Jan. 1978): 72-75, 78, 80, 82-83.

50. *Congressional Quarterly Almanac* (1977), 13; (1978), 12; (1980), 13; Vietor, *Energy Policy in America since 1945*, 259-62; Irving H. Siegel, *Fuller Employment with Less Inflation* (Kalamazoo, 1981), 9-12; John Palmer, ed., *Creating Jobs* (Washington, 1979); Ira C. Magaziner and Thomas Hout, *Japanese Industrial Policy* (London, 1980); Ezra F. Vogel, "Guided Free Enterprise in Japan," *Harvard Business Review* (May-June 1978). As passed, the Humphrey-Hawkins Act was little more than a symbolic gesture. It specified as provisional goals for 1983 the reduction of the unemployment rate to 4 percent and the inflation rate to 3 percent. But it allowed revision of the indicated schedules, and this was done at the earliest opportunity. In 1980 achievement of the employment target was deferred until 1985 and the price target to 1988.

51. Bruce R. Bartlett, *Reaganomics: Supply Side Economics in Action* (Westport, Conn., 1981), 139-47; John Quirt, "Aftershocks from the Great California Taxquake," *Fortune* 98 (25 September 1978):76-77; Kolkey, *New Right*, 336-37; Murray L. Weidenbaum, "A Way to Regulate the Regulatory Binge," *Business and Society Review* 20 (Winter 1977):4-5; James Miller and Bruce Yandle, *Benefit-Cost Analysis of Social Regulation* (Washington, 1979); Pertschuk, *Revolt against Regulation*, 64-92.

52. Vogel, "New Social Regulation," in McCraw, ed., *Regulation in Perspective*, 176-79; Pertschuk, *Revolt against Regulation*, 52-66; "Business Is Learning

How to Win in Washington"97 (*Fortune*, 27 March 1978):52-58; D. Quinn Mills, "Flawed Victory in Labor Law Reform," *Harvard Business Review* 57 (May-June 1979):92-102; Peter Slavin, "The Business Roundtable," *Business and Society Review* 16 (Winter 1976):28-32; Walter Guzzardi, Jr., "A New Public Face for Business," *Fortune* 101 (30 June 1980):48-52; McQuaid, *Big Business*, 289-301, 305.

53. See *Business Week's* special issue (30 June 1980) on "The Reindustrializaton of America," and the articles in *Time* 116 (1 September 1980):40-42, and *Newsweek* 96 (25 August 1980):59-60, and 96 (8 September 1980), 50-52.

54. "Reindustrialization of America," *Business Week* (30 June 1980):87-88, 146; Felix Rohatyn, "Strong Medicine," *Across the Board* 17 (May 1980):3-6; *Time* 116 (14 July 1980):42-43. The movement was also linked to a new current of thinking in the business schools. See particularly George C. Lodge, *The New American Ideology* (New York, 1975); Neil W. Chamberlain, *Remaking American Values* (New York, 1977); and Richard Eells, *The Political Crisis of the Enterprise System* (New York, 1980). On its appeal in business circles, see also Eugene Bardach, "Implementing Industrial Policy," in Chalmers Johnson, ed., *The Industrial Policy Debate* (San Francisco, 1984), 112-14.

55. *Newsweek* 96 (8 September 1980):51. See also *Time* 116 (8 September 1980):24.

56. Bartlett, *Reaganomics*, 1-11, 97-104, 114-23, 125-35; Irving Kristol, "Toward a New Economics?" *Wall Street Journal*, 9 May 1977; Paul Craig Roberts, "The Economics Case for Kemp-Roth," *Wall Street Journal* 1 August 1978; Walter Guzzardi, Jr., "The New Down-to-Earth Economics," *Fortune* 98 (31 December 1978):72-79; Martin Tolchin, "Jack Kemp's Bootleg Run to the Right," *Esquire* (24 October 1978):59-69; "A Stampede to Cut Taxes," *Business Week* (14 July 1980):36-37.

57. Kolkey, *New Right*, 334-44; Alan Crawford, *Thunder on the Right* (New York, 1980); Fred I. Greenstein, "The Background of the Reagan Presidency," in Greenstein, ed., *The Reagan Presidency* (Baltimore, 1983), 8-18.

58. Hugh Heclo and Rudolph Penner, "Fiscal and Political Strategy in the Reagan Administration," in Greenstein, ed., *Reagan Presidency*, 21-31; Congressional Quarterly, *Reagon's First Year* (Washington, 1982), 27-39, 51-53; Laurence I. Barrett, *Gambling with History: Reagan in the White House* (New York, 1983), 146-86.

59. Heclo and Penner, "Fiscal and Political Strategy in the Reagan Administration," in Greenstein, ed., *Reagan Presidency*, 31-41; Barrett, *Gambling with History*, 336-71; George Gilder, "What Ronald Reagan Doesn't Know about His Own Achievements," *National Review* (29 June 1984):22-25; Thomas E. Weisskopf, "The Elections and the Economy," *Dissent* (Fall 1984):397-400.

60. Heclo and Penner, "Fiscal and Political Strategy in the Reagan Administration," in Greenstein, ed., *Reagan Presidency*, 44-46; Richard P. Nathan, "The Reagan Presidency in Domestic Affairs," in Greenstein, ed., *Reagan Presidency*, 58-63, 73-77; "Reining in the Regulators," *Time* (15 June 1981):62-63; Martin and Susan J. Tolchin, *Dismantling America: The Rush to Deregulate* (Boston, 1983); Trammell E. Vickery, "Current Antitrust Developments," *Business Lawyer* 36 (March 1981):799-807; Mueller, "The Anti-Antitrust

Movement," *Antitrust Law and Economics Review* 13 (3 November 1981):59-91; Victor Kramer, "Antitrust Today," *Wisconsin Law Review* (1981):1287-1302; Lawrence A. Sullivan, "Monopolization: Corporate Strategy, the IBM Cases, and the Transformation of the Law," *Texas Law Review* 60 (April 1982):587-647; Donald and Beverly Baker, "Antitrust and Communications Deregulation," *Antitrust Bulletin* (Spring 1983):1-38; Alan Pearce and Philip Verneer, "Some Policy-Oriented Reflections on the A. T. & T. Antitrust Settlement," *Federal Bar News and Journal* 29 (November 1982):372-77. The "big" structural case that was not dropped and did result in major structural changes was that against American Telephone and Telegraph. Settled by a consent decree in 1982, it was hailed by most commentators as a victory for antitrust. But some were dubious. The divestiture plan, they noted, was essentially the one proposed by AT & T itself, and a major part of the settlement was the lifting of a 1956 decree that had barred AT & T from entering the data processing and informational services field.

61. Samuel P. Huntington, "The Defense Policy of the Reagan Administration," in Greenstein, ed., *Reagan Presidency*, 82-113; Bruce Bartlett, "Trade Policy and the Dangers of Protectionism," in Johnson, ed., *Industrial Policy Debate*, 171-72; Malcolm Baldridge, in *National Journal* (31 December 1983):2697; Juan Williams and Michael Schrage, "Reagan Names Commission on Industrial Competition," *Washington Post*, 5 August 1983; George Cabot Lodge and William Glass, "U. S. Trade Policy Needs One Voice," *Harvard Business Review* 83 (May-June 1983):75-83; Stephen J. Whitfield, "One Nation under God?: The Rise of the Religious Right," *Virginia Quarterly Review* 58 (Autumn 1982):557-74; Dick Kirschten, "Reagan Looks to Religious Leaders for Continuing Support," *National Journal* 15 (20 August 1983):1727-31.

62. Heclo and Penner, "Fiscal and Political Strategy in the Reagan Administration," in Greenstein, ed., *Reagan Presidency*, 43-46; Basking in Reagan's Troubles," *Time* (12 July 1982):14-15; "The Democrats Tout a New Tonic," *Time* (3 October 1983):47; "Debating Industrial Policy," *Time* (26 December 1983): 70; George Gilder, "American Industrial Policy: A Supply-Side Economics of the Left," *Public Interest* (Summer 1983):29-43; Aaron Wildavsky, "Squaring the Political Circle," in Johnson, ed., *Industrial Policy Debate*, 27-44; Robert Reich, *The Next American Frontier* (New York, 1983).

63. Louis J. Mulkern, quoted in Chalmers Johnson, "The Idea of Industrial Policy," in Johnson, ed., *Industrial Policy Debate*, 11.

The Third Energy Transition: Origins and Environmental Implications

Martin V. Melosi

During the nineteenth and early twentieth centuries, the United States passed through two energy transitions. The first—from wood and waterpower to coal—occurred in the mid-nineteenth century; the second—from coal to petroleum and natural gas—began about the turn of the century. In the late 1960s, the United States entered a third transition—from petroleum and natural gas to a wide array of alternative fuels. Despite the persistence of a petroleum-based culture in the United States, the control of oil by OPEC and other foreign powers forced Americans at least to explore alternative energy sources.

In several ways the transitions were similar: They all were accumulations of many smaller transitions in which older sources of energy were supplemented, complemented, or slowly displaced by new ones according to location and use. All of the transitions grew out of real or perceived energy needs arising from new technologies, new end-uses, and available supply and allocation of resources. Unlike the first two transitions, the most recent one has less to do with a shift from one major energy source to another, and more to do with a changing perception of the role of energy in the life of the nation (shaped by energy use and development patterns in the 1960s), the "energy crisis" in the 1970s, and the emergence of the modern environmental movement.

THE 1960s: PROLOGUE TO THE THIRD ENERGY TRANSITION

The International Energy Scene

In the wake of the "energy crisis" and the environmental movement, scholars have given too little attention to events of the early and mid-

1960s in setting the agenda for energy issues—including their environmental implications. A major reason for this oversight is that, as a contemporary issue, energy did not attract broad national concern. Other preoccupations—civil rights, an emerging counterculture, the Cold War, an escalating conflict in Southeast Asia—vied for Americans' time, thought, and attention. But this is only a partial answer. A more persuasive one is that energy was traditionally perceived as a local or regional question involving, for instance, development and use of a particular fuel. Government officials thus developed an array of fuel policies, but no broad energy strategy. From a historical vantage point, however, it is clear that a new perception of energy was on the horizon in the 1960s, and that the United States was moving through the end of an era in viewing energy in a narrow context. The beginnings of a changing context for energy in the 1960s are most clearly observable in the shift in control of international oil, the expansion of a national network of electrical power production, the commercialization of nuclear power, and the growing significance of the "environmental costs" of energy development and use as a national issue.

If a revolution occurred in the oil industry in the post-World War II era, it occurred in terms of developing nations in the Middle East, Africa, and Latin America acquiring greater control over their oil resources. The "Seven Sisters" had remained in control of world oil supplies in the 1950s,[1] but by 1961 the control of oil was being challenged by "independents" (as opposed to the large multinationals) venturing into the Middle East and North African oil regions; by host governments working out new arrangements with the oil companies and, in some cases, nationalizing their oil industries; and by competing cartels, especially OPEC. Also, in 1961, there was a great expansion in the volume of oil produced, and the flow of petroleum was more complex, with substantially greater production coming out of the Middle East, Africa, and the Soviet Union rather than the Americas.[2]

The creation of the Organization of Petroleum Exporting Countries (OPEC) in 1960 was the most visible sign of changing times. Founding members included Venezuela, Saudi Arabia, Kuwait, Iran, and Iraq. Jointly they represented 67 percent of the world's oil reserves, 38 percent of its production, and 90 percent of oil in international trade. Measured against its impact in the 1970s, the accomplishments of OPEC were modest in the 1960s. It moved cautiously, unsure of the extent of its strength, serving as a clearinghouse for information with a modest impact on oil revenues and price. The major oil companies were not immediately worried about OPEC, but snubbing the cartel was a momentary luxury. Like the American government in Washington, the majors could not grasp that the establishment of OPEC was but a symptom of broader changes in the Middle East.[3]

The so-called Six-Day War in the summer of 1967, in which Israel attacked Egypt to prevent a feared Egyptian assault, demonstrated how oil was becoming a potent instrument of political as well as economic power. Although largely ineffective, an oil boycott staged by Arab states against the United States and parts of Europe sent a signal only faintly understood in the West. In January 1968 the Organization of Arab Petroleum Exporting Countries (OAPEC) was formed by Saudi Arabia, Kuwait, and Libya. Although none of the countries participated in the Six-Day War, they intended eventually to unite the Arab world by using oil as a political and economic weapon.[4]

A more immediate harbinger of things to come occurred in Libya in 1969. The ultranationalist regime of Muammar Ghaddafi quickly increased oil revenues by juggling oil concessions among the various companies operating in Libya. While OPEC looked toward collective action to force changes in the international oil system, Ghaddafi played one oil company against another, ultimately driving up royalties and taxes on oil production in his country. The dramatic ploy induced the majors to seek new arrangements with other African and Middle East producers. By 1970 most oil-producing nations were receiving a 55 percent tax rate and higher posted prices on their crude. Libya's victory was an object lesson not only for the oil companies, but also for OPEC.[5]

The Energy Market at Home

At home, recognition that the change in the world oil market would ultimately affect domestic energy interests was slow in coming. Like their predecessors, John F. Kennedy and Lyndon B. Johnson tended to look to the future through the eyes of the present. Both administrations tried to cope with the immediate oil problem—linked to excess capacity—while overlooking the possibility of a future period of scarcity.

Focus remained on the mandatory oil import quotas imposed by the Eisenhower administration in 1959. The United States had become a net importer of oil in 1947, signaling a crucial change in the relationship between the domestic and international oil industries. Most business and government leaders regarded the continued good fortune of the domestic companies as synonymous with the economic health of the nation. They were concerned about domestic producers losing markets to cheap foreign oil, but they also feared that oil supplies might exceed demand, driving down prices for American crude. A national security argument was also being formulated, stressing that secure petroleum supplies could only be obtained through domestic sources—a persuasive argument in the early years of the Cold War. The import quotas had temporarily stabilized the U.S. oil industry, but they created an artificial energy environment where oil prices failed to respond to the prevailing market, and where consumers footed the bill from propped-up domestic oil.[6]

With the economy operating sluggishly in the early 1960s, the Kennedy administration was more concerned with demand deficiencies than the long-term effects of over-supply. One economist referred to the Kennedy energy policy as a "strategy of studied inaction"[7]: it included several energy studies, but made little real effort to establish a national energy policy. The Johnson administration, in much the same way, was unwilling to rethink the goals of its energy policies—especially the quota system. Murmurings about inflation, national defense, and protectionism were smothered by the administration's increasing preoccupation with the Vietnam War and the Great Society. The 1967 Arab-Israeli War and the subsequent Arab oil embargo were ignored as danger signals.[8]

Beyond the important place of petroleum in the life of the U.S., the expanding national electrical network and the commercialization of nuclear power fostered confidence in available, abundant, and cheap sources of energy in the 1960s. Belief in unbridled material progress was linked to visions of a high-technology society where every family drove a new car, had a modern ranch-style home, and accumulated every appliance that could be plugged into a wall socket. Utility companies put their faith—and their money—into large, centralized energy systems. Economies of scale dictated that the unquenchable demand for energy made larger generating units profitable, and thus, desirable.

In 1970 the electric utility industry was the largest industry—in terms of capital assets—in the United States, generating more than half of all electricity in the world. The trend toward centralization began in the 1920s, but the electric utility industry had become even more monolithic in recent years. In terms of actual numbers of power systems (between 3,300 and 3,500 in 1970), the industry was fragmented. However, as few as 250 to 300 privately owned utilities and two major federal systems produced approximately 90 percent of the nation's electricity. Along with growth in individual units there was a continual growth in the interconnection of systems.[9]

"Power pools"—or the combination of utility interests—grew out of the interconnections, but went beyond interconnections toward integration of systems, sometimes with federal support and encouragement. The number of power pools with unaffiliated corporate members increased from four in 1960 (12 percent of the nation's capacity) to seventeen in 1970 (50 percent of national capacity). This trend was viewed as an efficient means of delivering energy to consumers, but it was also a way to encourage concentration and monopolistic practices within the industry.[10] An unanticipated side-effect was the increased potential for massive blackouts, such as the one that plunged much of Canada and the eastern United States into darkness for as much as thirteen hours in November 1965.[11] In line with the relatively optimistic energy outlook of the 1960s, the Kennedy administration promoted the interconnection of systems. But after the 1965 blackout, a task force appointed by President Johnson recommended regional planning and integration of systems rather than moving toward a national network. Like its predecessors, the Nixon administration was conditioned by a long history of energy abundance in the U.S. and strongly supported the growth of energy industries without much serious attention to evaluating the state of those industries.[12]

In the case of electrical power generation, some observers were talking about an industry crisis in 1968. Primary fuel supplies, which earlier had been predicted as stable, became increasingly expensive and in short supply by the end of the decade. Technical improvements in the systems had not advanced rapidly enough to offset increased fuel prices. Managerial problems also undermined the effectiveness of the industry. By as early as 1964, the hope for rapid and continued expansion was being replaced by expectations of modest growth. Brownouts and blackouts, short supplies of natural gas, and environmental controversies provided hints of things to come.[13]

The promotion of nuclear power in the early 1960s, in part at least, benefited from problems faced by the electrical power industry. The development of commercial nuclear power had been modest in the 1950s, but advocates hoped that the Kennedy administration would provide more aggressive leadership in developing nuclear power. Kennedy's Cold War rhetoric buoyed those spirits, but the hopes were not fulfilled. After the successful launching of the Russian satellite Sputnik in 1957, it became apparent that if the U.S. may have been ahead in the development of nuclear weapons, it had slipped behind in rocketry. Having come to power in part because of this "missile gap" issue, the Kennedy administration thus directed research funds to missile development and the space program, rather than to nuclear power.

In 1962 the Atomic Energy Commission issued a report claiming that nuclear power was now commercially viable. Yet the report was more a hope than a reality. In 1961 two-thirds of the reactor programs still emphasized weapons and other military applications. But the AEC and congressional supporters of nuclear power continued to promote commercialization and began achieving results. Despite the fledgling industry's errors in estimating capital costs, demand for nuclear power facilities was on the rise in the mid-1960s. High coal prices and growing sensitivity to pollution associated with coal burning made nuclear power more attractive to utility companies. The great Northeast blackout of 1965 also stimulated interest in nuclear power generation. By the end of 1967, American utility companies planned to construct seventy-five nuclear plants; about half of all power plant capacity ordered was nuclear. By the end of 1969, ninety-seven nuclear plants were in operation, under construction, or had been contracted. For the moment, the future of the young industry looked bright. [14]

Energy and Environment in the 1960s

Although national energy policy showed few signs of change in the 1960s, the environmental implications of energy development and use acquired greater significance. The increased utilization of coal, oil, and nuclear fuels, due to the scale of electric-power production and the rising demand for energy, drew attention to the exploitation of natural resources. The commercial viability of nuclear power raised questions about radiation, the siting of nuclear plants, and reactor safety. And the ubiquity of air pollution—especially from automobile emissions and stationary fossil-fuel burners—moved policy makers toward more effective clean air standards. Although these issues were treated as separate and unique problems for most of the sixties, they were significant enough in scope to bring the relationship between energy and environment to national attention.

Since coal-fired steam plants were abundant in the 1960s, an environmental controversy emerged over the mining of coal and the contribution of coal to air pollution. The rationale for turning to strip mining was economic. In order to compete with cheap imported oil and natural gas, mining companies sought this less expensive means of acquiring coal. By the late 1960s, the economies of scale turned a labor-intensive operation into a cheaper capital-intensive operation in several eastern fields and some western fields.

Strip-mining, or surface mining, became a much-publicized national issue. In strip-mined areas community disruption led to almost 18 percent loss of population. By 1961 hundreds of miles of streams and thousands of acres of land were disturbed or ruined by strip mining. A 1969 report by the Appalachian Regional Commissioner stated that approximately 5,700 miles of streams had been polluted in the Appalachians, and the water quality of 10,500 miles of streams was affected. By that time thousands of acres of land had been stripped and not reclaimed ("orphan lands"), much of it in the Appalachians.[15]

Despite the environmental implications of strip mining, few restrictions were placed on the practice until the 1970s. Coal producers and their trade associations, electric utilities, the United Mine Workers, and companies with strong mining interests (including oil companies and railroads) united in their opposition to stringent environmental laws or sanctions. In 1961 Pennsylvania became the first state to pass a surface-mining reclamation act, but enforcement was inadequate. In states that followed Pennsylvania's lead, the results were the same.[16]

Air pollution became a national problem because of criticism of coal-burning by utilities and other industrial users and also because of a rising concern over smog. Through the encouragement of health officials and academics, the Department of Health, Education, and Welfare (HEW) sponsored the first National Conference on Air Pollution in 1958. The theme of the conference was cooperation between industry and government to reduce air pollution, but it attracted few people from the coal industry and few conservationists. By the time of the third Conference on Air Pollution in 1966 both coal and environmental interests were well represented. In the mid-1960s a relatively innocuous earlier law—the Clean Air Act of 1955—underwent several revisions potentially injurious to the coal and electric utility industries. The 1955 law affirmed that air pollution was a local problem. The 1967 revision changed the emphasis somewhat, conjuring up the spirit of cooperation between industry and government. In the broadest sense, these revisions brought industry into the policy-formation phase of air pollution legislation, resulting in a Clean Air Act that was "coal's law." Only with the Clean Air Act of 1970 would significant strides be made toward a national policy of air quality not tied so inextricably to the coal interests.[17]

A relatively new source of air pollution—automobile emissions—posed different problems. Los Angeles, the "smog capital of America" in the 1950s, became a living laboratory for studying massive doses of auto emissions. In 1959 eye irritation was reported in Los Angeles County on 187 days; in 1962, 212 days. A typical car produced in 1963 was found to discharge 520 pounds of hydrocarbons, 1,700 pounds of carbon monoxide, and 90 pounds of nitrogen oxide annually. Fed by thousands of cars, the smog problem in LA was critical.

It became apparent in the 1960s that smog was a national problem requiring the attention of the federal government. The 1963 Clean Air Act for the first time gave Washington limited enforcement power over interstate pollution. An amendment in 1965 recognized the need to control motor-vehicle pollution on a national scale and empowered HEW to establish and enforce air pollution standards for new motor vehicles. The 1967 Air Quality Act was the first piece of federal legislation designed to control lead emissions. But the automobile and oil industries resisted tougher standards, and though the public paid homage to clean air, it resented carrying the burden of responsiblity through higher costs and reduced automobile performance.[18]

Exploitation of oil resources also became intertwined with the question of "environmental costs" in the 1960s. No event riveted attention on the environmental dangers of oil production more than the Santa Barbara oil spill of January 1969. In 1955 the California legislature had passed a law barring drilling in specified "sanctuaries" within the three-mile limit, to preserve the seascape. Beyond that limit the federal government controlled the leases, granting its first one in 1963. By the time of the spill in January 1969, 925 wells had been drilled along the coastal tidelands from Santa Barbara to Los Angeles. The world-famous spill originated at Union Oil's well A-21 in the "federal zone" on January 28, and within days oil coated five miles of beach. The leak eventually released 235,000 gallons of crude, creating a slick of 800 miles.

This was not simply a local crisis. The Nixon administration responded to the spill with investigations and studies,but offered little immediate relief to Santa Barbara. Private lawsuits against Union Oil, as well as a lawsuit against the federal government, soon followed. Citizens' groups protested the remaining oil operations, but Union Oil resumed offshore production, and not until the end of March were the worst leaks plugged.

The resolution of the episode was mixed. Union Oil assumed liability for the blow-out, but the financial settlements were well below the total damage costs. Congress revised the Outer Continental Shelf Lands Act by tightening regulations on leases and making offshore operators liable for cleaning up spills. The worst fears about permanent harm to the California beaches and wildlife were not realized, but the spill helped to stimulate the growth of the modern environmental movement and moved the federal government toward the passage of the National Environmental Policy Act (NEPA) in 1969.[19]

Another environmental crisis arose in the late 1960s as opponents of nuclear power seized on its health and safety risks. Nuclear safety had been a secondary issue in the early development of nuclear power. The race to produce the bomb, the quest for strategic superiority engendered by the Cold War, and the determination to commercialize atomic energy received top priority. Questions of health and safety were raised as early as the 1950s, but they neither upstaged nor restrained the development of nuclear power. One of these issues—fallout from atmospheric testing—attracted world attention. The other—reactor safety and siting of reactors—received less publicity but was no less significant.

A mechanism for dealing with safety issues had been established within the AEC as early as 1947, but AEC leaders—convinced that the chance for a major accident was remote—regarded safety as an engineering problem. Controversy over safety was dramatized by a partial fuel meltdown in an experimental breeder reactor in 1955. The passage of the Price-Anderson Act in 1957 also raised debate over safety questions. The best-known portion of the act was the indemnification measure, limiting the liability of an individual company producing nuclear power and providing governmental subsidies to cover liability above insurance coverage. Price-Anderson confronted the safety issue and stimulated commercial development, but seemed to be an admission that nuclear power posed risks that producers were unwilling to assume without federal backing. The AEC regulations for health and safety remained vague into the 1960s. Missing were an independent safety research program and specific safety standards, applied universally, for all reactor projects.

Nuclear power safety grew as a public issue in the 1960s, especially after a small test reactor exploded at the National Reactor Testing Station in Idaho Falls in January 1961. The AEC claimed that the resulting three fatalities were due to an electrical power-surge blast; union officials blaimed them on radiation. Nonetheless, the AEC established guidelines for siting nuclear reactors away from large urban populations, and in 1962 set up a procedure for relating plant size to distance from dense populations (the concept of "remote location"). Late in the decade, however, the remote location concept had still not evolved into a clear set of standards.

The glut of licensing requests after 1966 strained AEC's review system and further limited its efforts to order safety modifications in existing plants. A partial meltdown at the Fermi Plant in Michigan in 1966 sent a clear warning about the need for careful licensing and monitoring practices. In the case of the building of the Monticello reactor in Minnesota in the late 1960s, public protest focused on citizens' rights in licensing and siting of plants. In response to the protests, a symposium on Nuclear Power and the Public was held at the University of Minnesota. The tone of later protests in the 1970s was set in this symposium and in similar meetings in California, New York, and Vermont.[20]

Taken as a group, the energy and environmental issues of the 1960s offered serious challenges to the American people and their government. But a dramatic series of events was needed to focus national attention on them. The rise of the modern environmental movement and the advent of the energy crisis provided that focus.

THE 1970S: THE ENERGY CRISIS AND ITS AFTERMATH:

When Richard M. Nixon took office in January 1969, signs of a looming crisis were ample. The winter of 1969-70 was the coldest in thirty years. A predicted scarcity in natural gas became a reality. Brownouts struck most cities. Clashes between environmentalists and energy producers were intensifying. Signs of aggressiveness were coming from OPEC. These warnings increased executive and congressional dialogue over a possible national energy policy, but there was little unanimity of interest in Washington.

Several events soon forced President Nixon to give more attention to energy matters. In June 1971 he delivered his first energy message, probably the most comprehensive message of its type ever sent to Congress. The emphasis was long-term, calling for expanded programs in nuclear power, coal conversion, outer-shelf development, and oil-shale reserve leasing, and recommending the establishment of a Department of Natural Resources. But in the absence of an emergency, the message went largely unheeded. In April 1973 Nixon abandoned the quota program—after liberalizing it several times—because of its inflationary effect on the economy. By that time the program had already distorted the allocation of recources and made it difficult for the nation to adjust to domestic depletion of oil and the rising price of foreign crude. Energy policy became ensnared in the debate over combating inflation in 1973, while the Nixon administration itself was also enmeshed in the Watergate scandal. Design of a coherent policy became impossible.

Critical events in international oil set a tone of "energy scarcity" and impending crisis in the early 1970s. Libya's victory over its concessionaires in 1969 was a prelude to OPEC's rise to power. By 1973 the producing countries of the Persian Gulf and North Africa virtually completed the process of controlling their own oil supplies, thus strongly influencing oil prices. The OPEC cartel was not omnipotent, nor did the international companies wither away. But the days of cheap energy were being replaced by an era of rising prices; an oil industry dominated by private companies made way for increased governmental domination.

The Yom Kippur War of 1973 provided a catalyst for OPEC's emergence as the world's oil leader. Coming on the heels of global price inflation, rising nationalism in the Third World, and the shift in oil production to the Middle East and North Africa, it was the proverbial straw that broke the camel's back. On 6 October 1973, Egypt and Syria launched a coordinated attack against Israel, as Egyptian leader Anwar Sadat attempted to carry out a promise to recover lands from Israel lost in the Six-Day War of 1967.

Acting on anti-Zionist views and an unwillingness to be isolated from a united Arab front, King Faisal of Saudi Arabia warned the United States that it faced serious consequences, particularly the loss of oil supplies, if it continued to aid Israel. Oil did not simply finance an attack on Israel but provided an opportunity to enhance OPEC control, and for the Arab members at least, a chance to influence diplomatic relations with the West. When the Nixon administration failed to heed the warnings, the Saudis supported an OAPEC boycott of oil against the United States and other supporters of Israel. The embargo lasted six months; in 1974 the price of Arabian oil delivered to the U.S. was $12.25 per barrel as compared to $3.65 a year earlier.[21]

When the Arab oil embargo was announced in October 1973, the Nixon administration was unable to meet the crisis effectively. On November 27 the President signed the Emergency Petroleum Allocation Act, which jettisoned voluntary oil and gas allocation measures, instead embracing governmental regulation as a way out of the crisis. The act established a new allocation plan, provided authority for gas rationing, and maintained price controls. In addition it established Project Independence, a rather diffuse plan designed to free the United States from reliance on foreign oil by 1980.

The embargo had established a new order in international oil. However, between 1974 and 1978 the world oil market remained relatively stable. This stability was broken in the late 1970s by events outside the control of either OPEC or the multinationals: in 1978 the Shah of Iran was forced into exile and replaced by the Ayatollah Khomeini, leader of an Islamic Revolution bent on toppling royal secular control and western influence in Iran. Oil exports from this important producer dropped quickly. Rapidly rising oil prices—coupled with the Soviet invasion of Afghanistan in December 1979 and concern about further Russian advances along the Persian Gulf—produced a renewed sense of disequilibrium.[22]

At home the phrase "energy crisis" was widespread after 1973. But even the jarring impact of higher energy prices and limited supplies was short-lived. It would take the Iranian crisis and a whole new round of rising prices and supply scarcities to reinforce the notion that the era of cheap energy was coming to an end.

Consumption and production trends in oil and natural gas in the early 1970s were strong indicators of the predicament the United States might face if its energy supplies were cut. Oil production steadily declined in the lower forty-eight states. For the first time, more natural gas was sold than was discovered. Practically all the increases in consumption of both energy sources after 1970 came from imports. In 1970 foreign oil accounted for approximately 22 percent of consumption; by 1973, 36 percent. Rising consumption was key to the potential disruption of the economy. In 1970 the average American consumed more than three times the energy of his forefathers in 1900. By 1977 petroleum and natural gas furnished 75 percent of the nation's total energy needs. Energy-hungry technologies, energy-intensive consumer goods, and the rise of the automobile accounted for much of this increase.[23]

The flurry of activity over the energy crisis in Washington was not sufficient to assuage the anxieties of Americans. Complicating the situation further were shifting combinations of states and other interest groups pushing for or contesting specific programs. As several commentators pointed out, the impact of the embargo was perhaps as much psychological and emotional as practical. By November some gasoline stations were shutting down because of short allocations; in metropolitan areas—especially automobile-dominated California—lines of vehicles waiting to fill up stretched around the block. Gas-guzzling cars were becoming pariahs and Detroit girded itself for hard times. Car-pooling and the sad state of mass transit were subjects of animated discussion.

The embargo was short-lived and not as calamitous as feared. But if not a crisis of dwindling supplies, it exposed a crisis of control, sustained by wasteful consumption and short-sighted energy policy. The 1973-74 crisis was most significant as a forceful demonstration of the changed status of the world oil industry and the value of oil in the world economy. But the fact that many Americans chose to believe that the shortages were manipulated and the crisis artificial made it difficult to move toward a coherent energy policy.[24]

When Gerald R. Ford became president, he faced many serious challenges not the least of which was responding to decontrol of oil and gas, security of the nation's oil supply, debate over alternative energy sources, and various environmental issues. Economic constraints and conflicting vested interests worked against a solution to the decontrol controversy. National interest overrode the goal of international cooperation in enhancing oil-supply security. Similarly, the Ford administration gained little ground clarifying what the federal role should be in developing new energy sources. While calling for private development of alternatives, the administration was not prepared to give up its control of vast public lands and their resources or to relinquish its leadership in nuclear power development. The only significant structural readjustment was establishment of the Energy Research and Development Administration (ERDA), the Nuclear Regulatory Commission (NRC), and the Energy Resources Council. The responsiblity formerly held by AEC, which was abolished in 1974, was divided between ERDA and NRC. The Energy Resources Council was meant to coordinate the formulation and implementation of national energy policy, but never achieved that goal.[25] As historian Robert A. Divine has noted, "The inability to come to grips with the energy crisis was Ford's gravest failure as President."[26] But blame for the administration's failure to take a tough stand on energy or develop long-term solutions must be shared by Congress. Like the administrations before it and after it, the Ford administration was saddled with an uncooperative Congress that did little to provide a comprehensive energy strategy. Rampant inflation in the 1970s also complicated policy-making with respect to energy.

The administration of Jimmy Carter faced the difficult task of confronting a new era of high energy costs and possible changes in American lifestyle. But Carter did not intend to confront the energy crisis with the tools of his predecessors. Though never successfully taking administrative or political control of the nation's highest office, he moved the United States closer to a holistic view of the energy problem. Yet in the end the Carter administration was more successful in changing the tone of the debate on energy than in changing the substance of the policy.

On 18 April 1977, Carter announced his National Energy Plan (NEP), describing the energy situation as "the moral equivalent of war." At the heart of the NEP was the notion that the U.S. was facing its third energy transition. The goal of the plan was to ease into the transition, to give the country sufficient time to implement major changes. This was interim planning rather than mere crisis management. In all, the plan included about 100 proposals ranging from incentives for conservation to new information systems, from development of alternative fuels to transportation studies. At its heart was the Crude Oil Equalization Tax (COET). In general the administration hoped to reduce dependence on imported crude, retain domestic price controls with a new pricing system, and bring supply and demand of natural gas into balance. The COET was meant to raise oil prices sufficiently over three years to reduce demand, while diverting the increased revenues to the government for use in various programs.

As anticipated, the NEP drew fire from many sources. After bogging down in the Senate, however, the National Energy Act passed in 1978. The plan as enacted included many of the original provisions, but the COET was killed in committee, and a proposed tax on industrial users of oil and gas was excluded. The act's major shortcoming was absence of provisions for oil pricing. In fact OPEC was never mentioned.[27]

In addition to the National Energy Act, the Carter administration raised the energy issue to Cabinet-level importance. In March 1977 the President submitted legislation to create a Department of Energy (DOE). The idea for a Cabinet-level department was the logical conclusion of what the Nixon and Ford administrations had been working toward, with roots even farther back. But the translation of the idea into reality created many problems. DOE did not get off to a good start because energy officials simultaneously tried to formulate NEP and construct the department. The first secretary, James Schlesinger, faced a "department in disarray"; as *Time* noted: "Though DOE was set up to bring order, drive and direction to the uncoordinated activities of the 50 federal agencies involved in energy matters, Secretary Schlesinger's superagency has been sinking into a bureaucratic stupor."[28] The "dual track" of legislation and administration was too much, too soon. Where previous administrations had dragged their feet on energy questions, the Carter administration failed to tie its shoes before marching off.

No sooner had the new legislation and the new department come into existence than the administration faced its own energy emergency. The Iranian crisis sent new shock waves through the U.S. In addition, double-digit inflation reappeared in the spring of 1978. Consumer prices had doubled since 1967, and the dollar was continuing to decline in international monetary markets.

The impact of the 1979 crisis was more tangible and easily as dramatic as the embargo of a few years before. Weekend and even weekday closing of gas stations hit several large cities. At one point 90 percent of New York City's stations were shutting down early or were closed. California was hit the hardest; in May it took drivers up to five hours to fill their tanks. By the summer shortages struck other populous states. Rationing systems cropped up in several states as gasoline prices nudged toward $1 a gallon—unheard-of levels in the United States at the time. Again, panic psychology as well as real shortages aggravated the crisis, and many people continued to believe—with some justification—that the shortages were contrived.

President Carter called for less driving and more attention to thermostat settings in the home and at work. He also tried to use the crisis to recoup losses in his original energy plan. He outlined a new plan for phased decontrol, accompanied by a windfall profits tax for oil companies. The tax would be used to subsidize mass transit, develop "synfuels," and give energy-assistance funds to the poor. As leverage with a public suspicious of the oil companies, Carter noted: "Just as surely as the sun will rise the oil companies can be expected to fight to keep the profits they have not earned. Unless you speak out, they will have more influence on Congress than you do." The timing of the new proposal insured success. However, Carter had to shoulder the onus of higher prices due to decontrol, and the new Windfall Tax Act of 1980 was predictably unpopular with the oil companies (and others in the business world who saw it as an unsettling precedent). Neither businessmen nor government leaders had much to be optimistic about in 1980.[29]

Energy and the Environmental Movement in the 1970s

The embargo and the Iranian crisis raised serious questions about the supply and price of oil, but the onset of the "energy crisis" rested on more than these issues. Since the 1960s the environmental implications of energy had taken on major proportions, and the views of Americans had broadened. As Samuel P. Hays has pointed out, "The term 'environment' in contrast with the earlier term 'conservation' reflects more precisely the innovations of values."[30] Local protests led to the emergence of an organized movement. An emphasis on quality of life issues—greater appreciation of natural environments, more attention to health matters, and a better understanding of pollution—complemented or replaced narrower concerns over the squandering of resources.

More than in the past, public concern about the effects of environmental degradation was accompanied by interest in causation. Environmentalists, warning about "eco-disasters," questioned the economic, political, and social structure that produced these problems. As a counterweight to such protests, others—notably business leaders, government officials, and economists—warned about energy shortfalls, threats to national security, and the deterioration of the standard of living.

The roots of the modern environmental movement that arose in the 1960s were imbedded in the European and American pasts—conservation, preservationism, naturalism, antipollution, and public health campaigns. More recent origins of the movement can be found in "natural" environment issues such as outdoor recreation, wildlands, and open space; in concerns over environmental pollution; and in the maturing of ecology as a science. Its rise is also linked to the "sixties generation," in that some have argued that political and economic elites sponsored or supported environmental activities as a way of distracting protesters from antiwar, antipoverty, or civil rights activities. The political and social turmoil of the 1960s, on the other hand, presented an opportunity for raising questions about environmental protection and provided willing supporters. But the environmental movement was grounded in more than youthful idealism, functioning politically as a coalition of groups that cut across class lines and varying interests. Older preservationist groups—the Sierra Club (1892) and the National Audubon Society (1905)—experienced a revival of interest in the 1970s. More recent groups with corporate backing, such as Resources for the Future (early 1950s), promoted efficient utilization of resources. Legal remedies received attention from groups such as the Environmental Defense Fund (1967).[31]

Nothing epitomized the appeal of the environmental movement better than the celebration of Earth Day on 22 April 1970. On two thousand college campuses, in ten thousand high schools, and in parks and various open areas throughout the nation, as many as 20 million people celebrated purportedly "the largest, cleanest, most peaceful demonstration in America's history."[32] The Nixon administration gave its blessing to Earth Day. In his first State of the Union message, the President had declared: "Clean air, clean water, open spaces—these should be the birthright of every American."

On 1 January 1970—four months before Earth Day—Nixon signed the National Environmental Policy Act of 1969 (NEPA). The president initially had opposed the bill, but when it cleared the congressional conferees the administration embraced NEPA as its own. Though far from "the Magna Carta of environmental protection" that some people proclaimed, NEPA called for a new national responsibility for the environment. The "action-forcing" provision required federal agencies to prepare environmental impact statements (for public release) in advance of all major recommendations, reports, or actions on legislation germane to the environment. Also established was the Council on Environmental Quality to review government activities pertaining to the environment, to develop impact-statement guidelines, and to advise the President on environmental matters.[33]

In early 1970 a presidential council recommended the establishment of a Department of Natural Resources and the Environment to combine several departments and agencies. Nixon, though interested in streamlining the federal bureaucracy, was not prepared to accept the recommendation, but interdepartmental sniping between Interior and Commerce, and the rising tide of environmental politics, forced the President's hand. In June he authorized the establishment of the Environmental Protection Agency (EPA). It would not be granted cabinet status, but was given responsibility for antipollution programs and the evaluation of impact statements.[34]

By the end of 1970, environmentalism had gained national attention. For the remainder of the decade, however, the interplay between energy policy and environmental protection would be a key to the future of both. The energy crisis put into bold relief the conflict between increasing domestic oil and gas production and environmental protection. Questions of resource exploitation and conservation arose in response to concerns over long-term scarcity.

Exploring for oil in undeveloped regions—land and sea—set off debates over economic productivity versus preservation. The search for new sources of petroleum inevitably led to increased interest in offshore wells. Ocean drilling and greater tanker traffic also guaranteed more blowouts and spills like that off Santa Barbara. During 1975 alone there were twelve thousand reported spills resulting in 21 million gallons of oil dumped into United States waters.[35] In 1979 an explosion and fire at the Ixtoc well in the Gulf of Mexico created a spill that was the largest to that time and renewed the controversy over oil exploration along the continental shelf.

The major battle over oil production in the 1970s was fought on land, not in the sea—specifically over the Alaska pipeline. Atlantic Richfield struck a massive oil field at Prudhoe Bay in Alaska in 1968. In 1969 the federal government awarded leases in the area, but environmentalists fought hard against a pipeline projected to run 800 miles from Prudhoe Bay to the port of Valdez. The 1973 oil embargo undermined their case, and in that year Congress passed the Trans-Alaska Pipeline Authorization Act. The biggest blow to environmentalists was not the laying of the pipeline, however, but a provision declaring that a previous environmental impact statement—regarded as haphazard—satisfied the requirements of NEPA. The most pessimistic opponents of the pipeline bemoaned the weakening of NEPA. The more optimistic rationalized that the oil companies had been forced to modify their original plans to include environmental safeguards. [36]

Environmental protest against the petroleum industry and its allies extended to end-use. A general concern for clean air led to further revisions of the Clean Air Acts. A 1970 amendment dealt with both auto emissions and stationary sources of pollution, and became the most stringent air pollution law ever passed in the U.S. Implementation, however, was made difficult by a reluctant automobile industry. As a result of the 1973 energy crisis, the industry was given the help it needed to acquire an extension. Despite some minor adjustments, such as the mandated 55 mile-an-hour national speed limit to save gasoline, the energy crisis blunted enthusiasm for more stringest air pollution laws. [37]

Another dimension of the air pollution question involved the burning of coal. The energy crisis stimulated interest in America's most abundant energy source, but coal's environmental implications detracted from its possibilities as a panacea to the nation's energy woes. Two strip-mining control bills failed to get beyond President Ford's desk, but the Federal Strip Mining Control Act of 1977 was passed under the Carter administration. Ironically, the act passed at a time when the President was encouraging greater coal production to offset losses in petroleum supplies. [38]

About one month after enacting the strip-mining bill, Congress adopted a new set of Clean Air Amendments. Throughout the first half of the 1970s, postponements of mandated air-pollution standards, plus foot-dragging by utilities that burned coal, led to strengthening of the legislation. The most important change was the inclusion of the highly controversial "no significant deterioration" provision whereby reduction in air quality was not to be allowed in areas that currently had high air quality. Coal interests, utilities, and others fought the provisions, and further extensions for meeting the standards were granted. No clear winner emerged from this conflict between energy and environment. [39]

The conflict over nuclear power in the 1970s was an encounter between proponents of large, centralized systems and those suspicious of high technology and unrestrained economic growth. Both sides cited mountains of evidence; public debates and demonstrations were plentiful. This was warfare of a classic type.

The controversy developed on two levels: one centered on the nature of the energy source itself, the other on the role of centralized power. Debate on the first level revolved around the question of safety. To advocates, nuclear power had a spotless record; reactors incorporated the latest technology and were constructed under rigorous supervision. Opponents questioned these claims, arguing that accidents had occurred in the past but had been covered up—and were likely to happen in the future if the technology proliferated. Advocates stressed reactor safety, but opponents discussed the unreliability of technical safeguards and human error, looking beyond reactors to potential problems all along the production cycle from the mining of uranium to disposing of radioactive wastes.

On the second level, broader societal and institutional issues were at stake. Advocates touted nuclear power as an answer to the energy crisis and to OPEC's control of oil, characterizing dependence on coal as a greater environmental risk than nuclear power. But antinuclear groups, suspicious of centralized power production as manifest in large nuclear systems, argued that such production kept energy development in the hands of the government and big business and left consumers vulnerable to their whims. A move toward decentralized systems—especially solar energy—would not only reduce the need for nuclear power, but also weaken the trend toward corporate control of society.

Although the war of words grew more intense, environmentalists scored some important victories for the antinuclear cause. Interestingly, the Federal Court of Appeals nudged the AEC in the direction of greater attention to environmental costs. The case *Calvert Cliffs Coordinating Committee v. AEC* grew out of citizen protest against the Calvert Cliffs Nuclear Generating Station near Lusby, Maryland. In July 1971 the court found AEC procedures in violation of the NEPA mandate to make a detailed assessment of costs, benefits, and the environmental impact of nuclear power plants before licensing them. The decision expanded citizen input into the licensing procedure and forced the AEC to give greater latitude in serving the public interest as well as promoting the industry.[40]

The safety question still remained the most controversial, however. The AEC decision to push ahead with the breeder reactor raised serious questions about the production of highly toxic plutonium—a requisite ingredient in atomic weapons. Through the early 1970s the AEC had treated the safety program as an in-house matter, but this became more difficult as environmentalists demanded a public accounting. Particularly disruptive was an internal debate over the dangers of radioactivity that erupted after the 1969 publication of a report by Dr. Ernest J.

Sternglass. The report stated that radioactive fallout from atmospheric nuclear tests in Nevada in the 1950s could cause the deaths of 400,000 babies. Ultimately, the public furor over safety forced the AEC onto the defensive, leading to the Reactor Safety Study—or the Rasmussen Report (directed by MIT nuclear engineer Dr. Norman C. Rasmussen) in 1972. The AEC tried to give the study the appearance of independence, but it was largely an apologia for nuclear power. The Reactor Safety Study concluded that the risk from nuclear reactors was very small, and that chances of core melt-downs were particularly remote—1 in 20,000.

The AEC and industry officials broadcast the report's findings widely and received much favorable press attention. But criticism began almost immediately, challenging every aspect of the study from its methodology to its estimates. Contrary to AEC hopes, the Rasmussan Report raised more questions than it answered. But for nuclear advocates the report and the lack of any catastrophic accident was vindication or at least recognition that criticism of the safety program was unduly alarmist.[41]

If the Rasmussen Report proved useful in defending the safety programs of the AEC, the onset of the energy crisis offered the chance to promote nuclear power as a hedge against OPEC and the scarcity of oil. By late 1973 the five-fold increase in imported oil prices made nuclear power competitive again; one year later orders for light-water reactors reached a new peak. But almost as quickly as it rose, the nuclear power market collapsed. The drop in consumption in electricity as a result of the energy crisis was an ironic turn of events, reducing the need for new plants of any kind. The setback to the nuclear power industry was further aggravated by the break-up of AEC in 1974 and the division of its promotion and regulatory authorities. The nuclear power industry was also reeling in the wake of an accident at the Browns Ferry nuclear plant near Athens, Alabama, in 1975—the world's largest nuclear generating facility at the time—and an array of public protests by antinuclear forces at Seabrook, New Hampshire (1976), and elsewhere.

Whether the protests were effective in increasing support for the antinuclear cause is unclear. The economic realities of the mid-1970s may have been more significant in undermining nuclear power. Uncertainty about further construction of nuclear plants was aggravated by a growing number of safety problems at a variety of installations. Indicative that the whole issue of risk was in flux was NRC's announcement in January 1979 that, "The Commission does not regard as reliable the Reactor Safety Study's numerical estimate of overall risk of reactor accident." Changing circumstances in the nuclear power controversy since the issuance of the Rasmussen Report in 1975 was as responsible as anything for the NRC's change of heart.[43]

Under the circumstances the accident at Three Mile Island in March 1979 was not the departure point for a loss of faith in nuclear power, but the climax. America's worst nuclear accident took place at a plant located on Three Mile Island in the Susquehanna River about ten miles southwest of Harrisburg, Pennsylvania. Although no major catastrophe occurred, the aftermath of the accident was almost as dramatic as the event itself. As one observer noted, the accident was "red meat" for the press. Coverage was extensive and editorial responses were frequent and often strident. Public reaction ranged from relief to indignation. Antinuclear protesters held a new round of demonstrations. In May about 70,000 protesters staged an event at the Capitol to the strains of "Hell No, We Won't Glow!" Official response predictably came in a flood of investigations. Dartmouth president John Kemeny headed a presidential commission, which placed the blame on plant builders and managers, operators, and federal regulators, but fell short of recommending a moratorium on construction of new plants. Several congressional investigations followed.[44]

The accident seemed to have little effect, however, on the strongest proponents and opponents of nuclear power. Even an event as dramatic as the accident at Three Mile Island could do little more than leave the future of nuclear power uncertain, as it remained in the early 1980s. In 1979 seventy-two plants were operational, contributing only 14 percent of electrical production and only 4 percent of total energy consumption.

ALTERNATIVE ENERGY FUTURES

The debate over nuclear power is in part a microcosm of the much larger controversy over the role of energy in modern American society. Trying to determine what that role is and should be leads to questions about what society is and might become. Events of the 1970s resulted in vigorous soul-searching about "alternative energy futures." While the American public was mostly concerned with immediate energy needs, scholars, social commentators, scientists, public officials, and others produced numerous books, articles, reports, plans, scenarios, and strategies as guildelines for the passage through the third energy transition.

On a mundane level, the search for alternative energy futures led to a search for a new or little-utilized energy source to replace or complement those that were becoming scarce (or were perceived as scarce). Several untapped sources of fossil fuels were available, including the conversion of coal into gas or liquid, the liquefaction of shale to retrieve oil, the extraction of oil from tar sands, and efforts at tertiary recovery from oil deposits. Various forms of solar energy attracted considerable attention, as did geothermal energy, controlled thermonuclear fusion, the conversion of hydrogen into liquid, and other alternatives.

The debate over alternatives went beyond tangible issues of replacement of old fuels with new ones. As a Resource for the Future study stated, "Energy has become the testing ground for conflict over broader social choices." Several long-held values and traditions came under scrutiny. Issues no less monumental than individual rights and freedoms, economic equity, the preservation of the environment, the role of government, and world peace were introduced into the debate over America's energy future.

The convergence of the environmental movement and the energy crisis made economic growth a focus for debate. The issue was not new. In the 1960s population growth had become a highly publicized issue. Kenneth Boulding criticized unrestrained growth as reckless, and pioneered the concept of "spaceship earth." A "spaceship economy"—an economy of limited resources—took into account the finite nature of the world's resources, suggesting a move away from the idea of unlimited growth. This was an early form of "ecological economics," which placed emphasis on social and political equity as well as economic growth.[45]

With the onset of the energy crisis, the debate over growth moved beyond environmental issues to include energy issues. Of particular concern were alternative energy futures for the United States. Proponents of continued energy growth noted the past benefits—comfort, material well-being, high employment, and more leisure time. They maintained a faith in the market mechanism to adjust to scarce resources, to produce technical fixes in exploiting available energy sources, and to create or discover new sources. Opponents of unlimited growth questioned economic practices leading to more material goods, rather than better services or an improved quality of life.

Some critics stressed the social and political consequences of unlimited growth. Complex, centralized systems that produced and sustained growth might threaten personal liberty, even the democratic process. Several major adjustments might be employed to redress these potential and real inequities: steering growth away from resource-intensive industries, redistributing income, giving higher priority to quality-of-life interests. In essence the effort to limit growth would require a shift in values.

An important popularization of the more extreme no-growth or anti-growth view was E. F. Schumacher's *Small is Beautiful: Economics as if People Mattered* [1973]. Schumacher criticized governmental and economic bigness and centralization, and lauded communal, human-scaled, decentralized cultures. He blamed society's commitment to unlimited economic growth, high technology, and consumerism for the social and economic ills of the world.

Schumacher's message captured the spirit of the counter-culture of the 1960s. However, it did little more than pillory modern society in ways that it had been criticized before. Amory B. Lovins—a young American physicist living in Britain, representative of the Friends of the Earth and ardent opponent of nuclear power—focused the anti-growth debate on the energy issue with his article "Energy Strategy: The Road Not Taken?" published in *Foreign Affairs* in 1976. In his various works Lovins presented a critique of contemporary energy systems and offered a radical alternative. Lovins stated that the policy of sustaining growth in energy consumption and limiting imports was no answer at all. Instead, he recommended an "end-use orientation," that is, to determine "how much of what kind of energy is needed to do the task for which the energy is desired, and then supplying exactly that kind." [46] In Lovins's eyes the energy problem was not so much tied to the source as to the society that used it. A significant social change, he reasoned, was necessary to get off the "hard energy path" and onto the "soft energy path." Hard energy paths were "high-energy, nuclear, centralized, electric"; soft paths were "lower-energy, fission-free, decentralized, less electrified."[47]

Lovins's dichotomy between hard and soft energy paths attracted considerable attention and controversy. Some energy experts refined the construct or borrowed from it in touting their own energy strategies for the future.[48] Numerous other reports tried to promote alternative perspectives, including "consensus" positions, "balanced" energy programs, and so forth.[49]

Advocates of the hard path—or critics of the soft path (these were not necessarily the same)—questioned Lovins's defense of "appropriate" technology and his decentralist position. It was common for critics to characterize the decentralist approach as "romantic" or simply the promotion of "post-industrial pastoral society." Samuel C. Florman—engineer, commentator, proponent of centralization, and critic of "the anti-technological backlash"—responded to the decentralist argument in a chapter entitled "Small is Dubious": " 'Smallness,' after all, is a word that is neutral—technologically, socially, aesthetically, and, of course, morally. Its use as a symbol of goodness would be one more entertaining example of human folly were it not for the disturbing consequences of the arguments advanced in its cause."[50]

Extremes, whether posed by Lovins or his opponents, stimulated debate over alternate energy futures, but did not undercut more modest appraisals, especially by pragmatists who tried to emphasize the differences among short-term, intermediate, and long-term energy requirements and goals. In the modern era, energy issues were also worldwide in scope and impact. Some critics could not reconcile a decentralization plan with that fact. Several studies favoring a new direction did not begin with the premise that Lovins's view offered the only hope for the nation. Instead, they argued that United States energy prospects were not likely to change dramatically overnight, and thus goals for the immediate future were most pressing.

The nation faced confounding choices by 1980. The options were at once complex and specific, practical and revolutionary. A pessimist looked at the intensity of the energy debate and saw an insurmountable problem. An optimist saw in the energy debate the first real effort to come to grips with the nation's energy requirements, environmental concerns, and future needs. In contrast to the early nineteenth century, the place of energy in American life seemed gigantic, unwieldy, and imposing in the 1970s. In the age of abundance, energy had been easier to take for granted. The threat of scarcity took away that luxury.

RESURRECTION OF "AMERICA THE ABUNDANT"

The tone of impending doom that pervaded the nation in the 1970s seemed to subside almost as quickly as it rose. In the early 1980s, some commentators were trumpeting the declining consumption of oil and other fuels and the loosening grip of OPEC as signs that the energy crisis was fading. The report of the President's Commission for a National Agenda for the Eighties (1980), appointed by Carter, asserted that the nation's energy predicament was not yet resolved, but, it added, "Past reliance on the rhetoric of crisis has probably harmed the nation's ability to cope with its energy problems because Americans soon discovered that predictions of imminent catastrophe did not materialize."

In the aftermath of the energy crisis and in the midst of a cautious optimism about the nation's energy present, conservative Ronald Reagan became the thirty-ninth President of the United States. The new president offered the country "the elixir of 'supply-side economics' mixed with a strong draught of military spending" to cure its economic woes in 1981.[51] Reagan's approach to government was built on faith in the productive capacity of the United States—not a fear of future energy shortages.

Within the next few years, oil prices stabilized and even declined as a result of an international oil glut. Experts warned about the transitory nature of the consumers' boom—and the possible financial repercussions—but it was difficult not to breathe a little easier. When the American economy began to climb out of the recession, it seemed that the decade of the 1970s was eons away.[52] The National Energy Policy Plan, announced on 4 October 1983, formally abandoned the goal of U.S. energy independence set in the 1970s. Energy Secretary Donald Hodel asserted: "This plan does not contemplate total self-sufficiency. This contemplates working toward what I would call energy non-dependence, in which we continue to import where that makes economic sense, but not to the extent that an interruption undercuts our economy or our military capability."[53]

The return of optimism in the early 1980s may have been temporary, but it suggested that historic forces have had a stronger impact on the nation's energy present than the fading memories of the energy crisis. The United States did not move quickly toward a post-petroleum economy after 1979, and aside from some conservation of gasoline, electricity, and home heating fuels, Americans did not lose faith in America the Abundant.

During the energy crisis, policy makers were obsessed with the role of the United States as a consumer of energy. In the early 1980s, the Reagan administration attempted to swing the pendulum back by focusing on energy production, utilizing the economic hard times to justify more intense energy exploration and to deregulate private energy supplies. The primary force behind the administration's faith in private development of energy was a reaffirmation of the historic role of government as promoter of economic growth. What it rejected was the additional role of regulator and intervener. The Reagan administration's market orientation did not lead to unrestrained competition in the energy field. There was no attempt to tamper with the multinationals and large oil independents or to frustrate oil companies from diversifying into other energy sources—namely coal and nuclear power. The primary goal was to remove governmental impediments to corporate action in the hope of stimulating economic growth. Immediate decontrol of natural gas was put off, for example. And the administration jealously guarded the central role of the federal government in the promotion of nuclear power.

In some ways the Reagan administration tried to make good on its pledge to reduce regulatory impediments to energy production—as in the case of lifting controls on gasoline, propane and crude in January 1981—and to streamline the federal energy bureaucracy—especially by attempting to dismantle the DOE—but with little attention to long-range future energy needs. It clearly had an aversion to "planning" as a way of setting policy, placing faith in supply-side approaches to expanding domestic energy production.

Although energy and environment were inextricably linked as issues in the 1970s, the setting for debate changed markedly in the early 1980s. Environmental groups were well entrenched within the economic and political institutions of the United States, but their power and influence was still largely dependent on the tone and actions of government. In the 1960s and 1970s, the federal government may not have always led the way in environmental issues, but it had paid lip service to many environmentalist goals. The notion of "environmental costs" came to be included in almost every discussion of energy policy. The Reagan administration, however, demonstrated a cavalier attitude toward the environment, which some people characterized as antienvironmental. In some cases environmental risks from energy exploration and development were dismissed or ignored. Conquering recession and restoring American world prestige, the President believed, were more important than the wants of over-sensitive preservationists. The appointment of James G. Watt as Secretary of the Interior and Anne McGill Burford (formerly Gorsuch) to head the EPA were clear reminders of where the adminstration's priorities stood. Watt, in particular, symbolized the commitment to economic growth at all costs.[54]

Despite the return of a short-term view of energy policy under the Reagan administration, signs of the third energy transition did not totally disappear. Energy experts were quick to point out that the nation had experienced a "fuel" scarcity rather than a full-fledged "energy crisis" in the 1970s. In an absolute sense, there was plenty of energy to be exploited, but a fuel scarcity was a very serious matter. At least the energy crisis helped to dispel the notion that American energy sources were inexhaustible. It also was becoming apparent that energy-use habits over the years had strongly influenced American culture. Not only had the United States become a petroleum-based society in the twentieth century, but it had become the most energy-intensive society on earth. It was committed to a one-dimensional transportation system dominated by the automobile and utterly dependent on electrical power. Industry was increasingly mechanized and much less labor-intensive. Thus, the emerging culture was fragile in key ways despite its apparent strengths.[55]

That the transition was in its early stages in the 1970s is borne out by several contradictions. For example, higher fuel costs encouraged some conservation, but the United States continued to depend on foreign oil supplies. In 1980 imports dropped by 20 percent; between April 1981 and April 1982, by 36 percent. Yet imports still accounted for one-fourth of the nation's petroleum needs. The automobile continued as the mainstay of American transportation with no challengers. The control of oil by OPEC and other foreign powers forced the United States at least to explore alternative energy sources, but renewed optimism in the early 1980s worked against crash programs. This suggests the tentativeness with which Americans have entered the third transition. A quick rise in gasoline prices or a sudden drop in supply could revitalize the turn toward alternatives.

The onset of the third energy transition reveals some change in values—albeit subtle—linked to energy. The debate over centralized versus decentralized energy systems has been most revealing about changing attitudes. An intriguing example is the interest in local self-reliance and the generation of "neighborhood [electrical] power." While advocates of self-reliance overstate their successes, the activities of the Institute for Local Self-Reliance and similar groups gained national attention. Local self-reliance goes beyond energy questions, but the establishment of "humanly scaled" energy systems is an integral part of the program. Cogeneration technology—or the simultaneous production of electricity and usable heat—is at the heart of the self-reliance approach, which got an important boost when Congress passed the Public Utility Regulatory Act of 1978 (PURPA). To encourage the use of cogeneration and renewable resources for power production, PURPA required utility companies to purchase electricity from independent power producers and to provide backup power at low cost. Independent power producers were also exempted from state and federal regulation. Curiously, this unique movement captured the spirit of limited federal intervention advocated by the Reagan administration, but it was committed to the the decentralist view critical of the corporate interests that the administration supported.

Like previous transitions the latest has been gradual and sporadic in its early stages, but it is unique in one important respect: the sense of improvement, which accompanied the change from wood / water to coal and from coal to oil, is not as intense. Because the third energy transition grew out of a fear of oil scarcity, rather than through a change from one abundant energy source to another, maintaining the prevailing standard of living is a central concern. That the scarcity of oil was treated as a resolvable crisis and that oil continued to be regarded as essential to maintaining the status quo, indicate that long-held views toward energy are not so rapidly abandoned. The contradictions of the latest transition suggest its complexity as well as its potential for becoming the most significant in American history.

1. The following seven companies controlled virtually all of the reserves in less-developed regions of the world and a large share in developed countries: British Petroleum, Royal Dutch-Shell, Mobil (Socony-Vacuum), Exxon (Standard of New Jersey), Socal, Texaco, and Gulf.

2. Robert B. Krueger, *The United States and International Oil* (New York, 1975), 56-58; Mira Wilkins, *The Maturing of Multinational Enterprise: American Business Abroad from 1914 to 1970* (Cambridge, Mass., 1974), 315-16; Frank R. Wyant, *The United States, OPEC, and Multinational Oil* (Lexington, Mass., 1977), 20-27, 58-60.

3. Loring Allen, *OPEC Oil* (Cambridge, Mass., 1979), 54-57; Ian Seymour, *OPEC: Instrument of Change* (London, 1980), 53-54; Wyant, *The United States, OPEC, and Multinational Oil*, 65-69; Krueger, *The United States and International Oil*, 58-61; Wilkins, *The Maturing of Multinational Enterprise*, 366ff.

4. Benjamin Shwadran, *The Middle East and the Great Powers* (New York, 1973), 513-15; Ali D. Johany, *The Myth of the OPEC Cartel: The Role of Saudi Arabia* (New York, 1980), 6-7; Joseph S. Szyliowicz and Bard E. O'Neill, eds., *The Energy Crisis and U.S. Foreign Policy* (New York, 1975), 91-96.

5. Wyant, *The United States, OPEC, and Multinational Oil*, 70-72; Krueger, *The United States and International Oil*, 61-63; Johany, *The Myth of the OPEC Cartel*, 9-10.

6. See Douglas R. Bohi and Milton Russell, *Limiting Oil Imports* (Baltimore, 1978).

7. William J. Barber, "Studied Inaction in the Kennedy Years," in Craufurd D. Goodwin, ed., *Energy Policy in Perspective* (Washington, D.C., 1981), 287-335.

8. See James L. Cochrane, "Energy Policy in the Johnson Administration: Logical Order versus Economic Pluralism," in Goodwin, ed., *Energy Policy in Perspective*, 337-93.

9. Marc Messing, H. Paul Friesema, and David Morell, *Centralized Power: The Politics of Scale in Electricity Generation* (Cambridge, Mass., 1979), 19-29, 45-48. See also Charles J. Johnson, *Coal Demand in the Electric Utility Industry, 1946-1990* (New York, 1979).

10. Messing, Friesema, and Morell, *Centralized Power*, 48-62.

11. See A. M. Rosenthal and Arthur Gelb, eds., *The Night the Lights Went Out* (New York, 1965); William Rodgers, *Brown-out: The Power Crisis in America* (New York, 1972).

12. Goodwin, ed., *Energy Policy in Perspective*, 332-35, 364-67, 398-400.

13. Richard F. Hirsh, "Conserving Kilowatts: The Electric Power Industry in Transition," *Materials and Society* 7 (1983):295-305.

14. Steven L. Del Sesto, *Science, Politics, and Controversy: Civilian Nuclear Power in the United States, 1946-1974* (Boulder, Colo., 1979), 76ff; S. David Aviel, *The Politics of Nuclear Energy* (Washington, D.C., 1982), 30-41; Robert Perry, *Development and Commercialization of the Light Water Reactor, 1946-1976* (Santa Monica, Calif., 1977), 80-83; Wendy Allen, *Nuclear Reactors for Generating Electricity: U. S. Development from 1946 to 1963* (Santa Monica, Calif., 1977), v-x, 76-80.

15. Joseph M. Petulla, *American Environmental History* (San Francisco, 1977), 340-41.

16. Richard H. K. Vietor, *Environmental Politics and the Coal Coalition* (College Station, Tex., 1980), 58-84.

17. Ibid., 127-54. See also Johnson, *Coal Demand in the Electric Utility Industry*, 152-70; Gail Greenberg, *The Coal Industry: Where To?* (Stamford, Conn., n.d.), 121-25.

18. U.S. Department of Commerce, *The Automobile and Air Pollution* (Washington, D.C., 1967), 1-28; Rex R. Campbell and Jerry L. Wade, eds., *Society and Environment: The Coming Collision* (Boston, 1972), 145-62; Alfred J. Van Tassel, ed., *Our Environment: The Outlook for 1980* (Lexington, Mass., 1973), 336ff.

19. Edward W. Lawless, *Technology and Social Shock* (New Brunswick, N. J., 1977), 233-45; James Ridgeway, *The Politics of Ecology* (New York, 1970), 147-60. See also Carol E. Steinhart and John Steinhart, *Blowout: A Case Study of the Santa Barbara Oil Spill* (New York, 1972); Lee Dye, *Blowout at Platform A* (New York, 1971).

20. Frank G. Dawson, *Nuclear Power: Development and Management of a Technology* (Seattle, 1976), 176-96; George T. Mazuzan, "Conflict of Interest: Promoting and Regulating the Infant Nuclear Power Industry, 1954-1956," *Historian* 44 (November 1981):1-14; William Thomas Keating, *Politics, Technology, and the Environment: Technology Assessment and Nuclear Energy* (New York, 1979), 41-51; Robert Gillette, "Nuclear Safety: The Roots of Dissent," *Science* 177 (1 September 1972):771-76; Gillette, "Nuclear Safety: The Years of Delay," *Science* 177 (8 September 1972):867-71; Del Sesto, *Science, Politics and Controversy*, 76ff; Aviel, *The Politics of Nuclear Energy*, 15ff; Allen, *Nuclear Reactors for Generating Electricity*, 76-80.

21. Anthony Sampson, *The Seven Sisters* (New York, 1981), 274-380; John M. Blair, *The Control of Oil* (New York, 1976), 261-93; Neil H. Jacoby, *Multinational Oil* (New York, 1974), 257-307; Krueger, *The United States and International Oil*, 63-74; Wyant, *The United States, OPEC, and Multinational Oil*, 74-83; Szyliowicz and O'Neill, eds., *Energy Crisis and U. S. Foreign Policy*, 96-109, 208-10; Allen, *OPEC Oil*, 1-23, 67-104.

22. Johany, *The Myth of the OPEC Cartel*, 54-58; Sampson, *The Seven Sisters*, 381-93.

23. Goodwin, ed., *Energy Policy in Perspective*, 476; Sidney Sonenblum, "Patterns of Energy Consumption," in Melvin Kranzberg, Timothy A. Hall, and Jane L. Scheiber, *Energy and the Way We Live* (San Francisco, 1980), 45-46.

24. Richard H. K. Vietor, "Too Little, Too Much: Market Disequilibrium and Business-Government Relations in Oil Policy, 1947-1980" (Paper delivered at the Conference on Energy in American History, Mountain Lake, Va., 1982), 8-10; Wyant, *The United States, OPEC, and Multinational Oil*, 127-33; Neil De Marchi, "Energy Policy under Nixon: Mainly Putting Out Fires," in Goodwin, ed., *Energy Policy in Perspective*, 395-473; Roger M. Anders, *The Federal Energy Administration* (Washington, D.C., 1980), 1-4.

25. Neil De Marchi, "The Ford Administration: Energy as a Political Good," in Goodwin, ed., *Energy Policy in Perspective*, 475-545; Alice L. Buck, *A History of the Energy Research and Development Administration* (Washington, D.C., 1982), 2-3; Vietor, "Too Little, Too Much," 10-11.

26. Robert A. Divine, *Since 1945* (New York, 1979), 222-23.

27. Vietor, "Too Little, Too Much," 11-13; James L. Cochrane, "Carter Energy Policy and the Ninety-fifth Congress," in Goodwin, ed., *Energy Policy in Perspective*, 547-600; Council on Energy Resources, University of Texas *National Energy Policy Issues* (Austin, Tex., 1979), 1-50.

28. *Time*, 19 June 1978. See also Jack M. Holl, *The United States Department of Energy: A History* (Washington, D.C., 1982).

29. *Time*, 16 April 1979, 67; Joseph A. Yager, "The Energy Battles of 1979," in Goodwin, ed., *Energy Policy in Perspective*, 601-36.

30. Samuel P. Hays, "From Conservation to Environment: Environmental Politics in the United States Since World War II," *Environmental Review* 6 (Fall 1982):17.

31. Richard N. L. Andrews, "Class Politics or Democratic Reform: Environmentalism and American Political Institutions," *Natural Resources Journal* 20 (April 1980):221-41. For a contrasting view, see William Tucker, *Progress and Privilege: America in the Age of Environmentalism* (New York, 1982). See also Walter A. Rosenbaum, *The Politics of Environmental Concern* (New York, 1973); Odom Fanning, *Man and His Environment: Citizen Action* (New York: 1975); Allen Schnaiberg, *The Environment: From Surplus to Scarcity* (New York, 1980); Michael Allaby, *The Eco-Activists: Youth Fights for a Human Environment* (London, 1971).

32. National Staff of Environmental Action, eds., *Earth Day—The Beginning* (New York, 1970).

33. Public Law 91-190, 42 U. S. Code 4321-4347(1 January 1970). See also Lettie McSpadden Wenner, "The Misuse and Abuse of NEPA," *Environmental Review* 7 (Fall 1983):229-54; Richard A. Liroff, *A National Policy for the Environment: NEPA and Its Aftermath* (Bloomington, Ind., 1976); Frederick R. Anderson, *NEPA in the Courts* (Baltimore, 1973).

34. See John Quarles, *Cleaning Up America: An Insider's View of the Environmental Protection Agency* (Boston, 1976).

35. Joseph M. Petulla, *American Environmentalism: Values, Tactics, Priorities* (College Station, Tex., 1980), 162-64.

36. See Mary Clay Berry, *The Alaskan Pipeline* (Bloomington, Ind., 1975).

37. Donald N. Dewees, *Economics and Public Policy: The Automobile Pollution Case* (Cambridge, Mass., 1974), 1-37, 145-46; Ian G. Barbour, *Technol-*

ogy, Environment, and Human Values (New York, 1980), 136-41; James E. Krier and Edmund Ursin, *Pollution and Policy: A Case Essay on California and Federal Experience with Motor Vehicle Air Pollution, 1940-1975* (Berkeley, 1977), 199-247; Vietor, *Environmental Politics and the Coal Coalition*, 156-93.

38. Greenberg, *The Coal Industry*, 128; Vietor, *Environmental Politics and the Coal Coalition*, 112-26.

39. Vietor, *Environmental Politics and the Coal Coalition*, 197-226. See also Bruce A. Ackerman, *Clean Coal/ Dirty Air* (New Haven, Conn., 1981).

40. Daniel Ford, *The Cult of the Atom* (New York, 1982), 133-34; George T. Mazuzan and Roger R. Trask, *An Outline History of Nuclear Regulation and Licensing, 1946-1979* (Washington, D.C., 1979), 70ff; Del Sesto, *Science, Politics and Controversy*, 156-59.

41. Elizabeth S. Rolph, *Nuclear Power and Public Safety* (Lexington, Mass., 1979), 144-45; Norman Metzger, *Energy: The Continuing Crisis* (New York, 1977), 133-36; Desaix Myers III, *The Nuclear Power Debate* (New York, 1977), 92-105. Aviel, *Politics of Nuclear Energy*, 199-200; Dawson, *Nuclear Power*, 210-15; Ford, *The Cult of the Atom*, 137-73.

42. Duncan Burn, *Nuclear Power and the Energy Crisis* (New York, 1978), 82-92; Ford, *The Cult of the Atom*, 223-29; Del Sesto, *Science, Politics and Controversy*, 193ff; Perry, *Development and Commercialization of the Light Water Reactor*, 82-87.

43. Cited in Ford, *The Cult of the Atom*, 172.

44. See Philip L. Cantelon and Robert C. Williams, *Crisis Contained: The Department of Energy at Three Mile Island* (Carbondale, Ill., 1982); Daniel Martin, *Three Mile Island: Prologue or Epilogue?* (Cambridge, Mass., 1980); Daniel Ford, *Three Mile Island: Thirty Minutes to Meltdown* (New York, 1982).

45. See Hazel Henderson, "Ecologists versus Economists," *Harvard Business Review* 51 (July 1973):28-36, 152-57; Robert T. Roelofs, Joseph N. Crowley, Donald C. Hardasty, eds., *Environment and Science* (Englewood Cliffs, N. J. 1974), 113ff; Carl Solberg, *Oil Power* (New York, 1976), 222-25; Petulla, *American Environmentalism*, 75ff, 121-23; Mancur Olson and Hans H. Lansberg, eds., *The No-Growth Society* (New York, 1973), 1-13; William Ophuls, *Ecology and the Politics of Scarcity* (San Francisco, 1977); Barbour, *Technology, Environment, and Human Values*, 274ff.

46. Amory B. Lovins, *Soft Energy Paths* (Cambridge, Mass., 1977), 3ff.

47. Amory B. Lovins and John H. Price, *Non-Nuclear Futures* (Cambridge, Mass., 1975), xxii. See also Hugh Nash, ed., *The Energy Controversy: Soft Path Questions and Answers* (San Francisco, 1979).

48. See James Ridgeway and Bettina Conner, *New Energy* (Boston, 1975); Lewis J. Perelman, "Speculations on the Transition to Sustainable Energy," in Lewis J. Perelman, August W. Giebelhaus, and Michael D. Yokell, eds., *Energy Transitions: Long-Term Perspectives* (Boulder, Colo, 1981), 185-213; David Morris, *Self-Reliant Cities* (San Franciso, 1982).

49. See RFF, National Energy Strategies Project, *Energy in America's Future* (Baltimore, 1979); Robert Stobaugh and Daniel Yergin, *Energy Future* (New York, 1979); Energy Policy Project, Ford Foundation, *A Time to Choose:*

America's Energy Future (Cambridge, Mass., 1974); Committee on Nuclear and Alternative Energy Systems, National Research Council, *Energy in Transition, 1985-2010* (Washington, D.C., 1980).

50. Samuel C. Florman, *Blaming Technology* (New York, 1981), 96. See also Henry Petroski, "Soft Energy Technology is Hard," *Technology Review* 85 (April 1982):39.

51. William E. Leuchtenburg, *A Troubled Feast: American Society Since 1945* (Rev. ed. Boston, 1983), 283.

52. For example, see *Newsweek*, 18 May 1981, 32-33; 14 September 1981, 74-75.

53. Houston *Post*, 5 October 1983, D-1.

54. *Newsweek*, 5 January 1981, 17; *Time*, 14 September 1981, 18; 21 February 1983, 14-16; 28 February 1983, 17; *New York Times*, 27 March 1983, E5.

55. See John Tirman, "Investing in the Energy Transition: From Oil to What?" *Technology Review* 85 (April 1982):65-72.

America and the World Economy

Mira Wilkins

The world economy of 1960-62 seemed smaller, more compact, than ever in history. In 1958 the first commercial jet crossed the Atlantic, making foreign countries more accessible. The television set brought distant economic events into American living rooms. For the American traveler, prices abroad were low. The dollar was strong. America enjoyed military, moral, and economic leadership. The existing world system was an American creation.

After the Second World War, unlike the time following World War I when the United States had not joined the League of Nations, the country had taken the lead in the United Nations, in the specialized agencies associated with it, in the reconstruction of Europe, and in encouraging worldwide development. Those Americans who had lived through the 1930s and World War II knew what they wanted: a world that was materially affluent for their offspring. America was committed to an open world economy. Economic growth of countries abroad would provide an environment for democracy to flourish. It would aid U.S. economic growth, for as others developed, countries would buy more of our exports. There was little concern over imports. American industry, technology, and leadership seemed invulnerable. *Giant Among Nations*, the title of Peter Kenen's 1960 book on U.S. foreign economic policy, reflected Americans' perception of the nation's stature.[1]

In the early 1960s, Americans remained pledged to freer trade, increasing foreign aid, and more foreign investment. Free trade would assist the world economy. So would foreign aid. Other nations' growth would mean the economic pie would become larger and everyone would gain. Even more than foreign aid, Americans favored foreign investment, which came from the private sector (there would be no burden on the taxpayer). U.S. companies should be encouraged to invest abroad, contributing to the process of world development.[2]

In the post-World War II years, the United States led the world economy. At Bretton Woods in 1944, in planning for the peace, two organizations had been proposed that would become specialized agencies of the United Nations. Like the United Nations itself, they would be headquartered in the United States. They were designed to establish a framework for the growth of world trade and output. The first was the International Monetary Fund (IMF), which provided the rules for what became known as the Bretton Woods system. The IMF envisaged a world where each currency had a fixed par value and all were freely convertible. Each country would select a value for its currency and then move toward convertibility. The multiplicity of foreign exchange restrictions that had been introduced in the 1930s and during World War II would be lifted; convertible currencies (that is, convertible into one another) would provide ease of payments to assist the expansion of international trade. The dollar was central to the Bretton Woods system. The values of all currencies were to be set against the dollar, which in turn had its value set against gold at $35.00 an ounce. Currencies could be adjusted in their relation to the dollar; there was, however, nothing in the system that provided for an adjustment of the value of the dollar itself.

The Bretton Woods agreement established the International Monetary Fund to cope with short-term balance of payments problems and to help countries maintain fixed rates and convertible currencies. It set the basis for international monetary cooperation. The agreement had been drafted and prepared by an American (Harry Dexter White) and to a lesser extent by a Britisher (John Maynard Keynes). International collaboration would substitute for earlier autarkic policies. By the early 1960s, the major industrial countries had adopted fixed rates for their currencies and achieved convertibility.[3] The system was working. The IMF recognized that less developed countries could protect their currencies with exchange controls; what was important was that the major trading countries eliminate foreign exchange restrictions. Ease of payments and known values of currencies by the early 1960s were raising the volume of international trade. The dollar was central to the whole system—the key currency.[4]

The second Bretton Woods institution was the International Bank for Reconstruction and Development (IBRD), otherwise known as the World Bank. Whereas the IMF was to focus on short-term imbalances related to temporary payments difficulties, the World Bank had a broader mandate. European recovery was its first priority; economic development in the rest of the world, its second. It had not proved adequate to the immense task of European reconstruction, and American foreign aid, through the Marshall Plan, had offered the needed spur for European recovery. By the years 1960-62, European output far exceeded any past period. In 1957, with the Treaty of Rome, France, Germany, Italy, Holland, Belgium, and Luxembourg had joined in the European Economic Community (EEC), the Common Market,[5] and rapid economic growth seemed assured.[6] Likewise, by the early 1960s the American-assisted Japanese economic recovery had been completed and expansion was in process.[7] The World Bank was devoting itself to its second task, that of development. At the same time, American foreign aid was now going to less developed countries, in far greater amounts than the aid from the World Bank.[8] In 1961 the Latin American Free Trade Area (LAFTA) had come into being. LAFTA sought to encourage trade and development in that region. Americans were committed to the Alliance for Progress, which would complement Latin Americans' efforts on their own behalf. Just as the Marshall Plan had offered the stimulus for the growth of European prosperity, so, it was thought, the Alliance for Progress would provide that extra impetus for Latin America. Once again, Americans were in the lead, assuming responsibility.[9]

In 1948-49 plans had been made for a third specialized agency of the United Nations to deal with international trade. The IMF would handle payments; the World Bank, reconstruction and development; the International Trade Organization (ITO) would aid commerce. The U.S. Congress never approved America's membership in the ITO, and the latter never came into existence. While ITO ratification was pending, a General Agreement for Tariffs and Trade, which did not need approval by the U.S. Congress, went into provisional operation in January 1948. GATT was a loose arrangement, providing a forum for discussions on ways of reducing tariffs and other trade barriers.[10] It became the institutional basis for international deliberations on freer world trade. In the 1950s America was in the forefront in the various rounds of GATT negotiations. With the passage in this country in 1962 of the Trade Expansion Act, the United States provided an example to the world, taking the initiative in lowering its tariffs. Its trade liberalization policy received wide support in the United States from corporations, organized labor, and consumer groups.[11]

American business participated in the general consensus that saw the United States as the world leader. Many U.S. corporations had long had international investments. In the 1930s and during World War II, these American multinationals had experienced losses and frustrations.[12] In the immediate postwar years, they had had to rebuild their overseas organizations while meeting pent-up demands at home. The U.S. government approved of American companies participating in the reconstruction of Europe, developing oil in the Middle East (to meet western Europe's needs), and then partaking in more general business abroad.[13] By 1960-62 American enterprises did not require U.S. government support as they sought out opportunities. The new European Economic Community seemed especially promising. As one American executive, just back from Europe, remarked in May 1962, "People say there may be hydrogen bombs; there may be Russian expansion; there may be war; but no one says the Common Market may fail."[14] Thus, in 1960-62 American corporations were looking first and foremost to investments in thriving Europe; secondarily, they were also considering new stakes in less developed countries. In Europe they invested to meet rising demands. In less developed countries, governments were increasing (rather than lowering) the barriers to trade. If they expected to maintain or to enlarge their activities in those markets, companies would have to invest in manufacturing in countries to which they had earlier exported. Whereas for many years American enterprises had made their largest investments in the less developed world in primary products (from bananas to copper to oil), by 1960 in Latin America, U.S. businessmen already had bigger stakes in manufacturing than in agriculture or mining.[15]

In the postwar years, many less developed countries had cast off colonialism and become independent. The Philippines became independent in 1946, India in 1947, Indonesia in 1949. From the late 1950s, beginning with Ghana, numerous colonies in Africa became new nations. The giant empires of the British, Dutch, and French dissolved. America, itself once a colony, now a leader, strongly favored the decolonization process.

In short, in 1960-62, within the United States there was a buoyancy. At home the postwar years had been prosperous. The recessions of 1949 and 1954 were shortlived and far from serious; Americans had recovered

Reprinted with permission of the *Miami Herald*.

from the brief 1958 and even briefer 1960 downturns. Certainly all was not perfect in the world economy; there were large sections of the globe not part of the American-led world economy; China was isolated, Eastern Europe was in the Russian orbit, and Russia was threatening (with the Cuban missile crisis and the Berlin Wall). Deficits had appeared in the U.S. balance of payments in the late 1950s and were persisting. It was clear, moreover, that Americans could not always get their way even in friendly parts of the world. The principal oil-producing, less developed countries had joined together in the new Organization of Petroleum Exporting Countries (1960), and had succeeded in preventing the international oil companies from lowering the posted price of oil (the posted price was the one on which host country revenues were calculated).[16] The outcome of the Korean War (1950-53) and early difficulties in Vietnam provided warning signs that American leadership was not, and would not always be, accepted. Yet such signs failed to dilute the pervasive sense of progress, excitement, and optimism. Fifteen years after the end of World War I, America had been in the depths of depression. Fifteen years after the end of World War II, the country was affluent. The young and handsome John F. Kennedy personified America's greatness in the world economy. Americans who had fought in World War II and returned home to have large families were seeing their children grow up in comfort at home and in a world where American-stimulated economic progress was the norm. America was in the lead; from Britain to Brazil, from Germany to Ghana, from Italy to India, the American dollar, the American traveler, the American diplomat, and the American businessman were ubiquitous. Sputnik notwithstanding, America's overall technological and economic supremacy was unquestioned. Economic growth seemed eternal and inevitable.

THE 1960s

The world in the 1960s was a global village. America was committed to lead, to fight communism in Vietnam, and to aid less developed countries in their task of economic development. At home the country could have a Great Society, while American expenditures abroad financed the world economy. U.S. business investments in Europe were called the "American Challenge."[17] Some U.S. multinational enterprises had revenues greater than the gross national products of individual countries.[18] American business's accomplishment was that of superior management methods and technological advantage.

The 1960s saw more rapid world economic growth than ever in history. This was evident in industrial and less developed countries. Europe became awash in dollars, which aided economic expansion. These dollars became the basis for a Euro-dollar market, a market in which dollars (and then other currencies as well) were used outside their home countries. These monies helped finance the multitude of new ventures requiring capital.[19] By 1968 the European Economic Community was a success, with free movement of goods, men, and monies within the six-nation grouping. OPEC had prevented the lowering of the posted price of oil, but its market price had dropped. From Venezuela to Saudi Arabia, U.S. multinational companies raised oil output. Cheap oil made possible the vigorous economic growth. The 1960s was the first decade in history when, for the world economy, oil exceeded coal as an energy source.[20]

The United Nations called the 1960s the "First Development Decade." American expenditures abroad, new technology, U.S. management sent abroad through the multinational enterprise, and low cost oil resulted in unprecedented change in the Third World. New technology led by American scientists prompted increased agricultural production (the Green Revolution). In many Third World countries, import substitution became the norm, as nations replaced imports with domestic output. These nations believed that only through industrialization could they raise their standards of living. American multinational companies—unable to reach protected markets through exports—joined in assisting this industrialization process, investing in manufacturing facilities.[21] In the less developed world, it came to be assumed that progress was automatic.

In Japan economic growth was spectacular.[22] At the start of the decade Japan had depended on U.S. technology. Its companies had made numerous licensing agreements with American multinationals to obtain U.S. know-how. While the Japanese government restricted the entry of U.S. multinational enterprises, Japanese firms paid these same companies large sums for the very best of U.S. technology.[23] By decade's end Japanese business had become highly innovative, and very competitive.

In the 1960s the dreams of the Bretton Woods planners seemed realized. Under fixed exchange rates for the major currencies, world trade and production was expanding at an unprecedented pace. The major trading nations were dismantling restrictions on trade. With the completion of the Kennedy Round of GATT negotiations in 1967, these countries were pledged to a dramatic liberalization of international commerce. To be sure, less developed countries remained protectionist, and with their import-substitution strategies even more so than in the past, but it did not matter, since they were not the major trading nations. The United States and the Organization for Economic Cooperation and Development (comprising the largest industrial nations) began at the end of the 1960s to put strong pressures on Japan to reduce its barriers to trade.[24]

America in the 1960s was prosperous. Technological accomplishments reached a new peak at decade's end when American astronauts landed on the moon. The spread of American multinational enterprise reflected the U.S. technological lead. As American business invested in numerous countries, people talked of the Coca Colaization of the world. Not only American technology, but also American brand names symbolized the triumph. Brand names denoted desirable consumer goods from the most affluent society.[25] American business management was without peer. U.S. multinational enterprises were allocating resources on an international scale.[26] Through trade and investment, American material values became the model for rising aspirations worldwide. In America the baby boom generation grew up in homes that had television sets, dishwashers, hi-fi equipment, and electric toothbrushes. The young took these material comforts for granted. Abroad, leadership meant that Americans became ever more involved in Vietnam.

As world economic growth occurred in the 1960s, spurred by technological change and by America's commitments, Americans began to question the value of technology and to find flaws in the world system. The very desirability of economic growth underwent scrutiny. Did not technological advance and economic growth bring costs as well as benefits? The literature opposing technological development grew.[27] Pesticides might raise agricultural output, but what about the birds? Rachel Carson's *Silent Spring* (1962) had immense impact. What about the quality of life? Books by environmentalists proliferated. In addition there was concern over the "forgotten Americans," who did not share in the economic prosperity.[28] Why spend money on astronauts when there were poor at home?[29] Going to the moon was seen as a display—a mere symbol that the United States was technologically superior. Many thought the nation should spend the same monies on eliminating poverty. Americans could not do everything.

American products abroad were often seen at home as representing a cultural imperialism. Should America be a world leader? Vietnam, after all, was becoming a disaster. Moreover, as less developed countries struggled with development, they were unconvinced that the United States had their interests at heart; they wanted economic as well as political independence.[30] They doubted that the U.S. model was applicable to them.

As America played out its leadership role, chronic deficits appeared in its balance of payments. This became the dominant issue in international monetary politics. Throughout the decade, U.S. merchandise exports still exceeded imports, but the gap narrowed and expenditures abroad for Vietnam, foreign aid, and multinational enterprise expansion added to the deficits. The dollar was overvalued. The Kennedy, Johnson, and Nixon administrations worried about the U.S. balance of payments.[31] In the mid-1960s, the Johnson administration imposed restrictions on the outflow of private capital. Nonetheless, there remained faith in the dollar; thus the deficits did not matter; and they were financing the impressive world economic growth. In the late 1960s, however, concerns deepened. The postwar dollar shortages in Europe had been replaced by a huge dollar glut. How long could confidence in the dollar continue?

The years 1971-74 marked the end of the golden age of world economic growth and the awakening in the United States to the dangers of inflation.[32] In August 1971 came the "Nixon shock." When it appeared that American imports were going to exceed exports, and confidence in the dollar waned, Nixon surprised everyone by closing the gold window—that is, declaring foreign Central Banks could no longer exchange their dollars for gold. This in effect meant he devalued the dollar. He did so with no international consultation. The Bretton Woods system had provided for changes in the par value of all currencies, except the dollar, which, backed by gold, could not be devalued. No one anticipated that it would ever need to be devalued. In refusing to let foreign central banks exchange their dollars for gold, Nixon unilaterally undermined the entire system. In the next few years, Americans tried to find an appropriate par value for the dollar and with central banks abroad, tried to repair the shattered international monetary order, but it was all in vain. In 1973 everyone gave up, and the IMF and the United States agreed to let the dollar float, that is, to let the value of the dollar be determined by the market. The Bretton Woods system was dead.[33]

Many economists applauded the change, since they believed there would be no need to worry about international deficits and the dollar would find its appropriate level. The change meant, however, there was no longer a leadership currency.[34] The Bretton Woods system of accepted par values had been established to encourage international trade; participants knew the value of currencies; they traded in goods, using currencies for payments. With fluctuating exchange rates, those involved in international trade also had to trade in currencies—hedging and speculating and incurring costs and taking risks that did not exist in earlier years. Fluctuating exchange rates created uncertainties that the framers of the Bretton Woods agreement had hoped to avoid.

The second important occurrence in the 1971-74 period was what has come to be called OPEC I. The economic growth of the 1960s had been fueled by cheap energy. American (and to a lesser extent, European) multinational enterprises had developed oil properties on a worldwide basis and brought the oil into international trade. America had been a net exporter of oil until the early 1950s; then it had become a net importer and its imports had mounted. New oil resources had been discovered during the 1950s and 1960s, keeping the price low. But in the early 1970s, supply and demand conditions were such as to warrant higher oil prices. Host governments and multinational enterprises participated in discussions to raise the posted price. Oil companies recognized that an increase in the posted price was desirable, but they did not want it to be too high, since the posted price determined their payments to the host governments. Knowing the volatility of oil prices, they did not wish to be locked into higher taxes, since they believed the market price of oil would inevitably once more decline.

On 6 October 1973, the Arab-Israeli war broke out. Ten days later OPEC, for the first time, bypassed the negotiating table and hiked the posted price of oil from $3.01 to $5.12 a barrel. Executives of the multinational oil companies read about it in the newspapers. The American government, absorbed in issues related to the war, had no conception of the significance of what had happened. Then on 18 October, Arab countries put an oil embargo on nations that were showing sympathy toward Israel (including the United States); the U.S. government turned its attention to this matter, neglecting the far more important one—the unilateral price rise, which remained. In December, emboldened by their success, OPEC countries increased the price of oil to $11.65 a barrel, effective 1 January 1974. The oil embargo ended 18 March 1974 but high oil prices persisted,[35] contributing importantly to rampant inflation in the United States.

Between 1972 and 1974, there was also a worldwide food crisis. Higher food prices (owing to crop failures due to bad weather) produced a general concern as to whether the world would be able to feed itself. Russian harvests had been bad, and the Russians emerged as major food importers buying American grain, which pushed up world prices.[36] The food crisis proved temporary, but it offered the disturbing warning that population growth might come to exceed global food output. With the world food crisis, for the first time in American history, the disposable income of the U.S. farm population exceeded that of the nonfarm population![37] It was a social dilemma to the extent that it took world hunger to bring up American farm families' income.

In 1974 Third World countries demanded a New International Economic Order (NIEO). The old International Economic Order—the American-led system—they believed, benefited only industrial nations. Less developed countries, encouraged by OPEC's ability to defy the multinational corporations, thought they too could lift the prices of their raw material exports. They wanted the transfer of wealth to less developed countries. Working through the United Nations Conference for Trade and Development (UNCTAD), they would end "exploitation." The spirit was one of confrontation, not cooperation.[38]

In 1973 America met defeat in Vietnam, and the next year the Watergate affair cost the U.S. government further respect at home and abroad. American leadership was also being undermined by changes in domestic priorities. Once Americans had reached the moon, there had seemed no support for a continued expensive space program. Most Americans failed to realize how much this program had encouraged the training of engineers and the stimulation of technology. Those who did recognize it often viewed technology as destructive rather than progressive. Technological accomplishments were a given, whereas technological horror stories—nuclear disaster, Thalidomide, chemical waste, and pollution—became topics of discussion.

At this point the word *stagflation* came into the American vocabulary. In the 1960s prices had risen, but America had been experiencing growth and Americans had not worried about inflation, since wages were rising faster than prices. Companies had not been overly concerned over higher costs, since it seemed possible to pass them on to the consumer in the form of higher prices. Compared with what followed, price increases had been relatively moderate in the 1960s. In the early 1970s, inflation was accompanied by stagnation. America's economic policy to cope with downturns had been to stimulate the economy, to introduce more inflation. Yet, now such a formula would worsen part of the problem. America's ability to control the nation's future seemed unclear.

In 1973 the European Economic Community added the United Kingdom, Ireland, and Denmark, thus enlarging its size from six to nine. Relative to the United States, industrial Europe grew in economic importance. That year (1973), also, the Tokyo Round of GATT was inaugurated in an atmosphere where developed countries considered protecting their domestic industries. The United States still advocated freer trade, but many Americans had started to worry about home production. American labor, moreover, no longer favored lowering barriers to trade.

In the early 1970s, America was becoming a large importer of goods, including oil, steel, and automobiles—items that the country had once exported in great quantities. Between 1971 and 1974, U.S. imports of automobiles (excluding those from Canada) captured between 14.8 and 15.9 percent of the American market. In those same years, the steel imports into the United States ranged from 17.9 percent to 13.4 percent "of apparent supply."[39] America—still a creditor nation—was also importing capital. In other industrial countries (especially in Europe), multinational enterprises had come of age, and America was becoming a *host* nation to these corporations. In addition, by 1974 the profits of oil exporting countries were beginning to be invested in the United States, adding to inflation in the United States and abroad.

In 1972 Richard Nixon visited communist China, and a large isolated country started its reentry into the world community. Another change in these watershed years was the inauguration of the Conference on the Law of the Sea in 1973.[40] There was a recognition that the resources of the world were not only on land; it was necessary to develop international rules on the exploitation of the seas.

On 16 September 1974, the Annual Report Issue of the *IMF Survey* stated, "At mid-1974, the world economy was in the throes of a virulent and widespread inflation, a deceleration of economic growth in reaction to the preceding high rate of expansion, and a massive disequilibrium in international payments."[41] What the report did not say was there was nothing the United States could do about it.

THE NEXT DECADE

There was no world leadership during 1974-84. Exchange rates floated, and economists discovered that floating exchange rates did not automatically adjust disequilibria in payments.[42] The years saw inflation and (with some exceptions) slow economic growth worldwide, including the United States. In 1980 Lester Thurow described the United States as "an economy that no longer performs."[43] With the appointment of Paul Volcker as Chairman of the Federal Reserve Board in 1979, the Board started to restrain inflation with controls over the growth of the money supply. The results brought less inflation, but high interest rates.

Throughout the decade industrial countries, including the United States, sought to hold protectionism at bay, but commitments to freer trade increasingly eroded. At the conclusion of the Tokyo Round of GATT negotiations in 1979, Americans agreed to reduce tariffs by 30 percent, the EEC by 27 percent, and Japan by 22 percent. Yet, at the same time, various protectionist measures were introduced, of a non-tariff nature.[44] The U.S. government remained, verbally at least, committed to lowering barriers to trade, but as the country faced rising imports and strong pressures from American unions to protect jobs at home, the commitment was hard to maintain. Americans worried about the nation's competitive position in world markets and many American industries seemed in trouble. The titles of books such as Ezra Vogel's *Japan As Number One* shocked the public.[45] By 1981 five European nations—Switzerland, Sweden, Norway, Germany, and Denmark—

had a higher gross national product per capita than the United States.[46] It did not help Americans to be told, "The Russians have become our military and geopolitical equals despite a per capita income much lower than ours."[47] Nor did it do much for American morale or capacity for leadership when the country had stood helpless for over a year as Americans were hostages in Iran, symbolizing America's weakness.

In the 1970s Americans learned the importance of energy in maintaining a competitive position. Industries that had wasted energy because it was cheap now saw their costs soar. The American automobile industry that had built high-powered, gas guzzling cars was caught unprepared. With the Iranian revolution and the Iraq-Iran war had come OPEC II, another sharp rise in oil prices. After only moderate increases in the mid-1970s, in 1979 oil prices more than doubled.[48] By 1982 the OPEC price of oil was $35.00 a barrel. It was hard to recall that in 1973, a mere nine years earlier, the posted price of oil had been $3.01. During the intervening decade, the high price of oil had triggered inflation, thus increasing the difficulties of American industry and contributing to the general slowdown in the U.S. economy.[49] Finally, in the early 1980s, the "oil glut" (along with high interest rates) helped reduce the rate of inflation. By 1984 OPEC's oil price had declined to $29.00 a barrel.[50] Oil consumption had also declined.

During this decade the less developed world was divided into two basic categories: oil exporters and oil importers. Overnight, the major oil exporting nations became flush with immense wealth, and rapidly they took over oil producing activities within their national boundaries. High oil prices provided these countries with monies to acquire ownership of oil production facilities from the foreign (in large part American) multinationals. The importance of this transfer of ownership has been little recognized. Production shifted from efficient enterprises to government companies. The U.S. government—recognizing the right of sovereign states to nationalize—did nothing, nor could it do anything. This transfer of ownership has not been adequately discussed. It was dramatic and had major consequences. In 1970 the seven principal international oil companies (five of which had headquarters in America) produced 68.9 percent of world crude oil, while other international oil companies produced 22.7 percent. Host-country oil companies' output was a mere 8.4 percent of the total. By 1979 host-country state-owned companies produced 68.7 percent of world crude oil, the seven majors were responsible for 23.9 percent, and other international oil companies for 7.4 percent.[51]

Next, the oil exporting countries embarked on formidable economic development plans, involving massive spending. Overnight, millionaires emerged. The governments and the newly-wealthy within the nations could not spend all the money at home, and "petrodollars" (as they were called) flowed into American and West European banks to be merged with Euro-dollars and recycled (that is, reinvested by the banks, according to decisions made by those institutions).

Less developed importing countries faced high energy costs that frustrated their economic development plans. The governments in these nations also enlarged their roles in the economies, seeking to increase the price of other raw material exports, but discovered they had little success. They continued, however, to pursue development goals; petrodollars available in American and West European banks provided a supply of monies on which to draw. Governments of less developed countries far preferred such loans to equity investments by foreign multinationals, since loans went to the country, whereas a direct investment by a multinational enterprise carried with it control of the use of the monies by the foreign business. In less developed countries, there was (as there had been for many years) apprehension over multinational enterprises. Governments preferred to borrow from the banks. Thus, in this decade, international debts rose faster than direct investment in less developed countries. American banks, aware of the weakness of currencies in the Third World, denominated their loans in dollars. Increasingly, to protect the lender, they made interest rates adjustable. Variable (that is, adjustable) rate loans rose from less than 10 percent in 1970 to 40 percent in 1980 of the total lending. Borrowers initially welcomed the adjustable rates, since by eliminating the interest rate risk for lenders, the latter were prepared to make longer-term loans. By mid-1982 the majority of loans were at floating rates of interest—which rates were at record levels. And the maturities had shortened.[52]

With petrodollars available to be recycled, the size of world debt rose rapidly. By the 1980s OPEC nations themselves were borrowing to meet their development plan needs. The rise in U.S. interest rates in the early 1980s and the strong dollar created new burdens on less developed countries in the servicing of their debts, and a consequent problem for U.S. banks that faced the possibility of nonperforming loans.[53] At the end of 1975, the claims of American and European commercial banks on developing countries amounted to $89 billion; by the end of 1980 the figure was $299 billion; in mid-1982, $362 billion. Important non-OPEC borrowers included Argentina, Brazil, Mexico, and Korea.[54] By 1984 commentators described the global debt problem as "mind boggling."[55]

Between 1974 and 1984, because American economic growth was

slow, the U.S. government cut back on foreign aid at the very time less developed countries clamored for additional assistance. While lending by the World Bank and its affiliates expanded, the loans did not meet those nations' full needs. Likewise, while the IMF extended its lending, many less developed countries objected to the stringent rules imposed by the IMF. Thus, more and more of less developed countries' debt had come to be held by private banks (in large part American) at "market" rather than "concessionary" (below market) rates of interest.

As less developed countries asked for preference in U.S. markets, Americans worried about the loss of jobs and feared the influx of goods made by cheap labor. American multinational corporations curbed their expansion abroad because of the hostility they faced in some countries, but more important, a world of slower economic growth meant fewer market opportunities. No matter which broad category of countries—developing countries, industrial countries, and even high-income oil exporting ones—the average annual percentage growth in G.D.P. was lower in 1973-79 than in 1960-73.[56]

At home American multinationals became the targets of numerous investigations. Whereas in the 1960s, the primary U.S. anxiety about multinationals related to their impact on the balance of payments, now questions multiplied: Were American multinationals good for the U.S. economy? Did they add to national income? How did they affect the distribution of national income? Did they evade American taxes? Were they exporting jobs? Was their export of technology creating strong national economies abroad at the expense of the American economy? Did they lack loyalty to America? Did multinationals affect U.S. foreign policy in a deleterious manner?[57]

Between 1973 and 1976, the Subcommittee on Multinational Corporations of the Committee on Foreign Relations, headed by Senator Frank Church, conducted long hearings on the impact of U.S. multinationals on U.S. foreign policy. The Church Commitee reviewed ITT's role in Chile as well as the activities of the multinational petroleum companies.[58] In this decade the Burke-Hartke bill, first introduced in 1971, was discussed at length. The bill was designed to restrain U.S. multinationals in the interests of U.S. employment. Its advocacy by the AFL-CIO represented the shift of organized American labor from a free trade viewpoint to one of protectionism.[59] It never passed; nonetheless, it reflected the alarm of American labor leaders over the state of the economy for which they often blamed U.S. multinationals. The Overseas Private Investment Corporation (OPIC), which provided political risk insurance for U.S. multinationals, underwent piercing scrutiny: The issue was whether the U.S. government insurance of private U.S. companies was propelling the government into political controversies in which it should not be involved.[60] OPIC, however, survived and in 1981 it wrote $1.9 billion worth of political risk coverage; in 1983 its coverage came to $3.9 billion.[61] By the early 1980s, with the slowdown in the expansion of U.S. business abroad, public attention shifted from U.S. multinationals (industrial enterprises) to the role of American banks in international lending. The shift in attention was the result of the formidable expansion in international lending and the mounting worries about defaults on international debts. In the spring of 1984, the Federal Reserve was pressing American bankers to stretch out loans and lower interest rates for Third World borrowers.[62]

Meanwhile, U.S. imports were climbing. Every year from 1976 through 1983 (and anticipated for 1984) the balance on the U.S. merchandise trade was negative (Table 1). America's commitment to freer trade teetered. At first, some had argued that the trade deficits were caused by the fall in the value of the dollar (the United States was paying more for imports); as the dollar strengthened, Americans discovered what every economist knew: an overvalued dollar made matters worse. Now imports were cheap and Americans bought more; exports were not competitive. Europeans pointed out that although President Reagan talked in favor of free trade, with "voluntary" (and nonvoluntary) arrangements, his Republican administration had restrained imports of automobiles, steel, motorcycles, textiles, and other products "in a pattern of protection for domestic industry unmatched in decades."[63]

Between 1960 and 1980, the structure of U. S. imports had changed dramatically (Table 2). The relative and absolute rise in imports of manufactured goods and fuels was striking. In the category of manufactured goods, all the increase was represented by machinery and transport equipment. In 1960 machinery and transport equipment represented 10 percent of U.S. imports, and other manufactures, 31 percent. In 1980 the figures were 25 percent and 27 percent, respectively.[64]

Interestingly, while American manufactured products met stiff competition in world markets, U.S. agricultural exports expanded. In the 1960s about 14 percent of U.S. farm production was sold abroad. By 1980 the figure had reached 30 percent. U.S. agricultural exports rose on average 20 percent per year in the 1970s and totaled over $43 billion in 1981 (about 18 percent of U.S. exports). America was a breadbasket for the world.[65]

As foreign investment in the United States rose in the decade 1974-84,

TABLE 1
U.S. FOREIGN TRADE—1960-1983
EXPORTS AND IMPORTS OF MERCHANDISE

| YEAR | MERCHANDISE | | |
| | Millions of Dollars | | |
	Exports	Imports	Net
1960	19,650	-14,758	4,892
1961	20,108	-14,537	5,571
1962	20,781	-16,260	4,521
1963	22,272	-17,048	5,224
1964	25,501	-18,700	6,801
1965	26,461	-25,510	4,951
1966	29,310	-25,493	3,817
1967	30,666	-26,866	3,800
1968	33,626	-32,991	635
1969	36,414	-35,807	607
1970	42,469	-39,866	2,603
1971	43,319	-45,579	-2,260
1972	49,381	-55,797	-6,416
1973	71,410	-70,499	911
1974	98,306	-103,811	-5,505
1975	107,088	-98,185	8,903
1976	114,745	-124,228	-9,483
1977	120,816	-151,907	-31,091
1978	142,054	-176,020	-33,966
1979	184,473	-212,028	-27,555
1980	224,237	-249,781	-25,544
1981	237,019	-265,086	-28,067
1982	211,217	-247,606	-36,389
1983	200,203	-260,753	-60,550

SOURCE: *Economic Report of the President, 1984* (1960-1982), 332; *Survey of Current Business,* March 1984 (1983): 38.

critics worried about "Arab" takeovers of American industry. On 26 October 1974, the Foreign Investment Study Act of 1974 became law, requiring the U.S. Departments of Commerce and the Treasury to undertake comprehensive studies of foreign investment in the United States. The Department of Commerce study, *Foreign Direct Investment in the United States* (1976), was a nine-volume work. On 7 May 1975, a Committee on Foreign Investment in the United States (CFIUS) was established (pursuant to Executive Order 11858) to review investments in the United States that "might have major implications for United States national interests."[66]

TABLE 2
PERCENTAGE SHARE OF U.S.
MERCHANDISE IMPORTS 1960-1980

	1960	1980
Manufactured goods	41	52
Fuels	10	33
Food	24	8
Primary Commodities (excluding fuel and food)	25	7

SOURCE: Based on World Bank, *World Development Report 1983*, 169.

Petrodollars went principally into American banks, U.S. government securities, corporate stocks and bonds, and land and real estate. Other foreign investors also made portfolio investments and invested in land and real estate.[67] There were particular concerns lest foreigners buy up America's agricultural land.[68] Then there were the European, Japanese, and Canadian multinationals that came to the United States to sell in this country. These direct investments (that carried control of operations) increased far faster than U.S. business abroad (Table 3). The investments outside the country by American multinationals remained larger than those of foreign multinationals in the United States ($221.3 billion versus $101.8 billion in 1982), but the rapid growth of the latter attracted attention.[69] Economists wrote of "the internationalization of ownership of U.S. industry."[70] There was particular alarm in 1981 when the Kuwait Petroleum Corporation, a government-owned company,

TABLE 3
U.S. DIRECT INVESTMENT ABROAD; FOREIGN DIRECT
INVESTMENT IN THE UNITED STATES—INVESTMENT POSITION AT YEAREND
(BILLIONS OF DOLLARS)

Type of Investment	1970	1972	1974	1976	1978	1980	1981	1982
U.S. Direct Investment Abroad (book value)	75.5	89.9	110.1	136.8	162.7	215.4	226.4	221.3
Foreign Direct Investment in the United States (book value)	13.3	14.9	25.1	30.8	42.5	68.4	90.4	101.8

SOURCE: *Economic Report of the President, 1984*, 337.

made the $2.5 billion acquisition of Santa Fe International Corporation, an independent American oil and gas company.[71]

By 1984 the influx into the United States of goods and capital from abroad and the recycling by American banks of monies placed in their hands created an entirely different set of international economic relations from what had existed a decade, much less two decades, earlier. It was a paradox. Arabs and Venezuelans (and others) invested in the United States, seeking a secure place for investment. U.S. banks, searching for loan opportunities, dispatched these monies to less developed countries—particularly those in Latin America!

In less developed countries during the period 1974-84, the mood of belligerent confrontation (South versus North) that had characterized the NIEO became increasingly muted. In the early 1980s, most of these countries were less smug and less certain that development would be automatic. In 1983 the gross domestic product of Latin America as a whole *dropped* by 3.3 percent, following a decline of 1 percent in 1982. Population rose, so the per capita product *fell* by an estimated 5.6 percent in 1983, so that the per capita product of that region was down to the 1977 level.[72] Less developed countries faced an immense debt burden and in some cases an inability to meet their obligations.[73] For American banks there were major worries lest defaults on their international loans undermine the banks' solvency.[74]

All during the years 1974-82, the United States balance of trade with the European common market had been positive. In 1983 it looked as though there would be a negative trade balance with these countries.[75] Moreover, in 1984 the European Economic Community was in greater disarray than at any time in its history. Great Britain, which since its entry into the community had felt its financial burden was too large, continued to object to the size of its contribution. There was talk of bankruptcy of the Community.

On 15 December 1978, President Carter announced the normalization of U.S. relations with the People's Republic of China—and in the years 1979-84, U.S.-China trade and investment relations slowly resumed. This nation of practically one billion people was reentering the world economy, and American business perceived new opportunities. Yet, not all Americans were pleased. After U.S. textile makers objected to the bilateral textile agreement between China and the United States (August 1983), President Reagan agreed to provide new protection for the U.S. textile industry.

In 1973, as noted earlier, the Law of the Sea Conference had begun. Throughout the 1970s and early 1980s, negotiations had gone forward.

Then in July 1982 the Reagan administration had rejected the treaty, despite the fact that it had been approved by the United Nations. In this highly important sphere, there was little to show for a decade of work.[76]

Indeed, in the early 1980s, none of the optimism about the world economy that existed at the start of the 1960s remained. There was a crisis of confidence. No one was sure that the United States could cope with the new realities. The situation in the Middle East, especially, threatened to have grave economic consequences. Much of America's imported oil came through the Caribbean, and Americans were also nervous about developments in that region. No one took high international growth rates for granted any longer. At the start of 1984 the large U.S. government deficit, the level of unemployment, the "competitiveness" of American industry, the overvalued dollar,[77] and the still high real interest rates were key domestic issues. All were linked with America's international position.

The huge U.S. domestic deficit was in part caused by large defense expenditures, made inevitable by the tenseness of U.S.-Soviet relations. The deficit would have to be financed, which, many believed, meant little prospect of lower interest rates. High interest rates encouraged the inflow of foreign monies into the United States. High interest rates had made the dollar desirable and pushed up its value and this, in turn, increased U.S. power to purchase abroad. The higher valued dollar also meant U.S. exports were not competitive. Falling exports adversely affected U.S. jobs (the dollar value of U.S. exports declined 1981-83). Imports invaded the home market that Americans had long served with domestic output. Trade restrictions notwithstanding, the U.S. market remained vulnerable to imports.[78]

Some Americans expected that with inflation under control, and the economy recovering, interest rates might decline. There were, however, worries that if this occurred, the foreign capital that had poured in would just as rapidly flow out, causing a disruption in U.S. financial markets as well as in the domestic economy. Of course, such an outflow would serve to decrease the value of the dollar, making U.S. exports more competitive—assuming the exodus was lasting. Changes in exchange rates caused by movements of "hot money" affect America's competitive position; these rate changes had no relationship whatsoever to the efficiency of American industry. Although many economists continued to believe in floating exchange rates, there is no question that they created great uncertainties that, I believe, imperiled the domestic and the international economic system, making it virtually impossible to evaluate the real competitive strength of America in the world economy.

A FINALE

There are hopeful signs. The American economy in 1984 was still the strongest in the world, the losses in relative position between 1960 and 1984 notwithstanding. The U.S. gross domestic product was the world's largest. In 1981 the United States had a G.D.P. of $2.9 trillion; its nearest rival was the Soviet Union with a G.D.P. of $1.3 trillion in 1979 (the most recent available figure). Japan, with a G.D.P. of $1.1 trillion in 1981, had substantially less than half that of the United States.[79] American technology—in computing and in genetic engineering especially—was far from stagnant. There was renewed attention to space age ventures. The American economy was undergoing fundamental and radical changes. Americans were reevaluating the role of the state, with a new commitment to "less government" and to deregulation; what the impact of this will be on America's role in the world economy is unclear. Even more important, there has been taking place for many years a profound structural change in the United States from an industrial to a service sector economy.[80] How this change will affect the nation's role in the world economy is also uncertain. Will American initiative—is discussing liberalization of trade in services.[81]

The new technology—properly used—should be cost reducing. The potentials of the computer in speeding transactions and creating economies have barely been realized. The computer makes feasible large productivity gains in the service sector. Genetic engineering has revolutionary possibilities in raising world food supplies. The American consumer and American industry have learned to be more parsimonious in the use of energy. New automobiles and airplanes get better mileage with less gasoline. U.S. companies have sought out new energy sources. It is hoped that the oil glut of 1984 will not breed complacency. The 1970s should have taught Americans how vital low-cost energy is to economic growth. In early 1984, as this paper was being completed, important mergers were taking place in the U.S. oil industry. Some critics suggested this might lower oil exploration activities, but it seems likely that the price of oil and expectations on the price are the stimulants to exploration rather than any other considerations.

Although less than 3 percent of the American population in the early 1980s lives on farms (and less than 40 percent of that group's income comes from farm sources), American agriculture is the world's most efficient. American farmers now provide about two-thirds of all the grain and soybeans that go into world trade.[82]

International economic cooperation, if at times tenuous, is still fundamental in American public policy, as is the U.S. commitment to international economic growth. Americans continue to make large contributions to the IMF and the World Bank, and other specialized agencies of the United Nations, although what was reasonably automatic in times past is now subject to bitter debate. When late in November 1983 the U.S. Congress ratified the IMF's quota increase (the rise in U.S. contribution), the policy debate centered on whether the United States was providing a "bailout" for the U.S. banks that overextended themselves in lending to less developed countries.

U.S. multinational enterprises remain highly important in tying the United States into the world economy.[83] These enterprises are associated with some 84 percent of American exports and about 55 percent of American imports.[84] As a U.N. report correctly stressed, "Current modes of thinking and analysis have not yet absorbed the full implications of the fact that a large proportion of various international economic transactions takes place within transnational corporations."[85] In 1979 U.S. income from direct investments abroad equaled 15 percent of total corporate profits before taxes and over 22 percent of profits after taxes.[86] These income figures fluctuate annually, but in 1984 it was clear that income from U.S. multinational enterprises' operations abroad represented a substantial portion of U.S. corporate profits. American banks are key in financing world development. Foreign investors find the United States a safe haven. Multinationals headquartered abroad play an expanding role in many very basic American industries. Imports provide a competitive stimulus to U.S. industry and a greater variety of choices to the American consumer. Like it or not, what happens abroad affects the U.S. economy and constrains U.S. public policy options.[87]

So, too, what happens in the American economy still affects the world economy in a highly significant fashion. Economies are interdependent. When there is inflation in the United States, it spreads. When there are high real interest rates here, Americans suffer, but so does the world economy. When there is slow economic growth in the United States, it is not contained within the national boundaries. If history teaches nothing else, it demonstrates that a healthy and prosperous world economy has always been in the U.S. interest and vice versa. Interdependence limits independent national policy making, but has major offsetting advantages. The existence of a world economy opens up the possibilities of international specialization, of using world resources for everyone's benefit on an unprecedented scale and with new efficiency, and of significant economic leaps forward. Four decades after World War II, the world economy is more integrated than ever before in history.

1. Peter Kenen, *Giant Among Nations* (Chicago, 1960).

2. All these views are reflected in John Parke Young, *The International Economy*, 4th ed., (New York, 1963). On policies to encourage foreign investment, see, for example, Marina v. N. Whitman, *Government Risk-Sharing in Foreign Investment* (Princeton, N.J., 1965).

3. At least on current accounts—that is, major currencies could be converted into dollars for current, if not capital, transactions. In 1958 the principal European currencies had become convertible. Leland B. Yeager, *International Monetary Relations* (New York, 1966), 372.

4. There are many good studies of the IMF. For a brief description, see Yeager, *International Monetary Relations*. Details are available in Alfred E. Eckes, Jr., *A Search for Solvency: Bretton Woods and the International Monetary System, 1941-1971* (Austin, Tex., 1975).

5. On the Common Market, Emile Benoit, *Europe at Sixes and Sevens* (New York, 1961); W. O. Henderson, *The Genesis of the Common Market* (Chicago, 1962); George Lichtheim, *The New Europe* (New York, 1963); Finn B. Jensen and Ingo Walter, *The Common Market* (Philadelphia, 1965). There had also been the formation (in 1959) of the European Free Trade Area (EFTA)—comprising Great Britain, Sweden, Norway, Denmark, Switzerland, Austria, and Portugual.

6. M. M. Postan, *An Economic History of Western Europe 1945-1964* (London, 1967).

7. G. C. Allen, *A Short History of Modern Japan* (London, 1962), 170-91.

8. On the World Bank, Eugene R. Black, *The Diplomacy of Economic Development and Other Papers* (New York, 1963). For comparisons of World Bank and U.S. aid to less developed countries, Jan Tinbergen, *Shaping the World Economy* (New York, 1962), 25-26.

9. For background see Young, *The International Economy*, 612-33.

10. Ibid., 310-19.

11. Kent Higgon Hughes, *Trade, Taxes, and the Transnationals* (New York, 1979), 1.

12. Mira Wilkins, *The Emergence of Multinational Enterprise: American Business Abroad from the Colonial Era to 1914* (Cambridge, Mass., 1970), for the early history of American multinational business, and Mira Wilkins, *The Maturing of Multinational Enterprise: American Business Abroad 1914-1970* (Cambridge, Mass., 1974), for subsequent years.

13. Wilkins, *The Maturing*, chap. 12.

14. Quoted in Mira Wilkins, *American Business Abroad: Ford on Six Continents* (Detroit, 1964), 412-13.

15. Wilkins, *The Maturing*, 330. See also Lincoln Gordon and Engelbert L. Grommers, *United States Manufacturing Investment in Brazil: The Impact of Brazilian Government Policies 1946-1960* (Boston, 1962).

16. Wilkins, *The Maturing*, 366, and Zuhayr Mikdashi, "The OPEC Process," in Raymond Vernon, ed., *The Oil Crisis* (New York, 1976), 203.

17. J. J. Servan-Schreiber, *The American Challenge* (New York, 1968).

18. "Gross National Products of Countries and Net Sales of Companies Interspersed: Top 100 by Rank, 1960, 1965, 1970," in U.S. Sen., Select Committee on Small Business, Subcommittee on Monopoly, *Role of Giant Corporations, Hearings*, 92nd Cong., 1st sess. (1971), pt. 2, 1195-1202.

19. On the rise of the Euro-dollar market, see W. M. Scammell, *The International Economy Since 1945* (New York, 1980), 103-4.

20. Carlo M. Cipolla, *The Economic History of World Population*, 7th ed. (New York, 1978), 59.

21. For these developments in Latin America in the 1960s, Wilkins, *The Maturing*, 353-54. For a critical view, but one that shows the vast impact of multinationals on industrialization, Richard Newfarmer and Willard F. Mueller, *Multinational Corporations in Brazil and Mexico*, Report to the U.S. Sen., Committee on Foreign Relations, Subcommittee on Multinational Corporations, 94th Cong., 1st sess. (1975). There is a general absence in the development literature of sober appraisals of what clearly has been the sizable role of U.S. multinational corporations in the industrialization process. I agree with Richard Caves that most of the large literature on multinationals in less developed countries has been more of rhetoric rather than of scholarship. Richard E. Caves, *Multinational Enterprise and Economic Analysis* (Cambridge, Eng., 1982), 252, 277.

22. Its average annual growth of G.D.P. (gross domestic product) 1960-1970 was 10.4%, compared with 4.3% for the United States, 4.4% for Germany, and 2.9% for the United Kingdom. Less developed countries had higher rates of growth in this decade than the industrial ones, but only the oil producers, Iran (11.3%) and Libya (24.4%) surpassed Japan. See World Bank, *World Development Report 1983*, 151.

23. Wilkins, *The Maturing*, 348.

24. Ibid.

25. In Japan, for example, English brand names were often not translated. I asked, why? Could the Japanese read English? The answer was "no"; nonetheless "Revlon" lipstick, for example, had appeal.

26. In Professor Chandler's terms, "the visible hand," the management of business enterprise, was apparent worldwide. See Alfred D. Chandler, *The Visible Hand* (Cambridge, Mass., 1977). In a discussion of this paper with my colleague, J. F. Hennart, he pushed me—very legitimately—to include the extension of management.

27. Barry Commoner, *Science and Survival* (New York, 1963), set the tone.

28. Michael Harrington, *The Other America: Poverty in the United States* (Baltimore, 1963), had been reprinted nine times by 1968.

29. Bruce Mazlish, ed., *The Railroad and the Space Program: An Exploration in Historical Analogy* (Cambridge, Mass., 1965), was exceptional in its openness to new technology.

30. Wilkins, *The Maturing*, 352.

31. Fred Block, *The Origins of International Economic Disorder* (Berkeley, Calif., 1977), 140, presents figures (p. 145) showing a deficit in the merchandise trade balance in 1968; others give figures that indicate this important indicator

was positive until 1971. See statistics in *Economic Report of the President, 1981*, 348.

32. On the perils of inflation see Irving S. Friedman, *Inflation: A World-Wide Disaster*, new edition (New York, 1980). This book was first published in 1973.

33. See John Williamson, *The Failure of World Monetary Reform 1971-74* (New York, 1977) and David P. Calleo, *The Imperious Economy* (Cambridge, Mass., 1982), 67-107.

34. See Charles P. Kindleberger, *The World in Depression 1929-1939* (Berkeley, Calif., 1973), for the importance of having a leadership currency.

35. Vernon, *The Oil Crisis*.

36. Raymond F. Hopkins and Donald J. Puchala, eds. *The Global Economy of Food* (Madison, Wis., 1978).

37. Richard G. Lipsey, Peter O. Steiner, and Douglas D. Purvis, *Economics*, 7th ed. (New York, 1984), 117.

38. On the NIEO, Albert Fishlow, et al., *Rich and Poor Nations in the World Economy* (New York, 1978), and Jan Tinbergen, coordinator, *Rio. Reshaping the International Order* (New York, 1976).

39. On automobile imports see Mira Wilkins, "Multinational Automobile Enterprises and Regulation: An Historical Overview;" in Douglas H. Ginsburg and William Abernathy, *Government, Technology, and the Future of the Automobile* (New York, 1978), 255; on steel, see Walter Adams, *The Structure of American Industry*, 6th ed. (New York, 1982), 82.

40. Tinbergen, *Rio*, 45-46, 402-20.

41. *IMF Survey*, 16 September 1974, 289.

42. See James C. Ingram, *International Economic Problems*, 3d ed. (New York, 1978), 90-101.

43. Lester C. Thurow, *The Zero-Sum Society* (New York, 1980), chap. 1.

44. *Economic Report of the President, 1980*, 80. See also Sylvia Ostry, "The World Economy," *Foreign Affairs* 42 (1984) 3:584.

45. Ezra F. Vogel, *Japan as Number One* (Cambridge, Mass., 1979).

46. World Bank, *World Development Report 1983*, 149.

47. Thurow, *The Zero-Sum Society*, 6.

48. *Economic Report of the President, 1980*, 3.

49. Robert Stobaugh and Daniel Yergin, *Energy Future* (New York, 1979), became a best seller—so important were issues of energy.

50. When the price had been $35.00 a barrel, a number of countries had "cheated," i.e. sold at less. By 1984 OPEC countries were trying to restrict production and to monitor sales. The $29.00 a barrel price was a more realistic one. In historical terms, however, it was still very high. Moreover, it bore little relationship to the cost of production.

51. See Raymond Vernon, *Two Hungry Giants* (Cambridge, Mass., 1983), 27.

52. World Bank, *World Development Report 1983*, 21, and United Nations, Centre on Transnational Corporations, *Transnational Corporations in World Development* (New York, 1983), 4.

53. There is a large literature on the debt of less developed countries. See
World Bank, *World Development Report 1983*, 20-23, for a brief discussion.
See also Jonathan David Aronson, ed., *Debt and Less Developed Countries*
(Boulder, Colo., 1979); William R. Cline, *International Debt: Systemic Risk
and Policy Response* (Cambridge, Mass., 1983).

54. U.N., Centre on Transnational Corporations, *Transnational Corporations*, 4-5.

55. Ostry, "World Economy," 560.

56. World Bank, *World Development Report 1983*, 7.

57. These concerns are well summarized in C. Fred Bergsten, Thomas Horst,
and Theodore H. Moran, *American Multinationals and American Interests*
(Washington, 1978); see also Peggy B. Musgrave, *Direct Investment Abroad
and the Multinationals: Effects on the United States Economy*, prepared for the
U.S. Sen., Committee on Foreign Relations, Subcommittee on Multinational
Corporations, 94th Cong., 1st sess. (1975).

58. U.S. Sen., Committee on Foreign Relations, Subcommittee on Multinational Corporations, *Multinational Corporations and United States Foreign
Policy, Hearings*, 93rd Cong., and 94th Cong. (1973-1976), 15 parts.

59. Hughes, *Trade, Taxes, and the Transnationals*.

60. U.S. Sen., Committee on Foreign Relations, Subcommittee on Multinational Corporations, *The Overseas Private Investment Corporation, Report*,
93rd Cong., 1st sess. (1973).

61. *Miami Herald*, 30 January 1984.

62. *Wall Street Journal*, 12 March 1984.

63. Quotation from *New York Times*, 25 December 1983; see also ibid., 18
March 1984.

64. World Bank, *World Development Report 1983*, 169.

65. Lipsey, Steiner, and Purvis, *Economics*, 120.

66. For details on the CFIUS, see U.S. House, Committee on Government
Operations; Commerce, Consumer, and Monetary Affairs Subcommittee, *The
Operations of Federal Agencies in Monitoring, Reporting on and Analyzing
Foreign Investments on the United States, Hearings*, 96th Cong., 1st sess.
(1979), pt. 3, 280-532. This was the Rosenthal Committee.

67. Land and real estate investments are direct investments in that they carry
control, but they require little in the way of management and are often made by
the same type of investor who buys certificates of deposits or securities. Portfolio investments by foreigners in the United States are, and over the years have
been, far larger than direct investments. For recent figures see *Survey of Current
Business*, August 1983, 44.

68. See U.S. Sen., Committee on Agriculture, Nutrition and Forestry, *Foreign Investment in U.S. Agricultural Land*, 95th Cong., 2d sess. (1979) and Mira
Wilkins, *New Foreign Enterprise in Florida* (Miami, 1980), 67-69.

69. *Survey of Current Business*, August 1983, 44, 15, 31, 36.

70. Walter S. Salant, "*The American Economy in Transition*: A Review Article," *Journal of Economic Literature* 20 (June 1982), 578. Salant added, "How-

ever that may be, we have certainly been seeing increasing internationalization of the ownership of industry in the world as a whole."

71. The Rosenthal Committee held hearings when the acquisition was announced. U.S. House, Committee on Government Operations; Commerce, Consumer, and Monetary Affairs Subcommittee, *Federal Response to OPEC Country Investments in the United States, Hearings*, 97th Cong., 1st sess. (1982), pt. 2—Investments in Sensitive Sectors of the U.S. Economy: Kuwait Petroleum Corp. Takeover of Santa Fe International Corp. The hearings were held October-December 1981. They started with Rep. Benjamin Rosenthal announcing, "If the merger is approved, it will be Kuwait's fifth direct investment this year in a U.S. oil and gas enterprise." (p. 1). The acquisition did take place.

72. See "Preliminary Balance of the Latin American Economy in 1983," *Notas Sobre la economía y el desarrollo de america latina* (prepared by ECLA Information Service), January 1984, 1.

73. Ibid., 3-4, 9, 14, is excellent on the dimensions of the Latin American debt burden.

74. In 1982-1984 the worries were sporadic; they would "flare up" and then subside. Late in 1983 Brazil reached an agreement with IMF. All seemed well. In March 1984 the principal immediate concern was the Argentine debt. See *Wall Street Journal*, 9 March 1984. The *IMF Survey* regularly monitored the concerns.

75. *New York Times*, 25 December 1983. Greece joined the common market in 1981, but the figures on trade balances exclude Greece.

76. Explicit U.S. rejection came in July 1982. For chronology see *Foreign Affairs* 61 (1983) 3:743.

77. Early in 1984 the "overvalued" dollar attracted attention; by March the *Wall Street Journal* was headlining a story, "Whither the Buck?" (15 March 1984). With floating exchange rates, no one knew. "A bed of nails it is for currency forecasters," was one comment.

78. William Diebold, Jr., "The United States in the World Economy: A Fifty Year Perspective," *Foreign Affairs* 61 (Fall 1983) 1:98, 101-2.

79. For U.S. and Japanese figures, see World Bank, *World Development Report 1983*, 153. For the Russian figures, see *The Statistical Abstract of the United States 1982-1983*, 865. Note, however, that measured by G.N.P. per capita, America ranked 8th in 1981, after the United Arab Emirates, Kuwait, Switzerland, Sweden, Norway, Germany, and Denmark (Japan was number 17, by this standard). World Bank, *World Development Report 1983*, 149. Russia ranked well behind Japan by this measure. (In mid-1981 the population of the Soviet Union was 268 million, of the U.S., 230 million, and of Japan, 118 million). World Bank, *World Development Report 1983*, 149.

80. Already in 1960 4% of the U.S. G.D.P. was in agriculture, 38% in industry, and 58% in "services." In 1981 3% was in agriculture, 34% in industry, and 63% in "services." "Services" include that share of G.D.P. that was not fully allocated to either agriculture or industry. World Bank, *World Development Report 1983*, 153. Some of the implications of this change have been discussed in the popular literature: See Alvin Toffler, *The Third Wave* (New York, 1980) and John Naisbitt, *Megatrends* (New York, 1984), first edition, 1982.

81. United States International Trade Commission, *The Relationship of Exports in Selected U.S. Service Industries to U.S. Merchandise Exports* (Washington, 1982), was the first study of service sector exports.

82. Lipsey, Steiner, and Purvis, *Economics*, 116.

83. The size of some of these multinationals is extraordinary. In 1980 General Motors employed 746,000 persons, 31% outside the United States; Ford employed 427,000, 58% abroad; General Electric employed 402,000, 29% outside the country. The figures for IBM were 340,000, 43% abroad and for Exxon, 177,000, 52% abroad. U.N. Centre for Transnational Corporations, *Transnational Corporations*, 357.

84. Ibid., 382. These are my calculations based on 1977 figures. There is no reason to believe 1984 figures would be radically different.

85. Ibid., 6.

86. Salant, "The American Economy in Transition," 578. In 1980 75% of the net earnings of Mobil Oil Corporation came from abroad, 90% of those of General Motors, 53% for IBM, 42% for General Electric. U.N. Centre for Transnational Corporations, *Transnational Corporations*, 357.

87. In 1979-80 I prepared an article for the U.S. Joint Economic Committee Special Study on Economic Change, in which I discussed "The Effects of Foreign Government Intervention on the U.S. Competitive Position: A Perspective of Change" (published in the Joint Economic Committee, Special Study on Economic Change, *Government Regulation*, vol. 5, 96th Cong., 2nd sess., 1980, 121-40). I argued foreign government policies had a major impact on the American competitive position and advocated far more U.S. leadership in this interdependent world economy. The article was very disturbing to some readers.

EPILOGUE

The Vietnam Generation

John Wheeler

A group of people together can be like sand, assembled though relatively disconnected, and subject to being scattered by the winds of events. But shared memories and attitudes, or events like hard times endured in common, make a kind of moisture that can bond the group, giving it form and permanence. Events then shape rather than scatter the group, sometimes creating divisions within it. At some threshold of life-and-ideals in common the group itself takes on life, enabling the people together to be much more in sum than as individuals. They can mightily shape events, and adverse events not so much divide them as create wounds. The formative key is the intensity of common experience. Families can be examples, and in history some churches, armies, and nations have shown examples. The group, its power, and its wounds are a kind of superbiological fact.

Since the 1940s a new such grouping has emerged, the generation of sixty million Americans born during and right after World War II, and matured and defined by the Vietnam era. Never before have so many people been born at one time, with so many attitudes, experiences, and received parental values in common, and never before has there been television, radio, and telephone in such powerful combination to further bond people. Never before has it been so revealing and predictive to view a generation as a whole, as a unified factor in human life. The thesis of this essay is that generational studies, and of the Vietnam generation in particular, are an invaluable organizing device in studying societal choices.

It is people who make choices. So, in studying American choices through the year 2000 and into the next century, it makes sense to study the dynamics of the Vietnam generation, the largest age cohort in American history. Because of its numbers and shared experiences and attitudes, it will be an even greater governing factor in American life in the next thirty years than in the last thirty. Memory and experience govern societal attitudes and choices. The key question is how these sixty million baby-boomers born in the 1940s and 1950s were matured, transformed, and divided by their journey to adulthood through the great interconnected passages of the 1960s and early 1970s—John Kennedy's call to "pay any price, bear any burden . . . to assure the survival and success of liberty," the assassinations, the civil rights movement both before and after 1968, the ascendancy of the women's movement, the environmental movement, the Peace Corps, the military draft, the war protests, and the central and catalytic event of the era, the Vietnam War.

Study of the Vietnam generation is probably the most important new work facing American scholars, since it can lead not only to knowledge of ourselves but also, through knowledge, to healing—by means of diminishing the bitterness and divisions rooted in the trauma of the 1960s. If we understand how our past shapes us, we can govern how it shapes us. The work of achieving this is a new thing: it focuses on a generation's present and future, as informed by its past. It gives great attention to the interconnections in causes, effects, and personalities among the formative movements of the generation's youth. It is NOT a rehashing of the Vietnam War.

The personal and policy choices made by Americans during the Vietnam era created deep divisions and so chilled the idealism and sense of community within the generation that it may not fulfill the great potential for creativity and service that its members seemed to have when they were youths—when John Kennedy was inaugurated, and when it took the same idealism to join the Peace Corps as to join the Green Berets.

Scholarly discipline has a sensible presumption against personal example, since introspection can inhibit objectivity. But pausing briefly to reflect on our personal histories can serve to illuminate the depth and nature of the questions that need scholarly attention.

When my daughter Katie was born eight years ago, she had only a partially formed trachea. For six years she needed twenty-four hour nursing and breathed through a tracheostomy tube. Often my wife Elisa and I got no sleep. Medical bills were enormous. But Katie is healed. Christmas 1984 marked her first year without the trach tube and monitor. Only when she was near recovery did the question occur to me: Was I exposed to Agent Orange while in the Army in Vietnam? Did that cause Katie's unusual birth defect? I felt so disconnected from my past that it took six years to realize the question. The delay is especially odd because during those years I grappled daily with the national amnesia over Vietnam, first organizing construction of the Southeast Asia Memorial at West Point and then working as chairman of the Vietnam Veterans Memorial Fund in Washington, to build the new memorial on the Mall. Vietnam was traumatic: going in 1969 in the midst of war protest at home, taking a General Staff assignment with regular helicopter missions all over the war zone, receiving daily news of friends killed in battle, and returning to the erupting political and social scene in the states. At age forty I am just beginning to link the experience to my present life.

This kind of delayed assimilation of the experience of the 1960s and early 1970s is going on among many in the Vietnam generation, both women and men. It has been comfortable for all of us to avoid discussion of how the Vietnam era still affects us. Our choice has been silence and avoidance, and it has been one of the most important and unidentified choices we Americans have made in the last two decades. Yet the early 1980s have seen a reversal of this choice. Vietnam veterans themselves have led in the creation of a body of literature on the Vietnam War. On dozens of campuses there are now courses on the events of the Vietnam War, usually housed in the political science or history department.

To date, the literature and courses have focused on the past (what happened a long time ago), on the war zone rather than on America and on the American men in that war zone—so the others deeply touched by wartime events go unexamined. There is in this focus on a long time ago, far away, and upon others a kind of safe remove from difficult or even painful questions.

The key word now in thinking about these questions is *interconnections*, especially how cause and effect of the major events of the era interconnect and how our memories and attitudes as shaped then interconnect to influence our choices and preferences now. This line of contemplation leads to thinking about the Vietnam generation as a generation, and consequently to the study of generations as a useful new major field of scholarship—a field in which we can uncover some reasonably specific tasks that need to be done in order to understand the generation and to help it realize its promise.

[We] cannot live in associations with the past alone . . . if we would be worthy of the past, we must find new fields for action or thought, and make for ourselves new careers. But, nevertheless, the generation that carried on the war has been set apart by its experience . . . in our youth our hearts were touched with fire.—Oliver Wendell Holmes, Jr., Memorial Day, 1884

The Vietnam War lasted from 1959 to 1975, the longest war in American history. During that time most of the largest generation in our history, the World War II baby-boom, reached twenty-one years of age, and all its young men were subject to the military draft. Estimates and assumptions differ, but in rough terms the Vietnam generation includes sixty million people, thirty million women and thirty million men, the total comprising about one hundredth of the people on the planet and a quarter of all Americans. Of the men, about one-third served in the armed forces, and nearly one-tenth served in the war zone.

There is deep cultural awareness of the "baby boom" generation as a vast cohort with much in common. For decades, of course, marketers have tracked the needs and wants of the generation. *People* magazine epitomizes this, with its current "We're booming" ads, which announce the magazine as well-tuned to the generation. In the 1984 presidential elections, pollsters and columnists found themselves zeroing in on the thirty- to forty-year-old bracket as a natural analytical segment. It was the bracket that gave much of the leadership and support to Gary Hart's surge in the Democratic nomination race. In the councils of both major political parties, the dynamics of the Vietnam Generation have become a focus of analysis.

The labels for this generation deserve some thought. Of this body of people known as the baby-boomers, the higher income portion has come to be called "Yuppies" (Young, Upwardly-mobile Professionals). The cover of *Newsweek* of 31 December 1984 proclaimed 1984 as the "Year of the Yuppie," and the cover of *Fortune* of 15 October 1984 promised to answer "What the Baby-Boomers Will Buy Next." The artwork on both covers featured strikingly similar young couples, with the women in each wearing Nike-type tennis shoes. The focus of the articles was materialistic—what the members of the generation want to acquire or to do in order to create wealth for themselves. Not featured were passions, ideals, or the effects of passage through the events of the 1960s—the characteristics that are more certainly the aspects that define it and its behaviors.

The generation is best understood, however, in terms of the shaping events of the past, as the Vietnam Generation. From the point of view of the future, there is the generation's role and responsibilities in national life during the decades on each side of the turn of the century. Because of its numbers and positions in the middle and upper ranks of business, academic, and professional life, it is the inevitable source of leadership for the country's activities and institutions, from the mid-1980s into the 2020s. In this respect the generation can be thought of as the Century Generation.[1]

Regardless of the labels used, the progression of thinking in the culture is good news, because it points to a necessary step: to see the generation as a living whole. Such a view will help us understand the generation better in all its dimensions, not simply the political or economic dimensions. As an example, such a view shows that there are great divisions within the generation, caused or widened by the interconnected events of the Vietnam era. The divisions are hidden and so have not been greatly discussed. Listing and exploring some of them yields evidence of the need for and potential value of concerted exploration of the dynamics of the generation.

MAN DIVIDED FROM MAN

Many men who did not wear a uniform in the 1960s feel estranged from the men in their generation who did. Talking about this with a group of Vietnam veterans, *Atlantic* editor James Fallows said, "I think most of my college and graduate school friends are not happy talking about these things because they're afraid they're going to be yelled at. They're afraid that all of you are going to shake them by the lapels and say, 'You coward! You weren't there with us.' And that is why they don't want to talk about this stuff. They would then say, 'Well, you war criminal!' I think that maybe the fear is partly unrealistic, partly self-inflicted, but I think I have some experience in this vein, having written about this and having a fair collection of letters."[2] This feeling of separation is worse than it seems from the quotation because the men on either side appear to misinterpret each other. But if many men who wore the uniform think that the others look down on them, some polling evidence indicates that actually most Americans respect the Vietnam veteran.[3]

A more recent development is that there seems to be an emerging popular view that service in Vietnam marks a man as strong and good. The television hero Magnum in "Magnum P.I.," portrayed by Tom Selleck, is a Vietnam veteran. Similarly, the Vietnam vets in "The A-Team" television series are portrayed as modern-day Robin Hoods. There is political and emotional voltage here. Bruce Caputo's 1982 campaign for the Republican nomination for a U.S. senate seat from New York ended when he acknowledged that his campaign literature incorrectly claimed he had served in Vietnam. More recently, in analyzing the 1984 presidential election results political polling consultant Samuel Popkin wrote in the November 11 Washington *Post* about future Democratic presidential nominees: "Above all, the Democrats will have to nominate a man who, when he says 'we,' will be able to convince white men that he includes them too. In the context of the '80s such a candidate might have to be a Vietnam veteran, or someone too old to have dodged the draft. Only such a candidate will appeal both to the Democratic Party's new core of blacks and working women and to white men who espouse the new patriotism and extol the competitive spirit." In fact there is growing voter affirmation of Vietnam veterans: Charles Robb is Governor of Virginia, Larry Pressler is Senator from South Dakota, Bob Kerrey is Governor of Nebraska, and John Kerry has been elected Senator from Massachusetts, leaving his post as Lieutenant Governor. Meanwhile Gary Hart took grief for waiting until the 1980's to enter military service, being commissioned in the reserves. This evidence suggest that Vietnam service is a very touchy topic among men, since societal esteem and rewards appear to be linked to it.

Set in the context of such division, the experience of Vietnam veterans becomes understandable. The sequence of experience is familiar: we soldiers, sailors, fliers, and Marines went to the War Zone. The war experience was harsh, but the existing literature shows that we were well prepared for war and in fact did our job well.[4] The puzzle is what was going on in America, especially the reaction to the battle of Tet '68—a surprise attack that indeed was spectacular and unexpected, but in which the attacking Viet Cong was so mauled that thereafter the brunt of the war shifted to the North Vietnamese Regular forces.[5] Americans at home, however, seemed to be preoccupied with the brutality and surprises of war and seemed to the veterans to overlook the military victory in Tet. Instead, Tet '68 marked the beginning of a radically intensified antiwar protest. From the fighting man's point of view, it was as if in World War II the Battle of the Bulge or Iwo Jima had been reported, and accepted, as German and Japanese victories because of the great resolve and unexpected strength they showed. Just like the Viet Cong in Tet '68, the German or Japanese could have been accorded a political and strategic victory, depending on how Americans at home chose to see the reality.

The specific instance of Tet '68 is significant because it crystallizes the puzzle. The Vietnam vet and his sacrifices were lost in the shuffle, just as we were lost in the shuffle on our return home, made nonpersons as far as our service was concerned. Reasons abound (some allege high command perfidy in having failed to warn Americans that the Tet experience was a possibility—the crux of the famous 1982 CBS television exposé on Tet[6])but the reasons do not adequately explain the consistent public avoidance of the Veteran and what he had done.

But when we think about the generation as a whole, we see why men who did not go to Vietnam would feel uneasy about their choice. A woman who is a poet and a newspaper editor wrote me in 1984 about trying to raise the issue of the effects of Vietnam with a male friend whose draft lottery number kept him out of Vietnam: "It was infinitely revealing to me that this was the one topic that I couldn't get him to discuss." The earlier quoted James Fallows and Samuel Popkin point to a very gut-level reason for such studied silence, namely the raw question of manhood, keeping commitments, and courage.

This silence towards and about the Vietnam vet, however understandable, has tended to keep vets atomized, alone, and uninformed about a possible medical disaster—birth defects and cancer caused by their exposure to Agent Orange while in Vietnam.[7] This choice of silence also carried the possibility of further harm to vets. A unique court settlement of $180 million from Agent Orange manufacturers, issued in 1984, seems to carry the seeds of healing, however; an advisory panel of Vietnam veterans is helping the court fashion both compensation and, perhaps, an advocacy structure that will watch in coming years for signs of later-life cancer among Vietnam vets.[8] As in other fields of life, on this issue the vets have been self-starters: they brought the cases themselves, and the court has assembled its advisory panel from the ranks of successful vets.

WOMAN SEPARATED FROM MAN

Memories of wartime choices carry high voltage, and the strongest voltage may be sexual. The Vietnam veteran whom America despised in the 1960s and early 1970s is now a strong sex object—for example, Tom Selleck as Magnum. In fact a poetic, subcultural recognition of the strength of the man who served in Vietnam seems always to have been present. Even in the movie "Coming Home," the wounded veteran gently teaches Jane Fonda to make love to him, and in "Rage of Angels," a made-for-television movie, the writers make the protagonist political candidate a Vietnam veteran and create a scene in which the woman falling in love with him learns of his compassion when she over-hears him during a visit to a veterans' center counseling group.

The complexity here is that the concept of masculinity went into eclipse during the Vietnam era. Only now is society trying to rediscover and define it anew; the sexual discovery of Vietnam veterans is a sign that this is happening. During the Vietnam era on many campuses the soldierly quality of willingness to fight at the country's call was neither fashionable nor apparently attractive to women. At the same time, men started becoming "flower children," and "hip" couples proliferated, in which the men often had the longer hair. And simultaneously with the war protests, the women's movement found new energy, moving farther in the Vietnam era than in the century before. Something was going on in these events besides mere coincidence: in fact, it appears that the war protest both created the conditions for and fed the eruption of the women's movement and that as a society America became somewhat more feminine.[9] The price was paid by men, particularly those who went to war. Since men have always been seen as a culture's warriors, a rough poetic and psychological equation seems to have formed in Americans' subconscious that said, "Dirty war, dirty man." The environmental movement's eruption at the same time had a similar equation, "Dirty war, dirty country"—so America set about cleansing itself. The unleash-ing of the creative power of women to contribute to society, of course, is a positive result. But part of the price, which no one wished, was ban-ishment of the Vietnam veteran for ten years, within his own country. In rejecting the war, society rejected the warrior.

One easy place to find the price paid by Vietnam vets is on the profes-sional career ladder in their generation. The women who chose to be-come lawyers, doctors, accountants, MBAs, and elected and appointed government officials zoomed on up the ladder along with the men who did not enter military service. It is true that between those women and men there was competition. It is also true that many of the women got a boost from the pressure created by the women's movement, for exam-ple, in the banking industry. But the point is this: vets all started with several years' handicap. Chuck O'Brien is now a partner in the law firm of Pepper, Hamilton & Sheetz in Philadelphia. Due to battle wounds he lost his lower left leg as a platoon leader in Vietnam. At a congressional hearing in 1981 about the leadership potential of Vietnam vets, he said:

> I discovered I have natural affinity for Vietnam veterans. They are more disciplined, more generous, and cooperative under pressure. And I just like their company. I've worked in the state government and the private sector, and I know that to succeed requires hard work and discipline. These are

characteristics of the men who served in Vietnam. These men have labored under tremendous disadvantages. They've had two to four years taken from them. Persons my age who were not in the service are now partners in their firms. This is a fundamental inequity and yet one that can be worked around.[10]

Suzanne Woolsey, a senior official in the Carter administration, told a group that met to discuss the effects of the events of the Vietnam era, "I always suspected that during Vietnam the men I knew felt a little resentful of the fact that they had to go through the difficult decisions and contortions. It's a combination of that and fear; fear for the men we love and a fear for our children. And it is a very complicated set of reactions and frankly I'm not surprised that we find it difficult to deal with, because we haven't sorted out either personally or as a society how different men and women ought to be."[11]

The subject *is* complicated. It has to do with the whole generation as it is being shaped by its experience of the Vietnam era. It needs to be studied as a generational question. There is evidence of a strong wish to begin the work. Kathleen Palm, on the editorial staff of the Hartford *Courant*, wrote an article on 11 November 1984 entitled "We Are Your Sisters and We Forgot You." She says,

As one of 30 million women who came of age during the war, I am ashamed of the way we have failed the veterans in our generation. We who have expended so much energy in the last 15 years on the politics of housework and harassment, who have fretted endlessly about how to dress for success, have not yet begun to turn our thoughts and talents toward achieving reconciliation, in our own time, with our brothers. Yet what America did in Vietnam and failed to do afterward profoundly affected all 60 million of us who came of age together. The war tore us apart then—male and female—and like a shameful secret divides us still.

SELF DIVIDED FROM SELF

I am witness to this division, since it was not until 1975 that I began to realize the impact that my tour in Vietnam had upon me, so that I could begin to discuss it with my wife. And it was not until our daughter was six that I was able to see the obvious question of whether my possible exposure to Agent Orange was linked to her health problem at birth. As all Vietnam veterans should, I take pride in my service. We went into hell, and we went in true self-giving. But it took years for this self-affirmation to surface. Keeping such self-affirmation from oneself is a kind of separation of self from self. It is not healthy.

Men who did not serve also appear to be undergoing some such separation of self from self, as they take a hard look at their actions of the past two decades and consider the tasks and international dangers of the present and coming decades. In the September 1983 issue of *Esquire*, for example, editor Christopher Buckley authored an article entitled "Viet Guilt," in which he reported his second thoughts about his jubilation at being medically disqualified for military service during the Vietnam War. Michael Blumenthal, a poet, in the 11 January 1981 *New York Times*, reflected on dodging the draft by faking illness. He wrote that he still would not serve in war. Then, comparing Vietnam veterans to non-veterans he said: "To put it bluntly, they have something we haven't got . . . realism, discipline, masculinity (kind of a dirty word these days), resilience, tenacity, resourcefulness . . . I'm not at all sure that they didn't turn out to be better *men*, in the best sense of the word."

GENERATIONAL STUDIES AS A NEW SCHOLARLY DISCIPLINE

> The process of living seems to consist in coming to realize truths so ancient and simple that, if stated, they sound like barren platitudes. They cannot sound otherwise to those who have not had the relevant experience: that is why there is not real teaching of such truths possible and every generation starts from scratch.—C. S. Lewis, *Letters*

C. S. Lewis was not as pessimistic about youthful learning as the above extract suggests, for he gave much of his life to university teaching and to creating the *Narnia* chronicles, which have delighted youngsters for years. But he expressed the truth that there must be intentional reflection in each generation about how its experiences relate to the great values and beliefs of its culture.

What is new in the 1980s is that sociology, political science, anthropology, history, and psychology have progressed as disciplines to the point where generations can be studied as living entities, while the generation lives its life. One key development making this possible is the computer. The use of computers in marketing and political work shows how thorough and useful data on age segments can be.

Some years ago neonatal medicine was not a separate discipline. Then biotechnology and knowledge of infant care grew, and suddenly, through the 1970s neonatal intensive care wards started appearing in hospitals across the country. Neonatal medicine became a new, discrete field of knowledge and practice. Similarly, the study of the ecology of areas of the sea or of the seashore and barrier islands has been emerging as a discrete field of knowledge among the life sciences; fifty years ago the idea of such separate and large fields of environmental science had not emerged.

As in the case of neonatal medicine or environmental sciences, the emerging field of generational studies has precursors in the form of developed portions of research in existing fields. For example, age-group studies have been done in several academic fields. At the beginning of *The Inner Civil War*, historian George Fredrickson writes, "The collective trauma which polarized the nation's energies, thoughts and emotions . . . had consequences for the history of ideas which were comparable to its well-known political and economic effects." The same can be said about the effects that have shaped the Vietnam Generation.

THE VIETNAM VETERANS MEMORIAL AS SYMBOL

The Memorial reflects as a mirror reflects, so that when you find the name you're searching for, you find it in your own reflection. And as you touch it, from certain angles, you're touching, too, the reflection of the Washington Monument or the chair in which great Abe Lincoln sits.

Those who fought in Vietnam are part of us, part of our history. They reflected the best in us. No number of wreaths, no amount of music and memorializing will ever do them justice. But it is good for us that we honor them and their sacrifice. And it's good that we do it in the reflected flow of the enduring symbols of our Republic.

It's been said that these memorials reflect a hunger for healing. Well, I do not know if perfect healing ever occurs. But I know that sometimes when a bone is broken, if it's knit together well, it will in the end be stronger than if it had not been broken.

There were great moral and philosophical disagreements about the rightness of the war. And we cannot forget them because there is no wisdom to be gained in forgetting. But we can forgive each other and ourselves for those things that we now recognize may have been wrong.

> President Ronald Reagan
> Accepting the Vietnam
> Veterans Memorial on
> Behalf of the
> United States
> November 11, 1984

Acceptance of the completed Vietnam Veterans Memorial was President Reagan's first official act in Washington after his overwhelming re-election in 1984. He and the First Lady left California at the crack of dawn in order to arrive in Washington in time for the ceremony. They went directly from Air Force One to the Memorial site, not even stopping at the White House. Over 100,000 were gathered to hear the President and millions watched on television.

Often ten thousand people a day visit the Memorial. The Park Service reports that it is one of the three most visited sites in Washington, ranking with the Air and Space Museum and the Lincoln Memorial. The decision to build the Memorial, implemented in less than five years and solely with private contributions, represented another significant recent American choice—a choice to begin remembering, and to start by recognizing the pain of wounded, broken, and ended lives among all of us, and not least of all among the women and the men who did not wear the uniform.

What the memorial discloses is a great felt need for healing. Commenting on the three-day cathedral vigil in which each name on the Memorial was read by volunteers from across the country, Bishop John Walker of Washington wrote, "There was in those moments a profound unity and the impact on me was deep and eternal. My faith was strengthened and the certainty of God's healing love was demonstrated."

Great and complex societal wounds are an unmistakable call to research—a call for scholarly attention as a step in the hard work of healing. Such research often leads to surprising glimpses into how societies work. For example, the Vietnam War is popularly seen as all bad; but this overlooks certain societal outcomes of the trauma of the 1960s and early 1970s that can only be described as redemptive or compensatory: the growth of the environmental movement, women's equality with men in many fields of life, the emergence of many fine men who are Vietnam veterans as leaders in our national life.

There appears to be the promise of such a resolution in study of the Vietnam Generation. The redemptive aspect can be that, in the end, the generation will emerge stronger and more creative and united, with a mature idealism more enriched than if there had been no war at all. Such a hope is worthy of America's best academic institutions.

STUDYING THE VIETNAM GENERATION

> There was, I see in retrospect, much of which I was unaware, and to some extent my lack of awareness was not innocent; I despise admitting it, but upon reflection I find I am a scandal to myself.—W. Taylor Stevenson, *Anglican Theological Review Issue on the Effects of the Vietnam War*, January 1982

Two key directions have to be taken. One is dialogue within and about the Vietnam Generation. Martin Buber said that all great civilizations progress by means of dialogue. Classroom and published discussion is a perfect focus for developing such dialogue, and it is principally through dialogue that the divisions within the generation can be diminished. The other key direction is the expansion of scholarly knowledge about the dynamics and trends within the generation and of how the generation is shaped by its history and role. Creation of this knowledge will take the emergence of a new field with new resources, in universities, colleges, seminaries, and the many institutions for public policy research.

The first need is to hold a series of discussions on campuses about the divisions in the Vietnam Generation. Courses are offered in the area of study of the Vietnam era and its effects. Given the popularity of such courses, teachers could help form and plan discussion forums on the broader question of the era's effects, especially the crucial question of its effects on the Vietnam Generation.

Fostering this new scholarship is the purpose of the Project on the Vietnam Generation, housed in the Smithsonian Institution.[12] The development of knowledge will require two things—societal awareness and encouragement of the Vietnam Generation as a subject of study, and intellectual interest and financial support on campuses. These two requisites feed each other; societal interest spurs support, and new knowledge spurs societal interest.

Most importantly, scholars and academic leaders who have an interest in the study of the Vietnam Generation can contribute by contacting the Project so that work in the field can be correlated and disseminated promptly, and worthy proposed research projects can be identified and planned.

> War has always had an adversary who almost never comes forward as such, but does his work in the stillness. This adversary is speech, fulfilled speech, the speech of genuine conversation in which men understand one another and come to a mutual understanding.—Martin Buber, *Pointing the Way*

1. I develop this thought in *Touched with Fire: The Future of the Vietnam Generation* (New York, 1985).

2. A. D. Horne, ed., *The Wounded Generation: America After Vietnam* (Englewood Cliffs, N.J., 1981), 141.

3. Victor Fischer and Louis Harris and Associates, *Myths and Realities: A Study of Attitudes Toward Vietnam Era Veterans*, U.S. Senate Committee on Veterans' Affairs, Committee Print no. 29, 96th Cong., 2d sess. July 1980, table IV-4.

4. This argument is developed at length in *Touched with Fire*, chapter one ("Going") and chapter two ("The War Zone"). See also references in *Touched with Fire*, 253-55. Compared to the young soldiers in other American wars, our Vietnam troops were well trained and performed well, when allowance is made for the fact that any combat at the small unit level is ragged and confusing, not some perfectly executed ballet. Americans watching television broadcasts from Vietnam in the 1960s and 1970s did not have the benefit of the corresponding candid telecasts from Antietam, the Somme, Omaha Beach, or the Chosin Reservoir.

5. Peter Braestrup, *Big Story: How the American Press and Television Reported and Interpreted the Crisis of Tet 1968 in Vietnam and Washington* (New Haven, 1984).

6. The resulting celebrated defamation case brought by General Westmoreland against CBS was settled in 1985.

7. Comprehensive basic reading is contained, in succinct form, in the 25 September 1984 "Preliminary Memorandum and Order on Settlement" in the *Agent Orange Product Liability Litigation* issued by Judge Jack Weinstein of the U. S. District Court for the Eastern District of New York, 597 F. Supp. 740 (E.D. N.Y. 1984).

8. Judge Weinstein established the group in November 1984. The membership list and charter are available from the Special Master.

9. See *Touched with Fire*, especially 138-50.

10. U.S. House of Representatives Committee on Veterans' Affairs, *The Vietnam Veterans Leadership Program*, Committee Print no. 97-42, 97th Cong., 1st sess., 22 October 1981, 48.

11. *Touched with Fire*, 145; see also Horne, *The Wounded Generation*, 105-14, 191, 193-204; and the special issue on the effects of Vietnam era events on American life, *The Anglican Theological Review*, January 1982 (main issue) and January 1983 (reply article by the Reverend Robert Certain).

12. The Project on the Vietnam Generation, National Museum of American History, Smithsonian Institution, Washington, D.C. 20560; telephone 202/357-4258.

Notes on the Contributors

MARK I. GELFAND is associate professor of history at Boston College and the author of *A Nation of Cities: The Federal Government and Urban America, 1933-1965* (1975).

ELLIS W. HAWLEY is professor of history at the University of Iowa. His recent publications include *The Great War and the Search for Modern Order: A History of the American People and Their Institutions, 1917-1933* (1979) and an edited collection, *Herbert Hoover as Secretary of Commerce: Studies in New Era Thought and Practice* (1981).

STEVEN F. LAWSON is associate professor and chair of the history department at the University of South Florida. He is the author of *Black Ballots: Voting Rights in the South, 1944-1969* (1976) and *In Pursuit of Power: Southern Blacks and Electoral Politics, 1965-1982* (1985).

RONALD LORA is professor of history at the University of Toledo. He is the author of *Conservative Minds in America* (1971) and the editor of *America in the Sixties: Cultural Authorities in Transition* (1974) and *The American West* (1980).

MARTIN V. MELOSI is professor of history and Director of the Institute for Public History at the University of Houston, University Park. His most recent books are *Garbage in the Cities: Refuse Reform and the Environment, 1880-1980* (1981) and *Coping With Abundance: Energy and Environment in Industrial America* (1985).

LEILA J. RUPP, associate professor of history at the Ohio State University is the author of *Mobilizing Women for War: German and American Propaganda, 1939-1945* (1978). She has recently completed a book with Verta Taylor on American feminism since World War II.

VERTA A. TAYLOR is associate professor of sociology at the Ohio State University. She is coeditor (with Laurel Walum Richardson) of *Feminist Frontiers: Rethinking Sex, Gender, and Society* (1983) and, with Leila Rupp, has recently completed a book on American feminism since World War II.

JOHN WHEELER is Chairman of the Vietnam Veterans Memorial Fund, the group that built the memorial on the Mall in Washington, D.C. He is the author of *Touched With Fire: The Future of the Vietnam Generation* (1984), and currently serves as Secretary of the Securities and Exchange Commision. He is president of the Project on the Vietnam Generation, a nonprofit effort to foster scholarship on the generation's dynamics, housed in the Smithsonian Institution.

MIRA WILKINS, professor of economics at Florida International University, has written a two-volume history of American business abroad, *The Emergence of Multinational Enterprise* (1970) and *The Maturing of Multinational Enterprise* (1974). She is currently working on the history of foreign investment in the United States.

ALLAN M. WINKLER is associate professor of history at the University of Oregon and the author of *The Politics of Propaganda: The Office of War Information, 1942-1945* (1978).

Index